What Christ Suffered

WHAT CHRIST SUFFERED

A DOCTOR'S JOURNEY THROUGH THE PASSION

THOMAS W. MCGOVERN, MD

FOREWORD BY BISHOP JAMES CONLEY

Our Sunday Visitor
Huntington, Indiana

Nihil Obstat
Msgr. Michael Heintz, Ph.D.
Censor Librorum

Imprimatur
✠ Kevin C. Rhoades
Bishop of Fort Wayne-South Bend
September 1, 2020

Except where noted, the Scripture citations used in this work are taken from the *Revised Standard Version of the Bible — Second Catholic Edition* (Ignatius Edition), copyright © 1965, 1966, 2006 National Council of the Churches of Christ in the United States of America. Used by permission. All rights reserved.

Every reasonable effort has been made to determine copyright holders of excerpted materials and to secure permissions as needed. If any copyrighted materials have been inadvertently used in this work without proper credit being given in one form or another, please notify Our Sunday Visitor in writing so that future printings of this work may be corrected accordingly.

Our Sunday Visitor Publishing Division
Our Sunday Visitor, Inc.
200 Noll Plaza
Huntington, IN 46750
www.osv.com
1-800-348-2440

ISBN: 978-1-68192-576-9 (Inventory No. T2447)
1. RELIGION—Christian Theology—History.
2. RELIGION—Religion & Science.
3. RELIGION—Christianity—Catholic.

eISBN: 978-1-68192-577-6
LCCN: 2020946018

Cover and interior design: Lindsey Riesen
Cover art: Restored Traditions
Interior art: All images of the Shroud of Turin are copyright © Barrie M. Schwortz Collecton, STERA, Inc. All rights reserved.

Printed in the United States of America

To Sally, without whom both this book — and its author — would not be what they are

Contents

Foreword

A few years after I converted to the Catholic Church during my undergraduate years, someone gave me a copy of the slim little paperback work entitled *A Doctor at Calvary*, by Pierre Barbet, MD. Dr. Barbet, a surgeon who served on the battlefields of World War I, had access to photographic negatives from 1898 of the Holy Shroud of Turin, upon which he based a forensic analysis of the sufferings of Jesus Christ.

That groundbreaking book opened my eyes to the sufferings of the Lord.

Dr. Barbet wrote his book in 1950. Given the advances in science over the past seventy years, I have long hoped an updated study might be written. Dr. Thomas McGovern has done just that. His scientifically up-to-date analysis of the Lord's Passion and death has also incorporated the Christian anthropology of Saint John Paul II as it is articulated in his 1984 apostolic exhortation on suffering, *Salvifici Doloris.*

Dr. McGovern examines in minute detail the physiological aspects of the sufferings of Jesus, drawing upon the literature, both modern and ancient, as well as his own experience as a physician. McGovern has also traveled in the Holy Land extensively and has deep knowledge of the land where Jesus lived and died.

The inevitability of suffering is universal. It is something in which all humanity shares. And the question of suffering — and why we all have to suffer — is one that everyone must ask, at some time in their lives.

The world tries to run away from suffering because it sees suffering as meaningless. The world believes and teaches us that suffering is absurd and must, if possible, be eradicated. But Saint John Paul II, in the opening lines of *Salvifici Doloris*, points us to Saint Paul's Letter to the Colossians when he writes: "Now I rejoice in my sufferings for your sake, and in my flesh I complete what is lacking in Christ's afflictions for the sake of his body, that is, the Church" (1:24). This mysterious passage from Saint Paul is the key to understanding the meaning and purpose of suffering, and it provides the backdrop of Dr. McGovern's book.

Dr. McGovern does not stop with the physical sufferings of the Lord. He also reflects upon the mental and emotional sufferings of the Lord. He describes how the Lord experienced fear, sorrow, anxiety, and mental distress. Because the Lord is true God and true man, he willingly chose, in his Passion and death, to suffer the human sufferings that we all experience. These profound insights remind me of Saint John Henry Newman's famous discourse on the "Mental Sufferings of the Lord in His Passion." When a person suffers from some kind of mental distress, they can take solace in the fact that the Lord has been there too, and he understands this unique kind of suffering that is so common today.

Saint John Paul II often quoted a very famous passage from the Second Vatican Council's Pastoral Constitution on the Church in the Modern World, *Gaudium et spes*: Christ "fully reveals man to man himself and makes his supreme calling clear" (22). In other words, it is only in coming to know Jesus and growing in friendship with him that we discover our true selves and our mission in life. Dr. McGovern applies this to the subject of the sufferings of Christ. As we come to understand the full meaning and depth of Christ's suffering, we begin to make sense of our own suffering and that of others. Dr. McGovern concludes by telling us that Christ showed us how to suffer: "He gave meaning to suffering and offers us the profound gift of finding meaning in our own suffering."

Christ's suffering gives meaning to our suffering. Understanding the Lord's suffering helps us understand the meaning of our own. In *What Christ Suffered: A Doctor's Journey Through the Passion*, Dr. Thomas McGovern gives us insight into the Lord's suffering, and into his abundant and transforming love for us.

James D. Conley
Bishop of Lincoln

Author lectoring during Mass on Calvary, Lent 2018. The Rock of Calvary is visible through the glass behind the Missionaries of Charity. The altar behind the sisters is the Greek Orthodox altar that is located on the traditional site of the crucifixion of Jesus. (Thomas W. McGovern)

Introduction

God created me with a deep desire to connect ideas and people that at first might not seem to have anything in common. During my time in medical school, my love of biology, anatomy, and medicine met my love for Christ and his Church. One day, an experience not only touched my reason, which is my usual way of approaching the world, but also ignited my heart.

During my first year at Mayo Medical School, since I was teaching fifth grade religious education at my parish, I thought it would be a good idea during Lent to teach my students about the suffering that Jesus endured for them. So, after a pathology lecture in mid-March 1986, I approached my professor, Dr. William Edwards, who was known to be a Christian. I asked Dr. Edwards if he had any information on the crucifixion. He said, "Come back to me after class tomorrow, and I'll have something for you."

The following day, I eagerly approached Dr. Edwards, who handed me a nine-page article with vivid illustrations of the Passion. Seeing the title, "On the Physical Death of Jesus Christ," I thought, "Well, this certainly hits the nail on the head for my request." But as I looked more closely, I noticed the publication date: March 21, 1986. Dr. Edwards had given me the article the week before it was to be published. How could he do that? We had not yet reached the era when electronic publications could be available before the printed journal was.

And then I saw it. In his humility, Dr. Edwards "neglected" to tell me that he was the first author of the article; that's why he had a copy ahead of time! Clearly, our encounter was no coincidence. An intense joy welled up inside of me.

Dr. Edwards became my mentor during my required half-year research project in my junior year of medical school. My project dealt with heart pathology, Dr. Edwards's specialty, but he also gave me access to all his research materials and slides dealing with Christ's sufferings and patiently answered my many questions. His materials included the groundbreaking book *A Doctor at Calvary*, written by the French surgeon Pierre Barbet and published in French in 1950 and in English in 1953.

For about twenty years after that Lent of 1986 (when I also brought hand and foot bones from my freshman "bone box" to show my 10- and 11-year-old students where nails probably penetrated Jesus), I researched and gave multimedia presentations around the country on the sufferings of Jesus.

Then I stopped giving presentations. Why did I stop?

A good physician is supposed to keep up-to-date on the latest treatments for his patients; following this same rule, I kept up-to-date on research regarding Christ's sufferings. But many things I was reading created cognitive dissonance. At first I just brushed off the work of researchers such as Dr. Frederick Zugibe. But after a while, I couldn't reconcile the differences between what Drs. Barbet and Edwards had written — and how Dr. Zugibe and others challenged their ideas.

In typical male fashion, since I couldn't reconcile the differences, I ignored them for about ten years and stopped giving presentations. If you have ever firmly believed something for a long period of time and have been confident that you were right — and you have repeated those "truths" to hundreds or thousands of people — then maybe you can understand why I didn't want to face the fact that I had been wrong about so much. Better to forget it than admit I was wrong.

But then, in late 2014, my friend Dr. Matthew Bunson, chair of faculty for Catholic Distance University (CDU), asked me if I would write a course for CDU students about the medical and historical aspects of Jesus' suffering and death.

While deciding whether — and how — to pursue this project, I read a 2006 article critical of the many published efforts of physicians to explain how crucifixion victims died.[1] The study's authors, Matthew Maslen and Piers Mitchell, point out the following:

1. There are at least ten presented hypotheses as to the cause of Jesus' death on the cross. While each of these hypotheses appears plausible, on closer examination, they believe that evidence as of 2006 was insufficient to substantiate them.
2. No Roman-era instructions for crucifixion have ever been found.
3. We don't know why breaking the legs of crucifixion victims hastened death.
4. Very few prior authors quote crucifixion literature from antiquity.
5. Crucifixion reenactment information is of limited relevance.

Maslen and Mitchell conclude: "At present, there is insufficient evidence to safely state exactly how people did die from crucifixion in Roman times."

I agree.

However, that word "exactly" calls for a high level of evidence. While we cannot know exactly how Christ died, there is quite a bit that we can know about his suffering and death. To whet your appetite for what is to come in this book, here are my general responses to the five concerns listed above:

1. Some of the potential causes of death have a much higher likelihood than others. Throughout this book,

I will discuss various potential causes and state which are more or less likely given the current evidence.

2. A general (though not specific) set of guidelines for executioners and their employees in the time of the Roman Empire has been found inscribed in a wall in Italy.

3. There are several theories about why breaking the legs of crucifixion victims hastened death, and I believe that one makes more sense than others.

4. This book will delve deeply into ancient crucifixion literary references spanning the millennium from 500 BC to AD 500.

5. While reenactment information may be of limited relevance, it is still of some relevance, and I will point out what I think is helpful to our understanding of Roman-era crucifixion.

Regarding point 4, it is important to note that a common weakness of research literature in any field — medicine included — is that authors will often refer to an ancient quote as mentioned in a recent article rather than going back to the original ancient source to see what it said. When this is repeated, it becomes like a scholarly version of the children's game of "telephone." What the first player whispers into the ear of the second player comes out as something entirely different by the time the tenth player hears it from the ninth.

Therefore, I accepted the implicit challenge of the Maslen and Mitchell article to review as much ancient literature (and artwork and inscriptions) on crucifixion as I could. After several months researching multiple websites dealing with ancient Greek and Latin texts, I discovered that John Granger Cook, a Catholic convert, college professor, and theologian, had just published a 522-page tome called *Crucifixion in the Mediterranean World*. Through email correspondence, Professor Cook was extremely kind in helping me understand his research, which delineated everything he had found written about crucifixion dating back to the early fifth century BC.

After working intensely through all of 2015 amidst patient,

family, and apostolic commitments, I completed the online course for Catholic Distance University in time for Ash Wednesday of 2016. In a nod to the seminal work done on this subject by Dr. Pierre Barbet in *A Doctor at Calvary*, I titled the course "Another Doctor at Calvary."

The course contains many new findings about the Passion and death of Jesus Christ and corrects many misunderstandings. Once again, I started giving presentations to groups around the country about the Passion of Jesus. And then physician friends and listeners around the country asked if I would write a book on the topic. After long consideration, I said I would, as long as I could see how such a book could help others come to love Jesus more by moving this knowledge from their heads to their hearts.

As you read this book, I want your learning about the Passion of Christ to be more than just a mental massage, more than satisfying curiosity, even more than learning how to meditate more deeply on the Sorrowful Mysteries of the Rosary. I want this book to help you love Jesus more. I want your reading of this book to lead you to more effectively exercise your baptismal priesthood so that you can do good *by* your suffering. And finally, I pray that by reading this book you will be inspired to do good *to* those who suffer.

In his Passion, Jesus exercised his priesthood. The essence of priesthood is to offer sacrifice on behalf of others. In Jesus' Sacrifice he offers himself — his entire self — for us sinners so that heaven is opened to us. His Sacrifice has eternal consequences because the One who was sacrificed is eternal. By studying his Passion, we enter deeply into Jesus' Sacrifice, the same Sacrifice that is re-presented daily (except on Good Friday, when we recall the original bloody sacrifice) in an unbloody fashion on altars throughout the world.

In 1958, inspired by words written on his father's tombstone, Phil Spector wrote the oft-recorded song "To Know Him Is to Love Him." How much more could this be said of Christ, the One who loves us more than any other, God enfleshed as a man?

In learning more about Christ and his suffering, we also learn that, because we have been baptized in Christ as priest, prophet, and king, each of us is a priest. Few of us are ordained priests, but all who are baptized have a priesthood to exercise.

How do we exercise it?

By offering sacrifice on behalf of others, just like Jesus. Because he has united us to himself through the sacraments, our sacrifices are united with his. As his Sacrifice has eternal consequences, our sacrifices too can have eternal consequences when we offer them in unity with his.

For the last two decades, superheroes wielding various superpowers have graced the screens of theaters, televisions, laptops, and smartphones. While the superpowers of these characters are pretty impressive — strength, speed, time travel, mind reading, invisibility, and many others — Christ has given each of us a superpower greater than any of these. That superpower can be summed up in three words many Catholics grew up hearing daily (words at which they often roll their eyes): "Offer it up."

This was the challenge I first gave to the listeners at a 2017 talk on Christ's Passion in Toledo, Ohio. I asked them to offer up their daily sufferings, in unity with Jesus' sufferings, as a sacrifice for specific people and intentions. In the same way, I challenge you, dear reader, to "let no suffering go to waste" as you read this book.

Saint Peter connects the idea of Christ's Passion with our ability to "offer it up" in his first letter: "But if when you do right and suffer for it you take it patiently, you have God's approval. For to this you have been called, because Christ also suffered for you, leaving you an example, that you should follow in his steps" (1 Pt 2:20b–21).

Christ left us an example of how to suffer — "Christ also suffered for you" — and of what to do with our suffering: We can also suffer for others. When we enter into his Sacrifice, we can better understand that example. If we better understand that example, we can follow more closely in his steps — and this has an eternal impact not only for us, but for all souls.

Because Christ gives our sacrifices the power of his Sacrifice, we can offer up our sufferings for the good of the souls of others; we can help influence others to choose heaven over hell. Our actions can have eternal consequences, and no superhero power can do that.

Come, enter his Sacrifice, the one that gives your sufferings and sacrifices power.

CHAPTER 1

What Is Suffering?

During our journey with Christ and his sufferings, we will follow a parallel journey with Saint John Paul II, who suffered visibly before billions. And in his suffering, he taught in a vivid way the truths he wrote about in his 1984 apostolic letter *Salvifici Doloris* (On the Christian Meaning of Human Suffering).

In the very first paragraph of the letter, John Paul quotes Saint Paul: "Now I rejoice in my sufferings for your sake, and in my flesh I complete what is lacking in Christ's afflictions for the sake of his body, that is, the Church" (Col 1:24). I call this the "mystery verse" because it seems to be a profound mystery that the greatest thing we seek — joy — can be found through the worst thing in our lives — suffering. In this verse, Saint Paul declares that he has discovered joy and meaning in suffering because of its power to save, and he shares this discovery with everyone who seeks meaning in their suffering.

What could be better than turning suffering into joy? Joy is distinct from both pleasure and happiness, as Miroslav Volf explains in his Yale Divinity School project on the Theology of Joy and the Good Life.[1] Pleasure is the positive emotion we feel when life feels good. Happiness is the positive emotion we experience when life goes well. Joy, which may be experienced alongside pleasure and/

or happiness, is the positive emotion we receive as the reward for living life well. Living life well means becoming the best versions of ourselves — becoming holy.

And joy is the greatest reward Jesus offers his followers, as expressed in the parable of the talents: "His master said to him, 'Well done, good and faithful servant; you have been faithful over a little, I will set you over much; enter into the joy of your master'" (Mt 25:23). Notice that we do not just receive joy; we are in joy. The greatest joy is that of the beatific vision in God's presence, which will be our eternal reward in heaven. How remarkable that we receive a taste of it here on earth, even possibly as a result of suffering.

What is Saint Paul's secret? Notice that Saint Paul does not say that joy will remove suffering. Rather, he says we can have joy and suffering simultaneously.

Saint John Paul II wrote *Salvifici Doloris* in 1983 to celebrate and recall the 1,950th anniversary of the redemption of the world (AD 33) and to remind all people that Jesus' suffering on the cross was — and is — salvific (that is, capable of saving). Through John Paul's teaching in *Salvifici Doloris*, we will unpack how Jesus' suffering is linked to our salvation and how we can put this knowledge into action in our lives.

The Universal Experience of Suffering

All men in all times and places have questioned the reason for — and the meaning of — suffering. Atheist ethicist Peter Singer got it very wrong when he said, "In suffering the animals are our equals."[2] On the contrary, as Pope John Paul taught, while man sees animals suffer, what man experiences transcends animal suffering, and indeed suffering is "essential to the nature of man."[3]

All men, all women, all children, everyone who has ever lived has suffered. Everyone alive will suffer. It is the common bond of humanity, and because suffering is perhaps the most difficult place for man to find meaning, men and women of all philosophies and religions have tried to understand it.

God himself suffered as Jesus Christ. As Saint Augustine is reported to have said, "God had one son on earth without sin, but never one without suffering." In his public life, Christ united himself to our sufferings by experiencing them in his own human body. Here are just a few examples from the Gospels:

- He was greatly fatigued, so much so that he was able to sleep in a small boat tossed about by the waves of the Sea of Galilee (see Mk 4:37–40).
- He was homeless and had "nowhere to lay his head" (Lk 9:58).
- He was misunderstood, even by his closest friends, asking, "Will you also go away?" (Jn 6:67).
- He was isolated by the hostility of others: "After this Jesus went about in Galilee; he would not go about in Judea, because the Jews sought to kill him" (Jn 7:1).
- He anticipated his final suffering and death and spoke of it often to his followers: "You know that after two days the Passover is coming, and the Son of man will be delivered up to be crucified" (Mt 26:2).

Peter's Response to Jesus' Prediction of His Passion

Peter, Jesus' handpicked leader among the apostles, wanted to protect Jesus from suffering. Immediately after Peter pronounced Jesus to be "the Christ, the Son of the living God" (Mt 16:16), Jesus foretold his own suffering and death that were to take place in Jerusalem (16:21). Peter replied, "God forbid, Lord! This shall never happen to you" (16:22).

Later, in the Garden of Gethsemane, Peter made another attempt to shield Jesus from arrest and suffering when he drew his sword and cut off the ear of Malchus, a slave of the high priest (see Jn 18:10). Jesus told Peter, "Put your sword into its sheath; shall I not drink the chalice which the Father has given me?" (18:11). And then he performed his last miracle by restoring Malchus's ear. Despite spending about three years with Jesus, Peter did not understand the need for Jesus to suffer. And if we reflect on it, don't we want to protect those closest to us from suffering?

With the benefit of nearly 2,000 years of Christian hindsight, author Elisabeth Elliot was able to reflect on this reality: "Our vision is so limited we can hardly imagine a love that does not show itself in protection from suffering. ... The love of God did not protect His own Son. ... He will not necessarily protect us — not from anything it takes to make us like His Son. A lot of hammering and chiseling and purifying by fire will have to go into the process."[4]

Saint Peter would come to understand this, but only after he received the gift of the Holy Spirit at Pentecost.

The Universal Search for Meaning in Suffering

Even atheists view suffering as somehow "unfair," though if God does not exist, then "fair" and "unfair" would seem to have no meaning. Stephen Jay Gould, an atheist paleontologist who contributed to modern theories of evolution, writes, "We are the offspring of history and must establish our own paths in this most diverse and interesting of conceivable universes — one indifferent to our suffering, and therefore offering us maximum freedom to thrive, or to fail, in our own chosen way."[5]

While Gould seemed to think suffering had no meaning, the atheist Christopher Hitchens — who called Saint Teresa of Calcutta the most evil person of the twentieth century — wished that it did. He reflected during his losing battle with cancer, "I sometimes wish I were suffering in a good cause, or risking my life for the good of others, instead of just being a gravely endangered patient."[6]

Atheist philosopher Friedrich Nietzsche, who famously announced that "God is dead," also spoke about suffering. This comment, widely attributed to him, is surprisingly wise: "To live is to suffer, to survive is to find some meaning in the suffering."

Unlike the animals, man asks the question "Why?" when he suffers. Man wants to know the cause, the reason, the purpose, and ultimately the meaning of suffering. Man's questioning is what makes his suffering human suffering. If man does not find satisfactory answers to his questions about suffering, his suffering takes on a greater intensity.

The nominal Anglican and practical atheist George Orwell noted the inescapable fact of suffering: "Most people get a fair amount of fun out of their lives, but on balance life is suffering, and only the very young or the very foolish imagine otherwise."[7]

The atheist eugenicist philosopher H. G. Wells even saw that suffering could have meaning from an earthly perspective, as long as it served a purpose. He writes, "There's nothing wrong in suffering, if you suffer for a purpose. Our revolution didn't abolish danger or death. It simply made danger and death worthwhile."[8]

Suffering Is Inescapable

The redemption of man was accomplished only *through* Christ's cross and suffering, not *despite* his suffering. Thus, John Paul II writes that "'every man becomes the way for the Church' ... when suffering enters his life."[9] And no man escapes the experience of suffering. As C. S. Lewis writes, "Try to exclude the possibility of suffering which the order of nature and the existence of free-will involves, and you find that you have excluded life itself."[10]

The Trappist monk Thomas Merton writes in his spiritual autobiography, "The truth that many people never understand until it is too late, is that the more you try to avoid suffering the more you suffer because smaller and more insignificant things begin to torture you in proportion to your fear of being hurt."[11]

According to John Paul II, because man can always be found on the path of suffering, the Church must continually and in a special way meet man there. While suffering intimidates us, it also evokes respect and compassion. Our hearts need to overcome our fear of suffering, and it is through faith that they can do this. Yet, even though we can discover reasons for — and meaning in — suffering, "man, in his suffering, remains an intangible mystery."[12]

Suffering Bodies, Suffering Souls, Suffering People

More than any other human experience, suffering demands answers to questions about its nature and meaning. Physical suffering, or sickness, constitutes the best-known type of suffering, and modern medicine contributes its science and art to alleviate much of the pain of the body. However, even the most advanced medicine cannot alleviate the deeper and more complex problem of moral suffering, or "pain of the soul."[13] John Paul II describes these different areas of suffering: "Suffering has both a passive and an active character. Subjectively, suffering is something we passively endure or allow, or to which we submit or acquiesce. In its essence, suffering is something that happens to us and is therefore passive. However, suffering possesses psychological activity including 'pain, sadness, disappointment, discouragement or even despair.'"[14] Suffering of both the body and the soul has an accompanying psychological dimension, but moral suffering is greater than psychological suffering and less reachable by medical treatment.

The Old Testament portrays many types of moral suffering: danger of death, the death of one's children, infertility, persecution, mockery, loneliness, and seeing the wicked prosper and the just suffer, among others.[15] Yet Scripture shows that moral sufferings can lead to physical pain as well. Throughout the Bible, we read of certain moral sufferings causing pain in parts of the body such as the bones, kidneys, or heart. The reality is that any kind of suffering can affect all parts of a person. Here are just a few examples from the Old Testament:

- "My heart is broken within me, / all my bones shake; / I am like a drunken man, / like a man overcome by wine, / because of the LORD / and because of his holy words" (Jer 23:9).
- "When my soul was embittered, / when I was pricked in heart, / I was stupid and ignorant, / I was like a beast toward you" (Ps 73:21–22).
- "He slashes open my kidneys, and does not spare; / he pours out my gall on the ground" (Jb 16:13).

In the end, the whole person suffers — our bodies and our souls do not suffer in isolation.

What Is Suffering?

To better understand suffering, we must understand its cause: evil. "Why does evil exist?" is a question closely tied to questions about suffering. Saint John Paul writes that suffering "is always an experience of evil."[16] In fact, he goes on, the Old Testament identified suffering and evil together because the Hebrew language contained no separate word to express "suffering." But in the Greek language of the New Testament, man was able to express suffering as a situation in which man experiences evil.

So what is evil?

In its essence, evil is nothing. Saint Augustine of Hippo writes in his *Confessions*, "Evil, then, the origin of which I had been seeking, has no substance at all."[17] Evil is a "certain lack, limitation or distortion of good."[18] In other words, evil is not a thing in itself; it is only the corruption of the good things God has made. As evil is literally nothing, it is impossible for God to create it.

Evil is a lack of good, just as cold is a lack of the goodness of heat, dark is a lack of the goodness of light, and dryness is a lack of the goodness of moisture.

Solidarity among the Suffering

Each person experiences his own suffering and cannot transfer his suffering to another or experience another person's suffering. We only know what our own suffering feels like. However, all those who suffer experience a certain solidarity, become like each other, and know how to understand each other; they speak the same language of suffering. They persistently question the meaning of suffering and are challenged to a deeper communion and solidarity with others who suffer.[19]

As you read further, keep in mind that Jesus intends to live his suffering in solidarity with our suffering. The ramifications of this truth are literally life changing.

CHAPTER 2

The Stage for the Cosmic Sacrifice

Christianity is an incarnational religion. The Church's founding events were carried out by specific individuals at definite times in particular places. And more importantly, the Church's essential teachings are meaningless unless those events occurred. Christianity is a relationship with Jesus Christ, God become man, who entered time and did certain things that affect us for eternity. Our religion is by no means purely spiritual.

When Did Jesus Die?
Therefore, since these events are crucial (notice that "crucial" comes from the Latin word *crux*, meaning "cross") to our salvation and ultimate joy, there should be a long tradition of exactly when and where Jesus did certain things, especially his suffering, dying, and rising from the dead. For centuries, the Church has held that Jesus died in the year AD 33. As indicated by Saint John Paul II's decision to write *Salvifici Doloris* on the anniversary, the Church still recognizes that date almost 2,000 years later. The pope writes, "The theme of suffering — precisely under the aspect of this salvific meaning

— seems to fit profoundly into the context of the Holy Year of the Redemption as an extraordinary Jubilee of the Church."[1]

The concept of the jubilee comes from the Old Testament, and it was celebrated every fifty years. The Church has celebrated ordinary jubilees every twenty-five years since 1475, the last one being the jubilee year of 2000. Starting in the sixteenth century, the Church added occasional extraordinary jubilees. Pope Pius IX proclaimed one in 1933 "to celebrate 1900 years of Redemption," and John Paul II proclaimed another in 1983 to mark 1,950 years since Jesus' death and resurrection.[2]

But is the year 33 correct?

While there is debate among theologians and historians, I find the arguments of apologist Jimmy Akin[3] and French historian and archaeoastronomist Gérard Gertoux[4] persuasive. Let's use the Gospels to guide us to the answer that Akin and Gertoux determined.

First, we know that Caiaphas was the high priest when Jesus was crucified (see Jn 11:49). From Jewish historical sources, we know that he was high priest from 18 to 36.

Second, the Gospels tell us that Pontius Pilate was the Roman governor who condemned Jesus to death (see Mt 27:2), and Roman sources tell us that he served in that role from 26 to 36.

Third, Luke (see 3:1–2) tells us that John the Baptist began his ministry in the fifteenth year of the reign of Tiberius Caesar, which was 29. This means Jesus must have died sometime between 29 and 36.

Fourth, all four Gospels tell us that Jesus was crucified on a Friday:

- Matthew 27:62: "Next day, that is, after the day of Preparation, the chief priests and the Pharisees gathered before Pilate."
- Mark 15:42: " … since it was … the day before the sabbath … "
- Luke 23:54: "It was the day of Preparation, and the sabbath was beginning." The sabbath occurred on what

we call "Saturday," and Luke could say that "the sabbath was beginning" because the Jews reckoned a day's
start at sunset the night before.
- John 19:42: "So because of the Jewish day of Preparation, as the tomb was close at hand, they laid Jesus
there."

Fifth, we know that Jesus and his disciples ate the Passover meal on
a Thursday evening and that the Jewish authorities considered the
following day to be their Passover. John's Gospel notes that "they
themselves [the Jewish authorities] did not enter the praetorium [on
Good Friday morning], so that they might not be defiled, but might
eat the Passover [that evening after sunset]" (Jn 18:28). If Jesus was
indeed the Passover "Lamb of God, who takes away the sin of the
world" (Jn 1:29), as John the Baptist called him, it would be appropriate for him to die on the actual day of Passover. Since the death
of Jesus has been narrowed down to between 29 and 36, we can find
out from the Jewish calendar how many times in those years the
Passover began on a Friday evening. The answer: twice, in 30 and 33.

Sixth, the Gospel of John records three different Passovers
during Jesus' ministry (see Jn 2:13; 6:4; 11:55). Since his baptism
by John could have occurred no sooner than 29, there would have
been no way for Jesus to celebrate three Passovers by the year 30.
That means the year the Church has traditionally recognized as the
year of Jesus' death (33) is almost certainly correct. From the Jewish calendar, we know that in that year the Passover was celebrated
on the date that corresponds with April 3 on our current calendar.
(The Gregorian calendar that we now follow was not instituted until
1582).

Finally, the precise time of Jesus' death is recorded in the Gospels. Matthew (27:46), Mark (15:34), and Luke (23:44) tell us that
Jesus died at about the "ninth hour." The Jewish day began at sunrise, and the total daylight for a given day was split into twelve equal
"hours" that had variable lengths depending on the time of year.[5]
Since April 3 is about two weeks after the spring equinox, it has

more than twelve modern clock hours of daylight, meaning that each Jewish hour on April 3 would have been slightly longer than 60 minutes (about 62.5 minutes). The ninth hour would be the ninth hour after sunrise. Since sunrise on April 3 would be at about 6:00 a.m., the ninth hour would be at about 3:00 p.m.

According to the Gospels, combined with relevant information from Roman and Jewish history, Jesus died for our sins at about 3:00 p.m. Jerusalem time, on Friday, April 3, 33.

Importance of the Passion Events

Not only do the Gospels — cross-referenced with contemporary historical documents — tell us when Jesus died, but they also tell us how important the suffering and death of Jesus were to Christians. Taken together, the four Gospels contain eighty-nine chapters. Of these, twenty-five are devoted to the final week of Jesus' life (Matthew 21–27, Mark 11–15, Luke 19–23, and John 12–19). That means that fully 28 percent of the Gospels focus on less than 0.06 percent of Jesus' earthly life (assuming Jesus was at least thirty-three years old at the time of his death). And John's Gospel devotes seven chapters (13–19), or 35 percent of the Gospel, to the twenty-four-hour span from the Last Supper through the entombment of Jesus. Clearly, the Gospel writers understood that the suffering and death of Jesus are paramount for Christians.

Finally, it is worth briefly addressing part of the timeline of Holy Week. I trust the summary written by Pope Benedict XVI,[6] a world-renowned theologian even before he became a bishop, cardinal, or pope. He agrees with the evangelist John that the Last Supper was not a Passover meal. That year, the Passover meal was celebrated by the Jews on Friday evening, and therefore the Passover lambs were being slaughtered on Good Friday at about the ninth hour, the same time that Jesus, the definitive Lamb of God, was also slaughtered. It also explains why on Good Friday morning, the high priests would not contaminate themselves by entering the residence of Pilate. They wanted to be able to eat the feast on Friday evening after sunset. Benedict XVI sees the Last Supper as the fulfillment of the Passover and its transformation into the celebration of the Eucharist.[7]

Old City of Jerusalem seen from the Mount of Olives (from the east looking west). The Dome of the Rock is visible on the Temple Mount. Just to the right, the arrow shows the location of the Church of the Holy Sepulchre, the site of Calvary. The land area of the Old City (225 acres) is about twice that of Vatican City (109 acres). (Thomas W. McGovern)

Where Did Jesus Die?

Christian Tradition has always held that Jesus died in Jerusalem, in Judea. The Gospels attest to this: Matthew 23:37, Mark 15:41, Luke 23:7, and John 12:12.

The Roman historian Tacitus writes about people "called Christians by the populace. Christus, from whom the name had its origin, suffered the extreme penalty during the reign of Tiberius at the hands of one of our procurators, Pontius Pilatus, and a most mischievous superstition, thus checked for the moment, again broke out not only in Judaea, the first source of the evil."[8]

Pontius Pilate, as the Roman governor, lived on the Mediterranean coast in Caesarea Maritima, but it was customary for him to travel to Jerusalem during the major feasts of the Jewish year to maintain public order when the city swelled with pilgrims. In her work on Pontius Pilate, Helen K. Bond writes:

> On occasion, however, the governor did move to Jerusalem. This was especially important during festivals when

the crowds and religious fervor generated could potentially lead to rioting. The presence of the governor with his troops helped to check such outbreaks. Although there is some dispute over whether the governor's Jerusalem residence was the Antonia Fortress or Herod's Palace, the latter is probably the likeliest. The commanding position of the beautiful palace meant that it was convenient for maintaining law and order.[9]

Jesus died in Jerusalem. He also rose from the dead in Jerusalem. Located at 31.8 degrees north latitude, Jerusalem is about as far north as El Paso, Texas. Although near some hot, dry deserts, Jerusalem receives just under 22 inches of rain annually[10] and has a comfortable average daily humidity ranging from 38 to 60 percent. With a listed elevation of 2,474 feet, it is just over 200 feet lower than the Mount of Olives (2,710 feet).

How many people lived in Jerusalem at the time of Jesus? There is no way to know for sure (even though we read about biblical censuses). All scholars would agree with "tens of thousands," with estimates of 20,000[11] to 55,000[12] to 80,000.[13] The city, however, swelled considerably during the three major Jewish feasts of Passover, Pentecost, and Tabernacles. Joachim Jeremias makes an estimate based on the number of animals slaughtered at Passover. Ten people could presumably share in a slaughtered lamb, so if the number of lambs is multiplied by ten, that means about 180,000 people would have been present for Passover, including 125,000 pilgrims. For the era, it was a large city.

The ancient walled city of Old Jerusalem is incredibly small, only 0.35 square miles. And this includes a section that was walled off in the decade after Jesus died to enclose Calvary (Golgotha), since it was outside the city walls until Herod Agrippa extended the walls during his reign (AD 41–44).

Since its founding in the fourth millennium BC, "Jerusalem has been destroyed completely at least twice, besieged twenty-three times, attacked an additional fifty-two times, and captured and re-

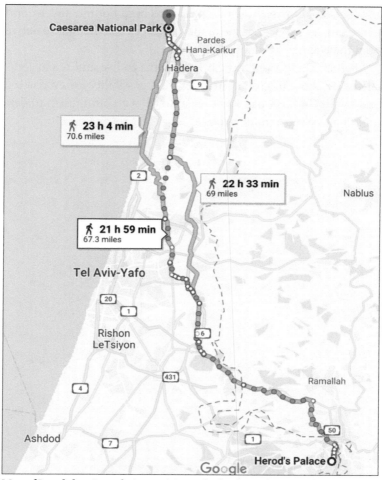

Map of Israel showing relative positions of Pilate's residence on the coast (Caesarea) and in Jerusalem (Herod's Palace).

captured forty-four times," according to Eric H. Cline's tally in *Jerusalem Besieged*.[14]

Jerusalem lies about thirty miles east of the Mediterranean and seven miles east of the Judean desert. It was crossed many times in history by travelers from the southwest (Egyptians and other Africans), the southeast (Arabs), the north (Syrians and Turks), and the east (Persians). Given how rare peace has been both in and around Jerusalem, it's ironic that the name "Jerusalem" is thought to derive from the Hebrew word for peace (shalom)!

Perhaps that is one reason Jesus came to live and die in Jerusalem: He chose to give all mankind the possibility for everlasting peace with God in what would seem to be — in our human understanding — a most unlikely place.

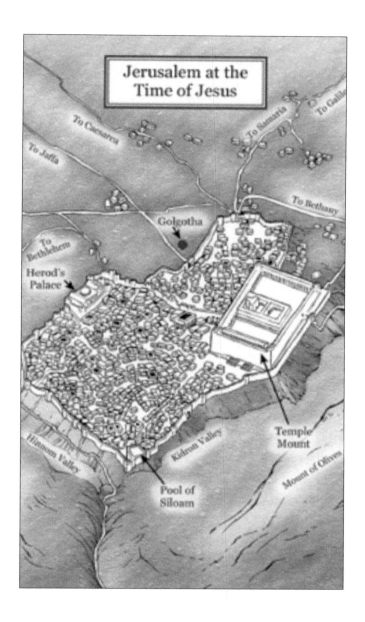

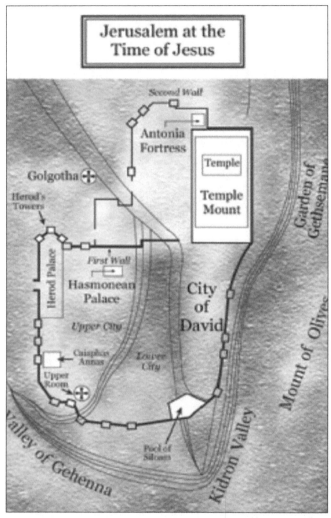

Maps of Jerusalem at the time of Jesus. (From from *The Execution of Jesus the Christ* by Dr. Mark Kubala, Westbow Press. Used by permission.)

CHAPTER 3

Bloody Sweat

Date: Holy Thursday, April 2, AD 33
Time: Between 9:00 p.m. and midnight
Place: Mount of Olives

Gospel Narrative

When Jesus had spoken these words, he went forth with his disciples across the Kidron valley, where there was a garden, which he and his disciples entered. (John 18:1)

And when he came to the place he said to them, "Pray that you may not enter into temptation." And he withdrew from them about a stone's throw, and knelt down and prayed, "Father, if you are willing, remove this cup from me; nevertheless not my will, but yours, be done." And there appeared to him an angel from heaven, strengthening him. And being in an agony he prayed more earnestly; **and his sweat became like great drops of blood falling down upon the ground.** And when he rose from prayer, he came to the disciples and found them sleeping for sorrow, and he said to them, "Why do you sleep? Rise and pray that you may not enter into temptation." (Luke 22:40–46, emphasis added)

O n an early April evening, with temperatures likely in the low-to-mid 50s Fahrenheit,[1] Jesus and his disciples walked east across the Kidron Valley from the Upper Room. During their half-hour descent into — and ascent from — the valley, they traveled about a mile. Jesus had just eaten and drunk for the last time, "until the Kingdom of God comes" (Lk 22:18).

We've heard the story many times: Jesus urges his disciples to pray in the Garden of Gethsemane on the Mount of Olives. They fall asleep. He wakes them up. They fall asleep. He wakes them up. They fall asleep again. Jesus asks the Father to prevent him from suffering

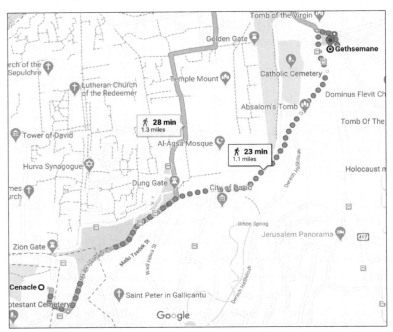

Approximate route of Jesus and his disciples from the site of the Last Supper (the Cenacle) to Gethsemane on the Mount of Olives.

Author next to the altar in the Grotto of Gethsemane where the apostles are thought to have prayed — and slept. (Note the sleeping apostles beneath the altar.) (Thomas W. McGovern)

and dying — but only if it is the Father's will. He sweats blood. He goes back to his disciples and wakes them up a third time. He is arrested. His disciples flee.

Good doctor Luke is the one who tells us that Jesus' sweat became like "great drops of blood falling down upon the ground" (Lk 22:44). Since Luke wasn't there, he must have gotten his information from an eyewitness (see Lk 1:2), which means that at least one of the disciples had to have been awake to see what was happening with Jesus.

We also know that Jesus was in intense agony — "sorrowful, even to death" according to Matthew, who was there (see Mt 26:38); and Mark (Mk 14:34), who was presumably present sometime that evening, as he is commonly identified as the young man who ran away naked after Jesus' arrest (Mk 14:51–52). It seems fitting that such agony should occur in Gethsemane. The name of the garden means "oil press," as it was where olives were crushed for their

Thousand-year-old olive trees in the Garden of Gethsemane. (Thomas W. Mc-Govern)

Rock of Agony in the Church of All Nations on the Mount of Olives. (Thomas W. McGovern)

life-giving oil. In the same way, Jesus felt crushed enduring his agony, which would be life-giving for us.

The primary event of Jesus' suffering that interests us now is his bloody sweat during his time of agony. According to *Strong's Concordance*, "agony" here can refer to both "a struggle for victory" and "severe mental struggles and emotions." In the garden, Jesus likely experienced both of these aspects of agony. It appears that he was living at the utmost of his human capacities during this struggle, and while doing so, something like great (Greek, *hósei*) drops of blood fell from him to the ground.

Claims

In each of the chapters describing the physical suffering of Jesus, I will share one or more quotes from other medical authors about Jesus' suffering. My goal is to give examples of the beliefs and understandings that seem to be most popular and accepted. I would like you, the reader, to consider whether this information is what you have read or been told. Then I would like you to put on your detective hat and read through the chapter to determine whether these beliefs are warranted based on the evidence. Toward the end of each of those chapters, you will find a short section called "Response to Claim(s)," which summarizes how those claims are supported or contradicted by the evidence I have gathered.

These are medical claims I have found regarding Jesus' suffering in the Garden of Gethsemane:

> [Jesus] was sorrowful even unto death. Such deep distress can bring on a phenomenon which is known to medical men, and of which St. Luke, who was himself a doctor, gives a perfect clinical description, which is most striking in its conciseness. This phenomenon, which is also extremely rare, **is provoked by some great mental disturbance**, following on deep emotion or great fear.[2]

Now this phenomenon, which is known in the profession

as hematidrosis, consists of an intense vasodilatation of the subcutaneous capillaries. **They become extremely distended, and burst when they come into contact with the millions of sweat glands which are distributed over the whole skin.** The blood mingles with the sweat, and it is this mixture which pearls over the whole surface of the body.[3]

His skin would be blood colored from the hematidrosis.[4]

Medical Analysis

When Saint Luke (a.k.a. "Doctor Luke") writes that Jesus' "sweat became like great drops of blood falling down upon the ground" (22:44), he uses two Greek words (*thromboi, haimatos*) that have given us English words. The first gives us "thrombus," our medical word for clot; thrombosis is what happens when a thrombus plugs up a blood vessel, as in a deep venous thrombosis (DVT), a blood clot in the deep veins of the leg. The second word (*haimatos*) is a form of the Greek word for "blood"; we see it in English words like hematology, the study of blood and its disorders, as well as hemophilia, hemoglobin, and hemorrhage.

In this passage, Luke describes something that looks like large drops of clotted blood falling to the ground. His description reminds me of a partially clotted hematoma (a collection of blood when bleeding doesn't stop under a skin wound stitched together) that is not quite solid and not quite liquid when expressed from under the skin.

Since the French surgeon Pierre Barbet suggested in 1950 that the mechanism of hematidrosis (also known as hematohidrosis) is that blood vessels in the skin swell, burst, and leak blood cells into sweat glands (see his statement in the preceding "Claims" section) has been repeated in medical articles up until the present time. But is it true?

Dr. Barbet did not reference another researcher or author for his statement, nor does he mention any of his own studies or reports of patients to back it up. As I learned from the one-eyed boxer-turned-Dominican-priest who taught me logic, "What can be freely asserted can be freely denied." But instead of freely denying Dr. Barbet's assertion, I want to see if we can come up with data to support or refute Dr. Barbet's claims. (It is only fair to disclose that I believed and taught Dr. Barbet's understanding of hematidrosis for over twenty years.)

Early Understanding of Hematidrosis

Dr. Barbet is correct in stating that there is a long history of reports — rare though they have been — regarding a condition called hematidrosis (bloody sweat). A 1996 review article summarized hematidrosis cases published until that date, and the most recent report was from 1962.[5] The authors found seventy-six proposed cases, but many occurred before 1900, and there were no photographs, no biopsies, and only one instance of examining the bloody sweat microscopically.

However, even this review called into question many of the writers who claimed that Jesus' skin was tender (a claim of Dr. Barbet) due to this phenomenon. While some patients had pain during or following bleeding, some had no pain at all. The most detailed pre-1996 report describes an 11-year-old girl in 1918 who would exude pink froth from her forehead during extreme stress; microscopically, the froth contained red and white blood cells at a lower concentration than in blood.

With great insight, the authors concluded that the fluid was more like "bleeding through unbroken skin" than blood passing through sweat glands and ducts. Perhaps the idea that the fluid passed through sweat glands and ducts came from Saint Luke's assuming that the fluid falling from Jesus was an odd sort of sweat. And who could blame him? What other fluid had people ever seen fall from the skin of an uninjured person?

Recent Multiplication of Hematidrosis Cases

Although no cases of hematidrosis were reported in medical journals for over forty years, at least thirty-two cases have been reported since 2004, and most of these have accompanying photographs.

But are these cases of the same thing Jesus endured in the Garden of Gethsemane? If we define hematidrosis, as Nicolas Kluger does, as "one or more episodes of spontaneous, bloody [fluid coming out] of non-traumatized skin,"[6] then we are talking about the same phenomenon. Strangely, even Kluger's proposed definition, from his article published in 2018, refers to hematidrosis as a "sweat disorder." Yet as I will show, there is no evidence that sweat glands have anything to do with it.

What can we learn from the thirty-two cases of "bloody fluid coming out of non-traumatized skin"? Quite a bit, actually.

While the reported patients ranged in age from seven months to seventy-two years, over half were girls ages nine to fifteen, and 84 percent were female. Over half (58 percent) of patients were from Asia (where 60 percent of the world's population lives), 19 percent from Africa (17 percent of the population), and 9 percent from Europe (10 percent of the population). None were from North America (5 percent of the population). The only two cases reported from the Western Hemisphere were from Brazil. The European cases were in Spain and Italy.

Appearance and Associations

According to the research on hematidrosis,[7] most patients experience a blood-colored fluid spontaneously passing onto the skin surface for 1 to 15 minutes. In 90 percent of patients, this occurs on the face, with 38 percent on the forehead, 41 percent from the eyes (inside the lids or tear ducts), and 38 percent from the ears. But all body surface areas, from scalp to toes, have been reported to release this bloody fluid. More importantly, many patients had bloody fluid discharge from areas where there are no sweat glands, including the tear ducts, inside the nose, the tongue, underneath the fingernails and toenails, and the lining of the gastrointestinal and urinary tracts.

Dr. Barbet wrote that hematidrosis is provoked by "some great mental disturbance."[8] Yet while 28 percent of the thirty-two recent patients with hematidrosis had a psychological diagnosis, 72 percent did not. Some of the patients even experienced hematidrosis in their sleep, and most had no symptoms or pain — except the pain of embarrassment and social isolation — when the fluid flowed. However, 28 percent of the patients had headache, abdominal pain, or even nausea and vomiting just prior to episodes.

Two patients had severe psychologic trauma prior to onset of symptoms: a 12-year-old girl who witnessed a beheading, and a 10-year-old girl who saw her sister abducted. Other patients were victims of child abuse. For instance, one young girl exhibited hematidrosis in front of a counselor when the emotional and physical abuse of her parents was discussed — in front of her parents. (She was receiving this abuse because she was "only" getting 90 percent scores on her math tests instead of 99 percent like her younger sister.)

Spontaneous episodes of hematidrosis were witnessed by doctors and/or nurses in 63 percent of cases, and 75 percent of cases had photographs of bloody sweat published.

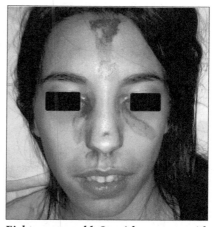

Eighteen-year-old Spanish woman with spontaneous bleeding from nose, tear ducts, and forehead. (Republished with permission of the American Society of Hematology [ASH], from "Hematidrosis: blood sweat," by Mora Elivra and Javier Lucas; permission conveyed through Copyright Clearance Center, Inc.)

In the 69 percent of cases where the fluid was examined, it always contained normal red and white blood cells in a fluid more watery than bloody. When doctors wiped this bloody fluid from patients' skin, they saw nothing abnormal (such as holes in the skin) underneath, even with magnification. Even more strange was that none of the patients had bruises of any size. It would make sense that, if blood is leaving the body through the skin, at least some of it would get trapped in the skin and make a bruise. But as we learned in medical school, "Diseases don't read textbooks." The lack of bruising suggests that virtually 100 percent of the red blood cells released from blood vessels in each episode reach the skin surface.

In eleven of the twelve skin biopsy samples taken, only normal skin was seen, except perhaps for some mild swelling in the middle layer of skin (dermis) that is comprised of mostly collagen fibers (the same protein that makes up leather).

But that twelfth biopsy shed some light, as we shall discuss a little later.

What Causes Hematidrosis?

To be clear, nobody knows for sure what causes hematidrosis. Nevertheless, I'll give you my best guess based on the evidence.

After spending over twenty years looking at hundreds of sections of skin under the microscope each day, I find it highly unlikely that blood vessels could burst and release their contents into sweat glands. There are just too many layers of intact cells in between, and further, how could all these blood cells — every one of them — neatly line up and enter the sweat glands instead of the surrounding skin to cause a bruise?

According to the referenced medical studies, every hematidrosis patient who was treated with anti-anxiety medications, mindfulness exercises, or beta-blocker drugs (like propranolol) improved. What do these treatments have in common? They depress the body's release of adrenaline. That's the chemical (also called epinephrine) that, with its cousin noradrenaline (norepinephrine), causes the "fight-or-flight" response in times of stress, fear, or danger.

Therefore, even in the patients who did not say they experienced stress, it is believed that the release of adrenaline was still important in the condition. (I'll use the term "adrenaline" for simplicity to refer to the combination of adrenaline and noradrenaline.)

The release of adrenaline affects all parts of the body. Blood flow is redirected to help us see better, think more clearly, and react with increased speed and strength. Adrenaline increases sweating

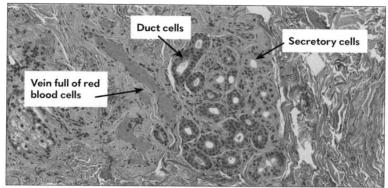

Eccrine sweat glands in the skin. Secretory cells make the sweat, and the ducts carry it to the surface. The clear areas within the cells contain sweat. (Hany Osman, M.D.)

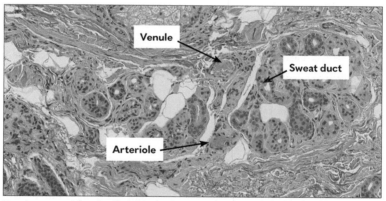

Eccrine sweat gland cells and nearby small blood vessels. This shows the multiple cell layers that blood cells would have to traverse if they were to mix with sweat in the glands or ducts in hematidrosis. (Hany Osman, M.D.)

(for all that muscular activity we are anticipating) and reduces blood flow to the skin (so blood can go to the muscles and brain). That's why our skin becomes cold and clammy when we get nervous. However, the blood vessels to the sweat glands stay open — all the better to provide the fluid to produce sweat.

As mentioned earlier, the skin in eleven of the twelve biopsies of those with hematidrosis was normal. But what about that twelfth patient? The patient was a 14-year-old girl from Thailand who had a biopsy of her scalp performed during a bleeding episode. This piece of skin was cut into very thin slices and put on many glass slides so that 100 percent of the biopsy sample could be examined under the microscope. What did the slides show?

First, the collagen protein fibers that make up the tough, middle layer of skin were spread apart more than normal. Of greater interest, there were red and white blood cells between these fibers. There were no blood cells in blood vessels, and none in sweat glands. These widened spaces in the dermis connected to openings in the surface of the skin where hair follicles met the normal skin. The surface cells apparently parted like the Dead Sea before Moses to allow the blood cells onto the skin surface.

I cannot explain why hematidrosis occurs in a vanishingly small percentage of the world's population in response to surges of adrenaline in their bodies. Some authors believe that after Jesus accepted the Father's will, his sympathetic nervous system calmed down and therefore stopped releasing high levels of adrenaline into his bloodstream. In turn, more blood flowed back into the skin, where a watery, bloody fluid exuded from his skin, primarily after his emotional and spiritual torment had passed.[9]

Medical Conclusions

Did Jesus sweat blood through his sweat glands? No.

Did Jesus have sweat and blood on his skin that fell to the ground? Yes.

With adrenaline flowing (as is the case with anyone in agony), he would have been sweating, but blood flow to most of the skin would have been reduced because adrenaline shrinks the blood vessels. Based on Luke's description, a bloody fluid was coming out of his skin. Jesus' blood and sweat mixed on the skin, not in the skin within the sweat glands.

Some authors believe that after Jesus accepted the Father's will, his sympathetic nervous system calmed down and therefore stopped releasing high levels of adrenaline into his bloodstream. With less adrenaline present, the blood vessels opened up wider to allow more blood flow into the skin. This provided more blood that could exude from his skin after his emotional and spiritual torment had passed.[10]

We have no idea how much blood and other fluid Jesus lost in the garden, but he lost some. This is important because he would lose a great deal of fluid, while drinking none, over the course of his Passion. Also, this fluid coating his skin on a dark night with temperatures below 50 degrees Fahrenheit would certainly not have been comfortable. And he would lose much more blood before his suffering ended.

Response to Claims

The first claim, that hematidrosis is "provoked by some great mental disturbance," is typically untrue based on recently reported patients, most of whom experienced no mental distress during episodes of hematidrosis.

In response to the second claim, there is no evidence that blood vessels swell and burst into sweat glands; red and white blood cells reach the skin apart from both the sweat glands and the blood vessels.

And finally, contrary to what would be reasonably expected, patients who experience hematidrosis have no bruising of their skin.

Fear in the Garden

"My soul is very sorrowful, even to death; remain here, and watch with me" (Mt 26:38). According to the Greek, Jesus was "encompassed with grief" or "exceedingly sorrowful." Jesus asked the Father to "remove this chalice from me; nevertheless not my will, but yours, be done" (Lk 22:42). Luke tells us that the disciples were sleeping, also "for sorrow" (Lk 22:45). Both Jesus and his disciples were sorrowful, but they reacted in startlingly different ways to their sorrow.

Saint Mark writes that in the garden, Jesus was "greatly distressed [*adēmonéō*] and troubled [*ekthambeīsthaid*]" (Mk 14:33). One meaning of the word *adēmonéō* is "to feel fear,"[11] while *ekthambeīsthaid* means "astonished" or "awestruck."[12]

Jesus felt fear and sorrow. The disciples were also fearful (later we read that they ran from the garden) and sorrowful (the reason for their sleep). In his agony, Jesus shows us how to derive great good out of the anxiety we experience.

Science shows that anxiety is meant to serve a good purpose. Fear and anxiety both anticipate suffering. "Fear is anxiety that is attached to a specific thing or circumstance,"[13] and this "specific thing" involves potential suffering. Yet modern psychology realizes that the unbidden emotion of anxiety can be a source of strength. "The problem of the management of anxiety is that of reducing anxiety to normal levels, and then to use this normal anxiety as stimulation to increase one's awareness, vigilance, zest for living."[14]

Therefore, the goal for those seeking counseling for anxiety is to reduce it, not eliminate it, because anxiety is meant to serve a positive purpose.[15] We are anxious when something we love is at risk and we fear losing it. We might fear loss of a family member or friend, a treasured item, a job, or physical health or comfort. The list of potential losses is extensive.

Dr. Kevin Majeres, a Harvard psychiatrist who runs the Opus Dei center in Cambridge, Massachusetts, spoke with me regarding the holy response God intends when we experience anxiety.[16] Jesus' actions in the Garden of Gethsemane serve as a prime example of how we can turn anxiety and fear into "something beautiful for God."

For about one-fifth of American adults today (and one-third of teens), anxiety is severe enough that it interferes with their living out their lives and doing the activities they value.[17] As a man, Jesus would have had a natural fear of the painful suffering and death he was about to undergo. He likely had an even greater fear of what it meant to bear the sins of all mankind. He even asked his Father if that cup of suffering could be removed.

While he was in the garden, Jesus' body was releasing high levels of adrenaline, the hormone that drives the fight-or-flight response. Adrenaline is released when we experience fear and anxiety, and we often interpret the anxiety induced by adrenaline as a negative thing. But adrenaline is given to us by God as a sort of superpower to help us, not to harm us. Sadly, those who suffer from anxiety disorders experience that adrenaline as harmful, as it gets channeled into worry and rumination.

Anxiety is an emotion that comes on its own and cannot be controlled, but we can learn to control our response to anxiety. The adrenaline released during times of anxiety is meant to help us meet and conquer a legitimate fear through action. While anxiety is experienced as a negative high-adrenaline state, it is meant to be transformed into a positive high-adrenaline state, which psychologists refer to as "flow."[18]

Psychologist Mihaly Csikszentmihalyi has defined flow as "being completely involved in an activity for its own sake. The ego falls away. Time flies. Every action, movement, and thought follows inevitably from the previous one, like playing jazz. Your whole being is involved, and you're using your skills to the utmost."[19] Dr. Majeres says that in flow, we love what we're doing and have dominion over our work and our actions. Colloquially, people refer to flow experience as being "in the zone." In anxiety, everything takes effort; in flow, everything seems effortless.

During flow, we are completely immersed in the present moment so that we can give all of ourselves to the task before us — whether it is prayer, work, chores around the house, or conversing with friends and family members. Adrenaline helps us to focus ourselves into whatever act of charity we are undertaking at any moment.

The adrenaline in our bodies is meant to give us a power to succeed, to perform at our best as the best versions of ourselves. Blood is shunted to the brain and muscles for better thinking and greater speed and strength. Dr. Majeres describes three steps that can transform the experience of anxiety into a flow state:

1. Reframing
2. Awareness
3. Challenge

When we are anxious, well-meaning people will often tell us to calm down. This never actually makes us feel better. With all that adrenaline flowing, calming down is not going to happen. So what can we do? We can reframe, considering the situation and its meaning in a different light. Simply put, reframing is a process in which we change the way we look at things.

In his agony, Jesus gave us the prime example of reframing in the face of great anxiety. We know from Scripture how he did it. (In fact, it isn't quite right to say that Jesus "reframed" his experience. Because he was perfect, he never had a "bad" frame for his experience, as we often do. But we can learn how to reframe by seeing how Jesus faced this situation.) First, he realized that he was not in control: "nevertheless not my will, but yours, be done" (Lk 22:42). He saw his situation as an opportunity to bring about the greatest love possible. And whenever we experience anxiety, we can reframe by asking ourselves, "What is the most loving thing I can do in this situation?"

Jesus "for the joy that was set before him endured the cross" (Heb 12:2). He did this so that "the world might be saved through him" (Jn 3:17). His agony was a far worse experience than any we can lay claim to, yet he gave it meaning. In reframing, one of the first things to say in the moment of anxiety is "Bring it on." This is because every experience of anxiety or fear is an opportunity to love. If we give in to anxiety, we are liable to act out of fear. But if we reframe and commit to endure, we will be able to act out of love, for "perfect love casts out fear" (1 Jn 4:18). When we reframe in this way, we can, like Jesus, say to the Father, "Not my will, but yours, be done."

The second step of transforming the high-adrenaline state of anxiety into flow is becoming aware of the present moment. This means that we feel and observe our anxiety — and the reality behind it — and accept it. So when we say, "Bring it on," the first thing we bring on is an honest awareness of the situation. We don't try to run from it or wrestle it to the ground, for the more we try to run away from or fight it, the worse it gets. As a wise counselor once said to me, "Sometimes, you just have to feel the pain." And the emotional pain of anxiety often passes in a few minutes if we accept it rather than fight it.

Jesus allowed himself to experience the pain of fear and anxiety in the garden; he didn't run from it, even though the Garden of

Gethsemane was on the escape route from Jerusalem into the desert in the east. He was completely willing to feel the pain in the garden, just as he would later feel the pain of the scourging and the pain of the nails when affixed to the cross. He told his disciples what he was feeling: "My soul is very sorrowful, even to death; remain here, and watch" (Mk 14:34). In fact, he felt the pain of anxiety and fear so intensely that his high-adrenaline state caused blood to flow out of his skin. He literally didn't hold it in!

After letting the feeling of anxiety, fear, and grief encompass him, he then answered the question that we should ask: "How can I act in a loving way right now?" He didn't let the negative thoughts of anxiety control him. He let his reframed, accurate thinking help him act. In reading the rest of the Gospels related to Jesus' Passion, we see that Jesus seems to live at a level almost beyond the rest of the actors in the story. He seems completely in control, even though he is the one suffering the most. On a human level, his adrenaline is working for him and the work he has come to do. Gone are whatever fear and doubts he had in the garden.

The final step of transforming fear into flow is to accept the challenge before you. Lean into it. Fulfill the next step of "bringing it on" by acting out of love. Now. The challenge for Jesus was to accept his Passion and death. Let the soldiers arrest him. Let his followers flee. Walk the painful road to Calvary and die. Because Jesus exercised love to the greatest level of his human capacity, we have been saved. Jesus had dominion over his work, the work of saving the world. He used his adrenaline to fulfill the Father's will that he should suffer, die, and rise again.

We can practice these three steps when we are tempted to give in to anxiety. The ultimate goal of transforming our anxiety is to exercise our abilities to their highest degree of excellence in acts of love. We can ask Jesus to help us imitate him by reframing our thinking (changing it to say "bring it on"), becoming aware of the present moment (silent observation and acceptance of our current experience and surroundings), and accepting the challenge (doing the most loving thing we can do in that moment).

CHAPTER 4

Sufferings in the Night

Date: Good Friday, April 3, AD 33
Time: Midnight to 6:00 a.m.
Places: Garden of Gethsemane, Kidron Valley, pit beneath the home of Caiaphas (modern Church of Saint Peter in Gallicantu), Sanhedrin Chamber of Hewn Stones in the Temple

---

Gospel Narrative

Midnight to 1:00 a.m. — from the Garden of Gethsemane to the home of Annas

First they led him to Annas; for he was the father-in-law of Caiaphas, who was high priest that year. ... The high priest [Annas] then questioned Jesus. ... Jesus answered him, "Why do you ask me? Ask those who have heard me, what I said to them; they know what I said." When he had said this, one of the officers standing by struck Jesus with his hand, saying, "Is that how you answer the high priest?" Jesus answered him, "If I have spoken wrongly, bear witness to the wrong; but if I have spoken rightly, why do you strike me?" (John

18:13, 19–20, 21–23)

1:00 a.m. — from the home of Annas to the home of Caiaphas
Annas then sent him bound to Caiaphas the high priest. (John 18:24)

2:00 to 3:00 a.m. — questioned at the home of Caiaphas
Now the chief priests and the whole council sought testimony against Jesus to put him to death; but they found none. … Again the high priest [Caiaphas] asked him, "Are you the Christ, the Son of the Blessed?" And Jesus said, "I am; and you will see the Son of man seated at the right hand of Power, and coming with the clouds of heaven." And the high priest tore his clothes, and said, "Why do we still need witnesses? You have heard his blasphemy. What is your decision?" And they all condemned him as deserving death. (Mark 14:55, 61–64)

3:00 to 5:30 a.m. — beatings beneath the home of Caiaphas
And some began to spit on him, and to cover his face, and to strike him, saying to him, "Prophesy!" And the guards received him with blows. (Mark 14:65)

Then they spat in his face, and struck him; and some slapped him, saying, "Prophesy to us, you Christ! Who is it that struck you?" (Matthew 26:67–68)

Now the men who were holding Jesus mocked him and beat him; they also blindfolded him and asked him, "Prophesy! Who is it that struck you?" And they spoke many other words against him, reviling him. (Luke 22:63–65)

Now Simon Peter was standing and warming himself. They said to him, "Are not you also one of his disciples?" He denied it and said, "I am not." One of the servants of the high priest, a kinsman of the man whose ear Peter had cut off, asked, "Did I not see you in the garden with him?" Peter again denied it; and at once the cock crowed.

(John 18:25–27)

6:30 a.m. (sunrise) — arrival at Sanhedrin meeting chamber in the Temple

When morning came, all the chief priests and the elders of the people took counsel against Jesus to put him to death. (Matthew 27:1)

When day came, the assembly of the elders of the people gathered together, both chief priests and scribes; and they led him away to their council. ... And they all said, "Are you the Son of God, then?" And he said to them, "You say that I am." And they said, "What further testimony do we need? We have heard it ourselves from his own lips." (Luke 22:66, 70–71)

How did the soldiers know where to find Jesus? With perhaps 180,000 people swelling the area of Jerusalem,[1] there were not enough inns to house all the people. Certainly, many of these pilgrims were sleeping under the stars, including on the Mount of Olives. Amidst all those people in the dark (although there would have been a nearly full moon that night[2] to shed some light), the soldiers went right to Jesus. Judas led them there. He knew where he had spent nights with Jesus and the other apostles in the past, and he knew that it would have been too late, after the Last Supper, for Jesus to return the six miles to Bethany, where he had spent the previous four nights, presumably with his friends Mary, Martha, and Lazarus.

Following his arrest in the Garden of Gethsemane, Jesus was bound and taken down the Mount of Olives and through the Kidron Valley to the home of Annas, where he was struck by an officer. While Annas had been appointed high priest of the newly named Roman province of Judea in AD 6, he had been deposed ten years later by the prefect Gratus.[3] Though removed from office, he remained influential both politically and socially.

Annas then sent Jesus bound to the home of his son-in-law

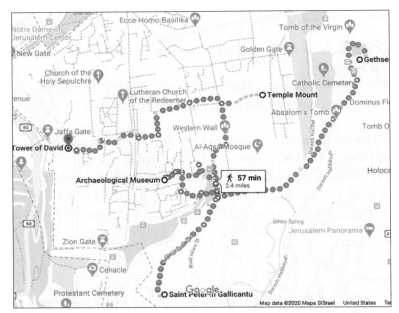

Nighttime travels of Jesus, from midnight to early morning on Good Friday. Jesus traveled from Gethsemane to the house of Annas (thought to be near today's Wohl Archaeological Museum), then to the house of Caiaphas (identified today with Saint Peter in Gallicantu Monastery). At sunrise he journeyed to the Chamber of Hewn Stones in the Temple to face the assembled Sanhedrin, and from there to Pontius Pilate at Herod's Palace complex (today's Tower of David Museum complex).

Caiaphas, the current high priest, where he was vigorously beaten during the night. Finally, Jesus greeted the sunrise on his way to the meeting chamber of the Sanhedrin at the Temple. In all, he walked 2.4 miles on dark, uneven, hilly terrain while bound and sleepless, hungry, and thirsty. And when the sun rose, with a temperature in the mid-40s Fahrenheit, he had lost yet more fluid through his nocturnal torture. Not only that, but while he was being tortured, his handpicked successor denied he even knew him.

During my first trip to Jerusalem in 2014, I was unaware of the traditional location of the beatings that occurred during the night after Jesus' questioning by Caiaphas. Saint Peter in Gallicantu (Latin

ABOVE: View from the Mount of Olives (the Garden of Gethsemane), showing locations of the Upper Room, the likely location of the Last Supper (red arrow), and Saint Peter in Gallicantu Monastery, location of the house of Caiaphas and the Sacred Pit (yellow arrow). (Thomas W. McGovern)

LEFT: Saint Peter in Gallicantu Monastery. (Thomas W. McGovern)

for "cockcrow") is a French Dominican monastery built over the site of what is believed to have been the home of Caiaphas, with its subterranean pit where Jesus was tortured by Caiaphas's soldiers. This dungeon is known today as the Sacred Pit.

While it is not definitively the house of Caiaphas, there is pilgrim testimony going back to AD 333 that the site of Saint Peter in Gallicantu was venerated by pilgrims and local Christians as the site where Jesus received his beatings in the early hours of Good Friday. No other site has stronger evidence. On the outside of the church, there is a mosaic that depicts Christ being trussed up by ropes to lower him down some thirty feet into the Sacred Pit. It is thought that he spent the night in this pit after being beaten and (as we shall see) perhaps even flayed.

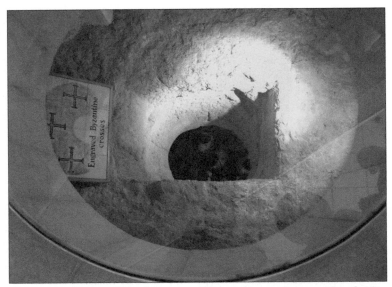

Entrance to the Sacred Pit with engraved Byzantine crosses venerating the site. (Thomas W. McGovern)

One of the many cells where prisoners were presumably tied while held and/or beaten beneath the house of Caiaphas. Note ropes at locations where prisoners were thought to be fixed. (Thomas W. McGovern)

Claims

In reviewing other works on the Passion of Christ, I found no claims regarding the events of midnight to 6:00 a.m. on Good Friday that needed adjusting in light of the evidence that I have uncovered. In this chapter, I want to share insights I gathered during my trips to Saint Peter in Gallicantu and reflect on what others have written about what may have happened to Jesus during that time. (This chapter requires no section called "Response to Claims.")

Medical Analysis

During the night, perhaps from midnight to 6:00 a.m. on Good Friday, the Gospels tell us that Jesus suffered various forms of physical abuse. He was struck (Greek, *rhapisma*)

Mosaic depiction on the outer wall of Saint Peter in Gallicantu. The image shows Jesus in a truss, which may have been used to lower him into the Sacred Pit beneath the house of Caiaphas. Note: Caption on the bottom right of the mosaic reads "Ps 87." This is the numbering in the Douay-Rheims, equivalent to Psalm 88 in other translations of Scripture. The French quotation means "They put me in a deep pit" (Ps 88:6). (Thomas W. McGovern)

by the hand of an officer at the home of Annas (see Jn 18:22). According to Mark 14:65 guards spit upon, blindfolded, struck, and showered blows on Jesus. Matthew 26:67 attests that Jesus was spit upon, struck, and slapped, while Luke 22:63–64 writes that he was beaten, blindfolded, and struck.

Think pragmatically about the guards. Most likely, they had been awake all day just like Jesus. Now, instead of going home to sleep, they have to stay up all night with this prisoner. It would not be surprising that they would take out their frustration on their prisoner rather than on their employer, the high priest. (Reflect on how much suffering we cause to others when we take our frustrations out on those who don't deserve it.)

Various Greek words are used in Scripture to describe Jesus' torture. The Greek *rhapisma* or *rhapizo* is translated in Matthew as "slapped"; in Mark as "received with blows"; and in John as "struck with his hand." According to *Strong's Concordance*, these words can also mean "to strike with a rod."[4] Although *rhapisma* and *rhapizo* possess this alternate meaning, all Bible translations I have found use the term to refer to slapping the face with the palm of an open hand.

The Greek word *kolaphizo* is translated in Matthew and Mark as "struck" and means to brutally strike with fists and treat with excessive force. Two different Greek words are translated as "struck" in Luke 22:64. The first, *paio*, means to strike or smite with a fist. The second, *typto*, also means to beat, strike, or smite. All three Synoptic Gospel writers tell us that Jesus was slapped and punched.

Does Luke Tell Us Something Extra?

As a bonus, though, Luke, the detail-oriented physician (for he told Theophilus how he wrote an orderly and accurate account for him [see Lk 1:1–4]), uses another word for Jesus' nighttime terror (22:63). As a dermatologist, I am impressed that Luke now brings up a second dermatologic detail about Christ's suffering. (The first was the sweat falling like drops of blood.) The word translated "beaten" is the Greek *derontes*, which comes from the same root — *der* — as derma, meaning skin (think "dermatologist" and "dermatitis"). *Derontes* primarily means to "flay the skin" and has a secondary meaning of "to beat." Since Matthew and Mark mention Jesus' being punched and slapped in the face, and since Luke also mentions this, Luke's use of this additional term *derontes* may indeed refer to something different.

Derivatives of this Greek word are used a total of eighteen times in the New Testament, as when Mark applies it to one of the punishments the wicked vineyard tenants mete out to representatives of the vineyard owner (see Mk 12:5) just before the owner sends his son. Forms of the *der* root are variously translated as "beat," "flog," "hit," "smite," and "strike," as in the treatment of the servants of the vineyard owner in the parable (Mt 21:35; Mk 12:3; Lk 20:10); the punishment of the unfaithful servants (Lk 12:47–48); and the beating of the apostles by the high priest and Sanhedrin (Acts 5:40). The commentary for Acts 5:40 in the Navarre Bible New Testament[5] refers to the punishment the apostles received (deirantes) as a Jewish scourging or flogging.

Vine's Expository Dictionary of New Testament Words states that *dero* means "primarily to flay, then to beat, thrash or smite." The entry goes on to say that "the significance of flogging does not always attach to the word [*dero*]," since derivatives of *dero* can refer to receiving a single blow rather than a series of blows. "The usual meaning is that of 'thrashing or cudgelling' [to hit with a short, thick stick], and when used of a blow it indicates one of great violence."[6]

According to the *Liddell-Scott-Jones Greek-English Lexicon*, *dero* could mean "to skin or flay an animal" or colloquially "to cudgel or thrash" a person.[7] *The Greek English Lexicon of the New Testament and Early Christian Literature* (BDAG) says that derivatives of *der* literally mean "skin, flay," but since the time of Aristophanes (446–386 BC) it has referred to "beat" or "whip" — significant damage to the skin, but not to actual removal of the skin.

There is a tradition still carried on in Jerusalem that there were two scourging pillars used for torturing Jesus: one used during the night below the home of Caiaphas and the one mentioned in the Gospels in or near the praetorium of Pontius Pilate (recently identified as Herod the Great's Palace near the current Tower of David in the Western portion of the Old City of Jerusalem — but more on that later). The former post resides in the Crusader-era Roman Catholic Chapel of the Apparition of Jesus to His Mother in the Church of the Holy Sepulchre, while the other is believed to be the one venerated in the Basilica of Santa Prassede in Rome.

Jewish Flogging in Antiquity

What can we make of this Jewish "flaying" or "beating" or "thrashing" or "cudgeling"? Was it different from the scourging that Jesus received upon the order of Pilate later on Good Friday?

This nighttime torture most certainly was a different torment than that meted out by Pilate's soldiers, and it hearkens back to the Book of Deuteronomy: "If the guilty man deserves to be beaten, the judge shall cause him to lie down and be beaten in his presence with a number of stripes in proportion to his offense. Forty stripes may be given him, but not more; lest, if one should go on to beat him with more stripes than these, your brother be degraded in your sight" (Dt 25:2–3).

According to the Jewish Virtual Library, there is no record of how floggings were administered in biblical times. Sometimes victims were whipped; other times they were beaten. "More than any other punishment, flogging is a means of correction rather than retribution, and, being a substitute for capital punishment which, in the rabbinic view, every violator of God's word properly deserves, it reflects God's infinite mercy."[8] Even though

Pilgrim venerating the pillar housed in the Catholic Chapel of the Blessed Sacrament in the Church of the Holy Sepulchre. Oral tradition in the region suggests that this is the base of the pillar to which Jesus was attached during his beating beneath the house of Caiaphas. (Thomas W. McGovern)

various Old Testament books mention instruments of beating, there is no evidence that any of these were used in floggings.

Jesus had warned his disciples that they would be flogged in synagogues. (Again, flogging does not necessarily imply a whip, though that may be our modern idea.) In Mark 13:9, Jesus tells his followers, "And you will be beaten in synagogues." The evangelist uses the Greek word *daresesthe*, which is derived from the same *der* root as Luke's term *derontes*. In Matthew 10:17, Jesus uses the Greek *mastigosousin*, meaning "they will flog" or "they will scourge." This referred to strapping a victim to a pole or frame and striking him with a *mastigos*, or whip.

If indeed Jesus' skin was flayed open in the early hours of Good Friday morning, it would have become exquisitely sensitive. The alternative meanings of *derontes*, however, still suggest a vigorous beating of the body, not the face; and whatever abuse he took to his body would have grown in pain as the hours passed and the inflammatory response progressed. Bruises would have been present on all the areas of his body afflicted with the punishments of soldiers at the house of Caiaphas. While there is no evidence that his "bloody sweat" made his skin more sensitive, these beatings and repeated "stripes" received beneath the home of Caiaphas certainly did.

While I will not use the Shroud of Turin to prove any of the points I make in this book, I find that most people want to know how my findings correlate with the Shroud (which I believe is a burial cloth of Jesus Christ). In this case, the Shroud not only demonstrates evidence of wounds inflicted by a Roman flagrum, but there is also a type of wound that could have been caused by a flagellum with leather strips. (Chapter 5 has more details on the evidence from the Shroud.) Since both the Romans and the Jews may have used such a flagellum, there is no way to know when the man in the Shroud received that separate beating.

On to the Temple

Luke tells us that after spending the night at the house of Caiaphas, the elders "led him away to their council" (22:66), most likely referring to the official meeting place of the Great Sanhedrin.[9] The seventy-one members of the Sanhedrin met in the Chamber of Hewn Stones in the Temple. According to the Jewish Virtual Library, the Great Sanhedrin met during the day, which would explain why Luke says that Jesus was brought there "when day came." They did not meet on the Sabbath, during festivals, or on festival eves — yet Good Friday was a festival eve!

This council was the final authority regarding any Jewish law, though there were smaller, local sanhedrins elsewhere in Israel. While the Great Sanhedrin did not have the authority to arrest, it judged accused lawbreakers. Two witnesses were required to convict a subject, and no attorneys were present, although the accused could call his own witnesses. This is what Jesus requested when he asked, "Why do you ask me? Ask those who have heard me, what I said to them; they know what I said" (Jn 18:21). Members of the Sanhedrin would question the accused and any witnesses. The members not only heard cases dealing with religious and Temple matters, but they also judged criminal cases. In addition to trials, the Great Sanhedrin solved difficulties regarding ritual laws, drew up the annual calendar, and prepared Torah scrolls. The Great Sanhedrin did not have authority to inflict capital punishment (this authority was removed from it around the time of Jesus), and it therefore had to get permission from the Roman governor. The Great Sanhedrin ceased to exist after the Temple was destroyed in AD 70.

Medical Conclusions

By the time the Jews handed Jesus over to Pilate, Jesus had lost an unknown amount of blood and sweat, beginning during his agony in Gethsemane. He had then been vigorously beaten by the guards who arrested him in the garden and who watched him overnight. By the time he reached Pilate early on Good Friday morning, he was exhausted and thirsty and had developed many tender areas of bruising and swelling on his face and body. His subsequent punishments would be magnified because the skin and soft tissues were inflamed and full of chemicals that mediate pain to the nervous system.

Christ's Life, Full of Suffering from Beginning to End

Today, pilgrims can descend steps into the pit where tradition holds that Jesus spent a painful, lonely night during and after his beatings. In the pit is a lectern, and Psalm 88 is printed on the lectern in many languages. Imagine being with Jesus in that pit as you reflect on the first eight verses of this psalm:

> O LORD, my God, I call for help by day;
> I cry out in the night before you.
>
> Let my prayer come before you,
> incline your ear to my cry!
>
> For my soul is full of troubles,
> and my life draws near to Sheol.
> I am reckoned among those who go down to the Pit;
>
> I am a man who has no strength,
> like one forsaken among the dead,
> like the slain that lie in the grave,
> like those whom you remember no more,
> for they are cut off from your hand.
>
> You have put me in the depths of the Pit,
> in the regions dark and deep.
>
> Your wrath lies heavy upon me,
> and you overwhelm me with all your waves.
>
> You have caused my companions to shun me;
> You have made me a thing of horror to them.
> I am shut in so that I cannot escape.

Such lonely suffering in the pit for hours before sunrise on Good Friday surely seemed meaningless to the guards who were beating Jesus. And Jesus himself certainly felt the Father's wrath lying heavy upon him as he took on the sins of all mankind — past, present, and future. Moreover, the very people who were supposed to protect, interpret, and promote the law and teachings of God were the very ones allowing God to be tortured!

Yet Christ's Passion was not his first experience with suffering. In fact, from what we know of his early private life, he seemed to suffer quite a bit, as did those closest to him:

- His very conception brought moral anguish to Joseph.
- The journey to his birthplace required a difficult journey for Mary.
- His birth took place in a cave without comforts.
- He had to flee as an infant to avoid slaughter by Herod.
- He had to live in Egypt as a young child for years until the threat of Herod the Great had passed.

And yet, when we pray the Rosary and consider these very events, what do we call them? The Joyful Mysteries! If such events happened in our own lives, "joyful" might be the last word we would use to describe them.

Furthermore, in his public life, Christ immersed himself in the sufferings of others:

- He healed the sick.
- He consoled the afflicted.
- He fed the hungry.
- He freed people from deafness, muteness, blindness, leprosy, and the devil.
- He restored the dead to life.
- He granted forgiveness of sins to those suffering in spirit due to their sins.
- He addressed his most famous sermon, the Beatitudes, to those suffering in various ways (due to poverty, affliction, insults, persecutions, hunger, etc.).

John Paul II writes, "Precisely by means of this suffering he must bring it about 'that man should not perish, but have eternal life.'"[10] Jesus could walk toward the cross because he knew that the suffering of his infinite love would have infinite power to redeem.

When Christ prophesied his own execution, Peter tried to prevent it (see Mt 16:22). When Christ was arrested in Gethsemane, Peter drew his sword (Jn 18:10). Both times, Christ told Peter that he must undergo this suffering. This type of sacrifice is beyond human experience and understanding. Thus, even Peter, one of Christ's inner circle, could not fathom it. Christ realized that his suffering had saving power; Peter did not yet realize it, but he would when enlightened by the Holy Spirit at Pentecost. Then he would realize that Christ suffered out of his love for the Father and for us. In his first sermon on Pentecost, Peter said that "whoever calls on the name of the Lord shall be saved" (Acts 2:21) because he "loved me and gave himself for me" (Gal 2:20).

CHAPTER 5

Scourging

Date: Good Friday, April 3, AD 33
Time: Late morning
Place: The praetorium — Herod's Palace near the Jaffa Gate, western side of the walled city of Old Jerusalem in the Tower of David complex

---

Gospel Narrative

Pilate then called together the chief priests and the rulers and the people, and said to them. ... "Behold, nothing deserving death has been done by him; **I will therefore chastise him and release him.**" (Luke 23:13, 15–16, emphasis added)

And Pilate again said to them, "Then what shall I do with the man whom you call the King of the Jews?" And they cried out again, "Crucify him." And Pilate said to them, "Why, what evil has he done?" But they shouted all the more, "Crucify him." So Pilate, wishing to satisfy the crowd, released for them Barabbas; and **having scourged Jesus**, he delivered him to be crucified. And the soldiers led him away inside the

palace (that is, the praetorium); and they called together the whole battalion. (Mark 15:12–16, emphasis added)

Early on Good Friday morning, after a brutally painful, sleepless night, a bound Jesus was brought about half a mile (800 meters) from the Temple's Chamber of Hewn Stones to Herod's Palace. The palace is where Pontius Pilate stayed when he traveled from the Mediterranean coast of Judea to Jerusalem to help keep the peace as the population swelled during Jewish feasts.[1]

This location is not where pilgrims today begin the Way of the Cross near the Church of the Flagellation. Instead, it is located on the west side of the Old City of Jerusalem near the Jaffa Gate and the Tower of David, about a quarter of a mile (400 meters) from Calvary.

Jesus was likely scourged outside Herod's Palace in a public place, for Roman punishment was meant to be seen by as many people as possible in order to deter further crime. His clothing was removed, and he was fixed naked to a pole or column during the scourging. (Some victims were simply thrown on the ground and scourged in that position. However, while the Gospels do not tell us Jesus' position during his scourging, the Church has an ancient oral tradition that a pillar was used.)

Claims

Here are three claims that I used to repeat during presentations on the Passion. The bolded words refer to areas where I have found support for a different understanding:

> We already know what the instrument of torture was like, the Roman 'flagrum,' the thongs of which had two balls of lead or a **small bone, the 'talus' of a sheep**, at some distance from their end.[2]

Since permission for an execution had to come from the

governing Romans, Jesus was taken early in the morning by the Temple officials to the Praetorium of the **Fortress of Antonia**, the residence and governmental seat of Pontius Pilate, the procurator of Judea.[3]

A flagrum found in the ruins of **Pompeii** consisted of three separate cords of leather tied together to a handle. Tied to these leather strips were sharp objects, such as **sharp bones, stones, glass, metal objects**, anything that would cut deep into tissue.[4]

The Praetorium

According to the Gospels (see Mt 27:27, Mk 15:16, Jn 19:9), the trial and scourging of Jesus took place in and adjacent to the praetorium (Greek, *praitorion*). The Jewish leaders came early on Good Friday morning to the praetorium (Jn 18:28) to present their case to Pilate, since Jews did not have the right to administer the death penalty. They conveniently changed their charge against Jesus from blasphemy (Mt 26:65) to sedition (rebellion against the government), by saying that Jesus claimed to be the King of the Jews, thus threatening Roman authority (Lk 23:2–3).

The word "praetorium" referred to both "an ancient Roman general's tent in a camp" and "the official residence of an ancient Roman governor," which would often be "a splendid country seat or a palatial residence."[5] The Way of the Cross that Christians have commemorated in Jerusalem since the sixteenth century begins in Jerusalem at the Franciscan Monastery of the Flagellation, located where, in Jesus' time, the Fortress of Antonia was attached to the Temple. From the fortress, some of the temporarily-deployed Roman soldiers could keep an eye on pilgrims overflowing the Temple during major Jewish feasts (such as Passover, when tens of thousands of pilgrims might be present.)[6]

However, Thayer's Greek Lexicon says that the praetorium was "the palace in which the governor or procurator of a province resided, to which use the Romans were accustomed to appropriate the

Exterior of the Franciscan Monastery of the Flagellation. This site, which marks the beginning of the modern Stations of the Cross in Jerusalem, is where Christians in the Middle Ages believed that the flagellation (scourging) took place. At that time, it was thought that Pilate would have judged and scourged Jesus at the Fortress of Antonia. That has now been demonstrated to be false. (Thomas W. McGovern)

Franciscan Monastery of the Flagellation, interior. (Thomas W. McGovern)

palaces already existing, and formerly dwelt in by kings or princes; at Jerusalem it was a magnificent palace which Herod the Great had built for himself, and which the Roman procurators seemed to have occupied whenever they came from Caesarea to Jerusalem to transact public business."[7] Therefore, even in the nineteenth century, biblical scholars came to understand that the traditional site of the trial before Pilate and the scourging was contradicted by the evidence of history and archaeology.

According to Dominican priest and biblical scholar Jerome Murphy-O'Connor, author of an archaeological guide to the Holy Land, the Antonia Fortress internally measured roughly 112 by 32 meters (or about 36,000 square feet).[8] That's enough room for a small garrison, but not a Roman legion (4,000 to 6,000 soldiers) as some have supposed. The fortress had a single watchtower that overlooked the Temple and connected directly to it. Murphy-O'Connor doubts the Antonia could have held even a cohort (480 soldiers) let alone a legion. And he says it would not have been considered a palace.

Murphy-O'Connor writes that Herod's Palace, as a luxurious and large complex of buildings, would have been where the governor and his large retinue would stay when in town. It is unlikely that Pilate would have stayed in the smaller military structure at the Fortress of Antonia near the Temple and let his second in command (Herod Antipas) occupy the best residence. According to Shimon Gibson, archaeological excavations show that the Antonia "Fortress" was not even a barracks; in reality it was no more than a watchtower.[9]

Philo of Alexandria (c. 20 BC–c. AD 50), a contemporary of Pilate, calls the palace of Herod the Great "the house of the procurators." He places Pilate at the palace shortly after his arrival in Judea in 26,[10] when he placed gilt shields bearing his name and the emperor's name facing outward on its walls.[11] When the Jews protested, the emperor had the shields removed to Caesarea Maritima, the seaside permanent home of Pilate.[12] It was from this same palace, between 64 and 66, that one of Pilate's successors, the procurator Gessius Florus, ordered many Jerusalem citizens scourged and crucified for mocking him.[13] Thus, Roman governors in Jerusalem were at Herod's Palace both before and after the year of the crucifixion.

You will note that Pilate is referred to as both a "governor" and a "procurator." "Prefect" was his official title, referring to the administrative governor of a region. Claudius, the second emperor after Tiberius, later changed the title from "prefect" to "procurator." Any of these titles can be used to describe Pilate's role during the time of the Gospels.

In 1999–2000, the foundation stones of Herod's Palace were uncovered in Jerusalem in the Tower of David complex, found in the western section of Jerusalem's Old City near the Jaffa Gate. Visitors may now tour the excavations that revealed these walls through the Tower of David Museum of the History of Jerusalem.[14] The museum holds an English-language tour of this area every Friday at 10:00 a.m.; it is called the "Kishle Tour" because these foundation stones were found beneath the Ottoman-era prison known as the Kishle.

TOP: Archaeologic excavation at site of Herod's Palace Complex in Jerusalem. View from ground-level entrance. Upper-level walls were constructed as part of the Kishle, a Turkish prison. The foundation stones of Herod's Palace were found beneath the Kishle. (Thomas W. McGovern)

MIDDLE: Foundation stones of Herod's Palace. There are multiple layers of foundation underground. (Thomas W. McGovern)

BOTTOM: Foundation stones of Herod's Palace, digging deeper underground. (Thomas W. McGovern)

Although it is not a religious site, one can experience a profound meditation there regarding the ill treatment of Jesus before Pilate — the scourging and the royal mocking.

The museum's tremendously detailed scale reconstruction of Jerusalem at the time of Jesus provides a reasonable estimate of the appearance of Herod's Palace as a complex of many buildings.

Location of the Ottoman Turkish prison known as the Kishle, beneath which the foundation stones of Herod's Palace have been found. Map shows relative locations of the Jaffa Gate, the Kishle (with red marker and Hebrew writing), and the Church of the Holy Sepulchre.

Therefore, it is easy to see how Pilate could have sent Jesus to Herod (see Lk 23:7) without Jesus' having to travel far. Herod Antipas was most likely staying in one of the other buildings within the complex that his father, Herod the Great, had built.

The Gospels also provide a clue to the location of Jesus' trial and scourging. In Mark 15:16, the New Revised Standard Version translates the Greek word *aule* as "palace," and no one would mistake a small military watchtower (such as the Fortress of Antonia) for a palace. Father Raymond Brown, in his tome *The Death of the Messiah*, postulates that the scene described in Matthew (see 27:27) and Mark (15:16) occurred "in the courtyard inside a palace, a place large enough to gather a whole body of troops."[15] In fact, Father Brown writes in a footnote, "The use of *aule* [in Mk 15:16] for the Roman locale may help to confirm that the tradition envisaged the Herodian Palace rather than the Fortress Antonia as the site of the Praetorium since Josephus uses *aule* for the former but *phrourion* or *pyrgos* for the latter."[16]

Matthew's Gospel provides one final piece of evidence that the

A 1:50 scale model of Jerusalem as it was thought to appear at the time of Christ. Herod's Palace complex of multiple buildings can be seen on the upper left where the orange-roofed buildings and three towers are located near the western wall of the city. (Thomas W. McGovern)

Closer view of the complex, taken from the left side of Herod's Palace from towers at the left. (Thomas W. McGovern)

Fortress of Antonia was not the praetorium: "Besides, while [Pilate] was sitting on the judgment seat, his wife sent word to him, 'Have nothing to do with that righteous man, for I have suffered much over him today in a dream'" (27:19). This strongly suggests that Pilate's wife was nearby, and there would be no reason to believe that when in Jerusalem, especially early on a Friday morning, his wife would be anywhere other than at the palace complex, let alone in a small military barracks and observation tower like the Antonia Fortress. (This passage is also warning to us husbands to listen to our wives!)

Scourging in Ancient History

Articles and books describing crucifixion state that scourging was routinely performed prior to crucifixion. William D. Edwards, Wesley J. Gabel, and Floyd E. Hosmer write the following in their 1986 article "On the Physical Death of Jesus Christ": "Flogging was a legal preliminary to every Roman execution, and only women and Roman senators or soldiers (except in cases of desertion) were exempt. The usual instrument was a short whip (flagellum) with several single or braided leather thongs of variable lengths, in which small iron balls or sharp pieces of sheep bones were tied at intervals."[17]

How accurate is this passage from Edwards et al.'s oft-quoted article? The quote references two books: Dr. Barbet's *A Doctor at Calvary* and Martin Hengel's 1977 book *Crucifixion: In the Ancient World and the Folly of the Message of the Cross*.[18]

First, Edwards et al. use the term "flogging." In ancient times, flogging was not only a Roman punishment but also a Jewish one. The Bible tells us precious little about Jesus' scourging; presumably, the readers of the Gospels were familiar enough with the punishment. Mark (15:15) and Matthew (27:26) use the term *phragellosas*, meaning "scourged." John (19:1) uses *emastigosen*, which can also mean "scourged," "whipped," or "chastised." Luke (23:16, 22) merely says that Pilate wanted Jesus "chastised" (*paideuo*) as a criminal who needed to be taught a lesson. In fact, only from Luke, the ever-careful physician, do we learn that Pilate meant the scourging to be Jesus' entire punishment: "A third time he said to them, 'Why, what evil has he done? I have found in him no crime deserving death; I will therefore chastise him and release him'" (23:22).

According to Father Raymond Brown, the Romans employed three types of flesh-beating corporal punishments.[19] They are listed here in order of severity from mildest to most severe:

- *Fustigatio* (beating). This chastisement constituted punishment for lesser crimes and served as a warning to teach the one punished not to cause further trouble. This is the type of punishment that Luke alludes to when he writes that Pilate said, "I will therefore chastise him and release him."
- *Flagellatio* (flogging). This chastisement bordered on inquisitional torture and was used to extract information from a prisoner to get him to confess. It could also be used preceding crucifixion.
- *Verberatio* (scourging). This chastisement was the typical prelude to crucifixion. It added to the suffering of

the condemned and enabled executioners to control how long the condemned would survive on the cross. Father Brown says that this is the punishment that Matthew and Mark mention in their Gospels.

Scourging before the Time of Christ

There are reliable ancient sources that describe scourging (*verberatio*) as early as the Etruscan era (eighth to third century BC) and the time of Plato and Xenophon (fourth century BC). Slaves and foreigners were the most common victims of scourging.

The earliest reported episode of scourging as an antecedent to crucifixion comes from the Greek historian Dionysius of Halicarnassus (first century BC), who writes about an event around 500 BC: "When the plot was revealed, the ringleaders were arrested and after being scourged [*mastixi*] were led away to be crucified [to crosses]."[20]

The Greek historian Xenophon (c. 430–354 BC) writes of an event around 400 BC in which one Cinadon "was straightway bound fast, neck and arms, in a collar, and under scourge (*mastigoumenos*) and goad was dragged about through the city and those with him. And so they met their punishment."[21]

Plato (428–348 BC) writes in his *Laws*:

> If he thinks that some stranger has struck him out of wantonness or insolence, and ought to be punished, he shall take him to the wardens of the city, but let him not strike him, that the stranger may be kept far away from the possibility of lifting up his hand against a citizen, and let the wardens of the city take the offender and examine him, not forgetting their duty to the God of Strangers, and in case the stranger appears to have struck the citizen unjustly, let them inflict upon him as many blows with the scourge [*mastigōsas*] as he has himself inflicted, and quell his presumption.[22]

The Greek mastigōsas used here by Plato has the same root as the word used in the Gospels to describe Jesus' punishment.

Flavius Josephus (c. AD 37–100) describes the persecution of the Jews by the Seleucid king Antiochus IV (Epiphanes), who forced Hellenistic religion upon the Jewish homeland. In 167 BC, Antiochus had his troops enter Palestine, and this attack led to the Maccabean Revolt described in the Old Testament books of 1 and 2 Maccabees. Josephus records: "Indeed, they were scourged [*masti-goumenoi*] and their bodies maltreated; while still alive and breathing they were crucified; and their wives and their children, whom they had circumcised against the policy of the king, they strangled by hanging them from the necks of their crucified parents."[23]

Marcus Tullius Cicero (106–43 BC) wrote *Against Verres* about a corrupt governor of Sicily who switched sides in a civil war waged in 88–87 BC. Cicero reports how Verres had a Roman citizen (Publius Gavius) scourged and crucified without a trial. In Cicero's description, Verres says: "What follows next? Scourgings [*verbera*], and burnings, and all those extreme agonies which are part of the punishment of condemned criminals, and which strike terror into the rest, torture and the cross?"[24]

Titus Livius ("Livy," 59 BC–AD 17) wrote about the Punic Wars (264–146 BC) between Carthage and Rome. During the Second Punic War (218–201 BC), the Carthaginian general Hannibal (famous for taking African war elephants through the Alps) had a guide crucified for taking his army to the wrong destination. Livy records: "And only when the guide had answered that he should lodge that night in Casilinum, did he perceive at last how the man had blundered, and that Casinum lay far off in another direction. Whereupon he scourged [*virgisque*] the guide, and, to terrify the others, crucified him [raised him to a cross]."[25] Livy uses the word *virgisque*, from *virgis*, from which we get virga, which was one of the lesser implements for inflicting the form of flogging known as *flagellatio*, or flagellation.

Livy also records that in 206 BC, Hannibal's brother Mago attempted to enter the city of Cadiz and complained that the gates were shut against him. He ordered the highest-ranking magistrates of the Phoenicians (Carthaginians) to a conference where he "ordered them to be scourged [*verberibus*] and crucified."[26] In this section, Livy uses the word *verberibus*, related to *verbera*, used by Cicero above. The Latin *verberare* means "to scourge." The English word "reverberation" is derived from this Latin term and gives us some indication of the recoil produced on the internal organs when *verberatio* was inflicted. This relates to the most severe of the three types of corporal punishment inflicted by the Romans.[27]

Livy also describes a 196 BC slave revolt put down by Manius Acilius Glabrio. The punishment meted out on the revolting slaves was this: "The ringleaders were scourged and crucified; the others sent back to their masters."[28]

The Lex Puteolana

Written evidence from the time of Jesus reveals that torture was not only carried out but actually regulated under the Roman state. A stone inscription, found in the modern Italian town of Pozzuoli (ancient Puteoli) just west of Naples, from the time of Augustus Caesar (who ruled from 27 BC to AD 14), details regulations for the hiring of people to torture or execute slaves, whether by court order or in response to an owner's request. These regulations are known as the Lex Puteolana (Law of Puteoli).

The inscription was found in three pieces between August 1955 and January 1957 in the public forum of Puteoli, with the heading "On the Public Undertaking Concession." This is the best example yet found of Roman law regulating scourging and crucifixion. While it contains no diagrams and far fewer details than we would like, this law sheds light on the ancient practice of capital punishment in Rome. We will delve more deeply into the Lex in chapter 7 and in appendix 2. However, one section of the Lex mentions the floggers (*verberatores*): "If [the private person] wants a *patibulum* put on the cross, the contractor has to furnish the cross-beam, posts, ties, ropes for the floggers as well as the floggers [*verberatores*]."[29]

Scourging during the Time of Christ

Lucius Annaeus Seneca (a.k.a. Seneca the Younger, c. 4 BC–AD 65) was a famous stoic philosopher and advisor to Emperor Nero. With Flavius Josephus, he furnishes some of the most vivid images of Roman crucifixion practice at the time of Christ. In his effort to provide solace to Marcia on the loss of her son ("On Consolation to Marcia"), he includes this passage: "I see crosses [*cruces*] there, not indeed of a single kind but different constructions by different people. Some had suspended their victims with the head toward the ground, others had driven stipes through the private parts of the victims, others had spread out their arms on a cross bar [*patibulum*]. I see cords, I see scourges [*verbera*], and for each limb and joint there is an engine of torture."[30]

First-century Jewish scholar and historian Flavius Josephus was born in Jerusalem and fought against the Romans until AD 67. After surrendering to Vespasian and becoming his slave, he was later freed in 69, assumed the emperor's family name of Flavius, and was granted Roman citizenship. He gives us the most details of the war in which Rome destroyed Jerusalem. His two greatest works are *The Jewish War* and *The Antiquities of the Jews*. He wrote in his mother tongue of Aramaic, but only Greek translations (probably overseen by Josephus) survive today.

Josephus writes that in AD 66, a Roman procurator, Gessius Florus, crucified individuals in an unruly crowd who had insulted him for pillaging the Temple treasury:

> Florus … had them first scourged [*mastixin*] and then crucified. The total number of that day's victims, including women and children, for even infancy received no quarter, amounted to about 630. The calamity was aggravated by the unprecedented character of the Romans' cruelty. For Florus ventured that day to do what none had ever done before, namely, to scourge before his tribunal and nail to the cross men of equestrian rank, men who, if Jews by birth, were at least invested with that Roman dignity.[31]

Josephus also relays the following episode from April or May of AD 70, when General Titus caught deserters from his army who were desperate to find food during the Siege of Jerusalem: "After they were accordingly scourged [*mastigoumenoi*] and subjected to torture of every description before death, they were crucified opposite the walls … that the spectacle might perhaps induce the Jews to surrender."[32]

The Greek word *mastixin* used in the first quote from Josephus means "by scourging" and is the same word used in Acts 22:24–25, which was probably written within a few years of the writing of *The Wars of the Jews*. The passage from Acts reads: "The tribune commanded [Paul] to be brought into the barracks, and ordered him to be examined by scourging [*mastixin*], to find out why they shouted thus against him. But when they had tied him up with the thongs, Paul said to the centurion who was standing by, 'Is it lawful for you to scourge a man who is a Roman citizen, and uncondemned?'"

Remember, John uses a word from the same root (*emastigosen*) to describe Jesus' scourging, although Matthew and Mark use a different word, meaning "flogged" (*phragellosas*).

From these biblical passages and from Josephus, we see that multiple words were used to refer to punishments involving whipping. In Luke (23:16), Pilate says that he plans to "chastise" Jesus and release him, referring to the mildest form of such punishment (*fustigatio*). Matthew and Mark refer to a type of flogging that can be translated as "scourged" or "flogged." In the above passage from Acts, Luke apparently refers to *flagellatio*, since it was to be used to extract information from a prisoner. We also learn from Acts 22:25 that Roman citizens were not to be whipped, flogged, or scourged without having been properly tried and found guilty.

Scourging Implements

Multiple types of scourging implements were used, depending on the degree of harm intended.

For less severe punishments, various types of flagella, such as the virga, were used. The virga was a small rod of elm or birch carried by lictors (bodyguards for magistrates in the Roman Empire) as a sign of their judicial authority. When used to its full extent, a virga in the hand of a lictor could kill a man. Cicero says that rods (*virgae*) were prepared for Gavius's scourging.[33]

In his *History of Rome*, Livy writes that Romulus instituted lictors, twelve attendants to the king. These lictors were usually lower-class, free-born Roman citizens. Romulus borrowed the idea from the Etruscans (eighth to third century BC).[34] The purpose of lictors was to increase the dignity of the king in the eyes of his subjects. Each lictor carried fasces, an axe bound with red thongs to a bundle of elm or birch rods (*virgae*), which served as a sign of the king's absolute power to seize and punish criminals. Not only did the king have lictors during the Republic and the Roman Empire, but impe-

Proposed model of scourging implement at the Shroud of Turin Exhibit, Notre Dame Center of Jerusalem. (Thomas W. McGovern)

rial magistrates (consul, proconsul, praetor, military tribune, dictator) also had them — both inside and outside of Rome.

Other flagella included the *scorpio* (a virga with nubby ends and quills that could inflict deep wounds) and the "Spanish cord," which had a handle with several leather straps attached.

The most severe beating (*verberatio*) was performed with the dreaded flagrum. Sometimes the flagrum is considered to have been the deadliest form of flagellum, but in the strict etymological sense, flagellum is the diminutive form of flagrum. The primary difference between a flagellum and a flagrum is that the end of the flagrum was fortified with lead or bone that could beat and rip flesh.

While the flagrum was the instrument usually associated with *verberatio*, this was only the case for slaves or foreigners: "In the case of slaves, the rule is observed that they are punished after the fashion of people of low rank. For the same reason that freeborn person is beaten with rods [*fustibus* — knobbed stick, cudgel, staff, club], a slave is ordered to be beaten with lashes [*flagellis* — whips, diminutive of flagrum] and returned to his/her master."[35]

The *Theodosian Code* that compiled all the laws of the Roman Empire from AD 312 to 429 includes talk of a lead-tipped scourge — *plumbatarum*, meaning "lead ball": "In that case the manager of the estate should be chastised with a lead-tipped scourge and consigned to perpetual labor in the mines. The leaseholder or chief-tenant was to be deported."[36]

Fasces that include a bundle of virgae (sticks), which could be used to whip or beat criminals, surrounding an axe. Here the fasces are held in a lion's mouth at Sheldonian Theatre, Oxford, England. (BabelStone, CC BY-SA 3.0)

The fourth-century Christian poet Prudentius, who lived in Spain, writes about a lead-tipped scourge:

> Let his back be beaten with many strokes, and his shoulders swell up with the blows of the leaded lash [*plumboque*] …
> So the martyr received that hail of blows.
> Amid the leaded strokes [*ictus plumbeos*] he voiced a hymn.[37]

Evidence from Archaeology

While no literary references to lead-tipped scourges before the time of Christ have been found, we do have archaeological evidence of lead-tipped scourges. In an 1859 issue of the *Bulletin of the Institute of Archaeological Correspondence*, an archaeologist specializing in the Etruscan era (768–264 BC) reported the recovery of a bronze scourge made of six long, thin chains attached to a handle; each chain was tipped with a small lead ball. The Guarnacci Etruscan Museum of Volterra in Tuscany purchased such an item in 1860. Sadly, the museum no longer has this in its possession.[38]

The city of Herculaneum was buried by the same eruption of Mount Vesuvius in AD 79 that buried Pompeii. Three dictionaries of antiquities possess pictures of items from xylographies (images carved into wood and then printed) of the nineteenth century. Sadly, once again, the museums (such as the Naples National Archeological Museum) that once held these could not locate them. The museum director pointed out that they may have been filed in their archives with a nomenclature other than "scourge," "whip," or "lash," and may have even been dismembered, as many examples of twisted chains, handles, and metal knobs are present, each of which could have been part of a flagrum.[39]

Fortunately, the Vatican Museums today preserve (but do not currently display) four objects classified as bronze Roman flagella; since they are tipped with metal balls, these flagella would appropriately be called flagra. These flagra were found in catacombs and were likely the instruments of martyrdom for some of the martyrs buried in the catacombs. Note that both round and triangular ends are present on these.

Possible Scourge Marks on the Shroud of Turin

The details of the Shroud are more visible in a photographic negative of the image. On the dorsal (backside) image, from the shoulder down the backs of the legs including the naked buttocks, round marks are visible, with a narrower band between them (dumbbell-shaped). On the frontal image, similar dumbbell-shaped marks

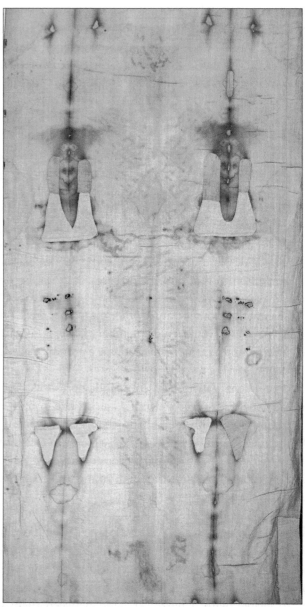

**Marks on the back of the man in the Shroud of Turin, pre-
sumed to be from scourging.**

are seen on the chest, abdomen, thighs, and legs. The head, neck, and groin are spared. Because of patches that have been sewn onto the Shroud, neither arm (shoulder to elbow) is visible. The forearms are visible on the ventral (frontside) image. Some believe that these demonstrate scourge wounds. Others (with whom I agree after viewing a 1:1 high-resolution image of the Shroud obtained from photographer Barrie Schwortz) believe that these have a different appearance, and therefore origin, from the dumbbell-shaped marks on other parts of the body.

During the Shroud of Turin Research Project study of 1978, researchers discovered that the dumbbell-shaped "scourge" marks were somewhat different from the other two types of blood images [flows and "piercings"]. Under UV fluorescence, they appear to be darker than the image and, also, to be much more sharply defined than they appear in visible light, as would be expected on the basis of the known spectral characteristics of iron porphyrin compounds. The geometric similarity of groups of these dumbbell-shaped marks is also quite striking. Fine "scratches" from the distal ends of these dumbbell-shaped marks appear in the UV-stimulated fluorescence photographs.[40]

To the naked eye, these marks have a reddish, diffuse appearance with darker spots within. However, under ultraviolet light, these marks are highly absorbing and resolve into parallel scratch-like lines in groups of three or four. According to Miller and Pellicori, the immediate areas bordering these dumbbell-shaped areas fluoresce and are consistent with the appearance of serum separating from blood.[41] The fine scratch marks are likely due to surface irregularities on the pieces of lead.

Sticky-tape samples from the different reddish-brown marks, including the dumbbell-shaped areas, reveal not only heme derivatives (suggesting presence of hemoglobin from red blood cells) but also bile pigments and albumin, major proteins found in serum (blood = serum + cells).[42] The finding of these nonheme proteins adjacent to blood images supports Dr. Pierre Barbet's contention, and Miller and Pellicori's findings, that the blood images signify

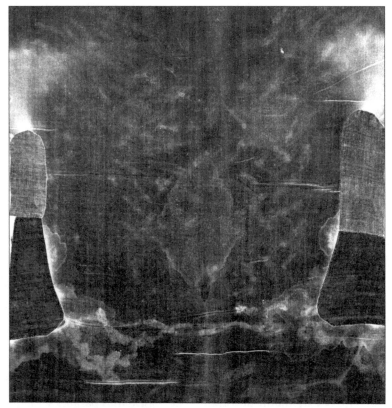

Closer view of torso on the Shroud, showing paired round marls thought to be caused by lead balls at the end of the scourging instrument.

clotted blood with "haloes" of serum that separated from the clotted cells.

Italian Shroud researchers Barbara Faccini and Giulio Fanti have proposed the presence of marks that correspond to two different types of torture instruments.[43] They count over 150 marks on the frontal (ventral) image and over 200 marks on the back (dorsal) image, which they believe are due to scourging either with a flagrum or with *virgae*. They provide a photograph of a proposed flagrum with two lead balls on each of three leather strips. Some of the Shroud images suggest two or three lead balls per leather strip, and the scratchlike images best seen under UV imaging could be due to the leather striking the skin, or even due to surface irregularities on the pieces of lead.

The most visible marks on the Shroud image that are ascribed to scourging are the dumbbell-shaped ones that appear to have been caused by small, ball-shaped, hard (metal) objects striking the skin. These are just under a third of an inch in diameter (for comparison, a standard pencil eraser is almost a quarter of an inch thick). When comparing the dumbbell-shaped marks of blood on the Shroud to scourging implements found in the catacombs, we can see that a tool existed in Rome to account for those marks on the man on the Shroud of Turin.

Other marks fit more with wounds inflicted by *virgae*. These marks on other parts of the Shroud image are covered by the dumbbell-shaped marks, indicating that they were inflicted before the scourge marks. Could these have been inflicted by the Jewish guards in the dungeon beneath the house of Caiaphas the night before? That would fit with a literal reading of Luke's (22:63) description of Jesus' beating, called *derontes* in Greek. However, there is currently no way to know with certainty. Because *virgae* were made of perishable materials, there is no ancient evidence of specific *virgae* used for torture.

Reconstructing Jesus' Scourging

Flavia Manservigi, an Italian scourging researcher, argues that we cannot know with any level of certainty in what position or with what implement Jesus was scourged. Her research has demonstrated that implements existed at the time of Jesus consistent with the marks on the Shroud of Turin. In a 2015 email to me, she wrote:

> The different words can imply a scourging with different tools, and the hypothesis that He was scourged with a flagrum is not safe; what I wanted to demonstrate with my research was that a type of scourging that could have left the marks visible on the Turin Shroud (so with flagra ending with heavy objects) was practiced in the Roman Era,

and could have been applied also [to] Jesus. Nevertheless, it is not possible to state definitely how Jesus was flogged or scourged … we can only try to do some hypothesis.[44]

The Pillar of the Scourging

Two pillars have been venerated since ancient times as those at which Christ was scourged. One pillar would have been in the Sacred Pit; the other would have been used for the scourging ordered by Pilate.

German historian Michael Hesemann believes that fourth-century pilgrims in Jerusalem venerated the pillar from the house of Caiaphas (now the site of Saint Peter in Gallicantu) as the pillar of scourging. This pillar was moved to its current location in the Church of the Holy Sepulchre in 614 after the Persians demolished the original Basilica of Saint Peter built on that spot. This pillar measures approximately 25 inches in height, but it is obviously broken at the top and could have been significantly taller. It is plausible that Jesus was tied to this pillar in the dungeon beneath the house of Caiaphas and beaten with rods such as *virgae.*[45]

Portion of a pillar venerated as the pillar at which Christ was scourged. This relic is housed in the basilica of Santa Prassede in Rome. **(Lalupa, CC BY-SA 3.0)**

In the late fourth century, a second pillar was revealed that had been hidden on Mount Zion after the Romans destroyed Jerusalem in AD 70. It was openly displayed to the public by 383.[46] It then traveled to Constantinople in 1009, was saved when Caliph Al-Hakim ordered the church housing it to be destroyed,[47] and in 1223 was transported to Rome, where it now sits in the Church of Santa Prassede. Made of Egyptian marble (Herod the Great was known to bring marble from Egypt during his building of the Temple), it measures 25 inches (63 centimeters) in height and 16 inches (40 centimeters) in diameter at the base, narrowing to 5 inches (13 centimeters) at the top. It has a place at the top where a thick, metal ring was attached to supposedly bind a prisoner.[48]

The Position of the Scourging

There is not enough evidence to reliably indicate the position that Jesus assumed during his scourging, for there is no artwork from the Roman Empire or ancient literature depicting or describing how victims were fixed to pillars during scourging. Jesus has often been pictured naked, facing a pillar with his hands tied above him and his feet barely touching the ground. However, he has also been portrayed shackled to a low pillar while bent over it, with his forearms resting on top of it.

In Acts 22:24–25, when Saint Paul is prepared to be "examined by scourging," it says that he was "tied … up with the thongs." The Greek for this passage uses the word *proteinô*, meaning to "extend before" or "stretch out," suggesting that the body was made tense for a more severe punishment that would cause a more exaggerated splitting of the skin. This reminds me, as a dermatologist, of when I tense the skin during surgery to make it easier to penetrate deeply and precisely with a scalpel. The sense of this word could refer to stretching forward over a pillar or tying up with hands up high.

The Damage of Scourging

If the Shroud of Turin truly represents Jesus, the person or persons wielding the scourge(s) (sometimes verberatores were employed on either side of the victim) never struck his upper extremities; there are no scourge marks present there. What would be the effects of *virgae* and a flagrum striking the back of a naked victim, particularly one who had been weakened by prior beating only hours before in the dungeon below the house of Caiaphas?

There was no legal limit to the amount of strokes a victim of Roman scourging could receive. Manservigi and Morini write, "In the Roman world the number of strokes that could be given was not fixed (different than the Jews); if scourging was just a punishment not connected to a death sentence, the executioners had to avoid the death of the sentenced. In the Jewish world, where the number of lashes was fixed to thirty-nine [forty minus one, in case there was a counting error] scourging could have various consequences, and they depended on the kind of tools that were used."[49]

Since we know Pilate initially meant the scourging to be Jesus' entire punishment (see Lk 23:16, 22), he would have been sure to inform the verberatores not to kill Jesus. If Jesus had been "flayed" or "flogged" with rods only hours before in the dungeon below Caiaphas's house, the flagrum would have rapidly removed the dried clots from his back, and fresh blood would have flowed quickly. The skin of Jesus' back, sides, buttocks, thighs, and legs would then have been damaged so that wheals (welts), purpura (large bruises), abrasions, lacerations, and bloody blisters formed.

While some have surmised that sheep bone fragments attached to the flagrum would have penetrated through the skin to the muscles of Jesus' back, this is unlikely. First, the flagrum was studded with sheep bone fragments only in non-Roman locations. Second, if the Shroud of Turin is the burial cloth of Christ, there is no evidence of tearing wounds. Therefore, it is unlikely that muscles would have been exposed, unless the beating with the metal balls was so severe that it turned the skin to a pulp that fell away from the muscles in areas. Nevertheless, there would have been profuse bleeding from the contused muscles, at least beneath the skin and likely through the skin to the surface in areas where the beating was most severe.

The angles of the scourge marks on the Shroud of Turin seem to make a fan pattern on the back; this could be achieved with the scourger to the side of Jesus while he was upright or bent over a low pillar. Regardless of his position, he was struck violently on the back with a metal-tipped flagrum numerous times. Then he was turned around — or perhaps flung on the ground on his back — and struck again across the front. Indescribable pain flooded Jesus' consciousness and possibly brought him to unconsciousness as he lost a significant amount of blood.

If the Shroud of Turin is the burial cloth of Christ, the image would necessarily underestimate his scourge wounds as Dr. Barbet surmised. The wounds that bled would appear in the image, but if a wound consisted only of deep contusions and bruising, it would not appear.

Physiological Effects of Scourging

Because it seems that Pilate wanted Jesus' scourging to be the full punishment, it is possible that his beating was more severe than a typical precrucifixion scourging. We know from the Gospels that Pilate was surprised (see Mk 15:44) at how soon Jesus died on the cross. Physician commentators such as Dr. Barbet and Dr. Edwards et al. believe that a very severe scourging was the main reason that Jesus lived such a short time on the cross, and they claim the reason was circulatory shock (see a more detailed discussion of shock in chapter 9).

The physical results of scourging are due to repeated blunt trauma. The skin would demonstrate widespread bruises and swelling with tissue fluid. With enough damage, shallow ulcers (open, bloody wounds) could form. After being struck repeatedly, swollen areas of skin would rupture and exude clear or bloody fluid. Blood could also pool in the muscles of the chest and any part of the body struck by the lead-tipped flagrum. Blood loss would occur through repeatedly ruptured skin. Blood would also be lost inside the body. As long as the blood is outside the blood vessels, it contributes to circulatory shock.

Severe pain increases oxygen consumption, which would require more rapid breathing and a higher output of blood from the heart. It would also stimulate the sympathetic nervous system (the "fight-or-flight" response mentioned in chapter 3), leading to profuse sweating and thus more fluid loss, among other signs.

Blunt chest trauma can lead to multiple problems:

- **Pneumothorax (collapsed lung)**. Blunt trauma can cause small tears in the lung that allow air to enter the chest (pleural) cavity between the lungs and chest wall. This compresses the lungs and reduces how much air a person can breathe into his lungs. Sometimes a lung will completely collapse.
- **Chest pain and splinting**. When the chest hurts (and Jesus' chest pain would have been grievous), the victim takes shallower breaths than normal. A deep inspiration causes the chest to expand fully, and this magnifies the sharp pain experienced during inspiration. "Splinting" refers to the reduced inspiratory effort of shallow breathing to reduce chest wall movement and therefore reduce pain.
- **Pleural effusion (with or without blood)**. Blunt trauma can cause breaks in small blood vessels of the lungs so that the blood leaks into the pleural cavity (between lungs and chest wall) and slowly fills up this space (hemothorax). At least 8.5 ounces (250 milliliters) of fluid are typically required before pleural effusion shows up on a chest x-ray of an upright person, and 17 ounces (500 milliliters) to be seen above the diaphragm.[50] In the figure with the ribs, heart, lungs, and diaphragm showing, notice that about one pint (500 milliliters) of blood will rise to the level of the space between the fourth and fifth ribs. This will become important when we consider the lance that pierced Jesus' side.

  Symptoms of pleural effusion and hemothorax include cyanosis (bluish skin); unequal rising of the chest if the hemothorax is only on one side; rapid heart rate; low blood pressure; and pale, cool, clammy skin.

The fluid around the lungs would compress the lung tissue so that there would be less surface area for exchange of oxygen and carbon dioxide. Therefore, each breath would deliver less oxygen to the blood and remove less carbon dioxide from it. To make up for this less efficient breathing, the breathing rate would have to increase to meet the needs of the body. And since each breath would have hurt Jesus more due to muscle and rib damage, staying alive would have required that he increase the pain of breathing by trying to breathe faster and deeper.

Pleural Effusion

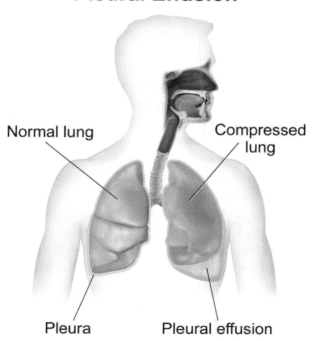

Normal lung

Compressed lung

Pleura

Pleural effusion

Pleural effusion — fluid in the space between the lungs and chest wall.

- **Flail chest**. When trauma causes multiple rib fractures, a portion of the chest may rise when it should fall and fall when it should rise; the damaged segment of the chest moves in the opposite direction from the rest of the chest. This condition, called flail chest, increases the work of breathing and is associated with significant pain. Flail chest probably could not occur without rib fractures, and according to Scripture and Church teaching, none of Christ's bones was broken (see Jn 19:36). Half of patients with flail chest die unless they receive rapid care. Therefore, it is almost certain that Jesus did not have flail chest, since there is no evidence that he had any fractures.
- **Pulmonary contusion**. Chest trauma can cause a bruise (contusion) of the lung itself. With damage to the smallest blood vessels (capillaries), blood and other fluids accumulate in the lung tissue and prevent normal exchange of oxygen into the blood and carbon dioxide out of it. Therefore, those suffering from pulmonary contusion experience chest pain, shortness of breath, and even hemoptysis (coughing up blood).
- **Shock or near shock**. How much blood did Jesus lose? We have no way of knowing. We do know that severe dehydration occurs when over 10 percent of body fluids have been lost. Sixty percent of a man's weight is accounted for by water. If Jesus weighed 176 pounds (80 kilograms), that means that 106 pounds (48 kilograms) was water; 10 percent of 106 pounds is 10.6 pounds, or 4.8 kilograms (10.6 pints; 5.3 quarts; 1.3 gallons). Losing a combination of blood and sweat equal to 1.3 gallons would have caused Jesus severe dehydration — not even considering the effects of trauma and pain.

  Note that severe dehydration with this amount of blood loss applies if a patient is lying down. If the person is upright, the effects of dehydration will be even more severe, due to the effects of gravity on body fluids including blood. Blood loss can also be internal. For instance, blood or fluid that leaves the circulatory system and enters the chest cavity or the lung tissue could contribute to shock, because this blood and fluid would no longer be contributing to a healthy blood pressure necessary to continue bringing oxygen to tissue and taking waste products away from the tissues.

- **Dehydration.** As Jesus was almost certainly dehydrated from his agony-induced sweating and bleeding (hematidrosis), beatings in the middle of the night, and lack of fluids to drink, he would have suffered a dry tongue sticking to the roof of his mouth, extreme headache, dizziness with light-headedness, confusion, palpitations (strong heartbeats felt in his chest), and muscle cramps. Jesus would have been very thirsty. This was the state Jesus was in when he spoke to Pilate, telling him that he would have no power over him unless it had been given to him from above (see Jn 19:11).

  Compared to a more normal blood pressure he would have had while lying down or even sitting, Jesus' blood pressure would have dropped significantly while he stood. Pilate sought to release this severely beaten man immediately (see Jn 19:12). Try to imagine how such nobility could overshadow the physical reality of his brutally beaten body to impress Pontius Pilate to ask for his release.

  Complications of dehydration include hypovolemic (low-blood-volume) shock with pale, cool, clammy skin; rapid heartbeat; and shallow breathing. Thirst increases, as does one's temperature.

- **Blunt cardiac trauma.** Chest trauma can damage the heart and its protective sac (pericardium). Today, injury to the heart from blunt trauma is most commonly seen in motor vehicle accidents, but assault injuries can also cause it.

- **Heart damage**. The heart can sustain damage to its four valves, the coronary arteries, and even the heart muscle itself. Injuries to the right side of the heart are more common than those to the much thicker-walled left side of the heart. The thinner right-side heart muscle can develop a partial tear that can temporarily be plugged by a clot; later disruption can lead to rapid death due to blood spilling out of the heart and into the chest cavity. Given Jesus' ability to walk to Calvary, it is unlikely that contusion of his heart muscle played a significant role in his death.
- **Pericardial injuries**. The pericardium (the sac surrounding the heart) can rupture, reducing the effectiveness of the heart in pumping blood. In severe instances, cardiac arrest (heart attack) may occur. Alternatively, a pericardial effusion may occur. This is similar to a pleural effusion, discussed above, in which fluid (including blood) can get into the cavity around the lungs. The cavity around the heart is contained within the sac known as the pericardium. When this sac fills with fluid, the heart cannot expand enough, and therefore each heartbeat will propel less blood into circulation, thus contributing to shock. If Jesus had had a significant pericardial effusion, it is unlikely he would have made it to Calvary, even without carrying the cross.
- **Hyperkalemia**. According to neurosurgeon and author Dr. Mark Kubala, the muscle damage Jesus suffered from the violent scourging would have led to release of potassium from muscle tissue. This would have increased potassium levels in his blood, a condition known as hyperkalemia, which can disrupt normal heart rhythms. In fact, intravenous injections of potassium are a common modern means of administering

the death penalty. The muscle damage from scourging also would have released a protein called myoglobin, which would have damaged the kidneys and prevented them from excreting excess potassium into the urine. For Jesus, hyperkalemia may have led to ventricular fibrillation of the heart as the terminal event in his mortal life.

Dr. Edwards et al. write that after his scourging, Jesus was in intense pain and had lost a significant amount of blood. If not in shock, he would have been in a preshock state. According to Edwards et al., his condition would have been serious and possibly critical. These terms are not particularly precise, but in general, "serious" means that the vital signs (pulse, blood pressure, respiratory rate) are unstable and outside normal limits.

From the practical standpoint of the Roman soldiers who had to execute criminals by crucifixion, the scourging weakened the victim so much that he could probably do little to resist being attached to the cross.

Response to Claims

The first claim at the beginning of the chapter suggests that sharp pieces of bone were used in the scourge. However, as we have seen, the evidence shows that only Greeks used sharp pieces of bone on scourges. Furthermore, the Shroud of Turin demonstrates no tearing wounds that sharp bones would have inflicted.

Secondly, it is often claimed that the site of the scourging was the Fortress of Antonia. However, multiple sources of evidence suggest that the scourging took place on the western side of the Old City of Jerusalem, within the complex of Herod's Palace.

Finally, Dr. Kubala stated that a scourge with sharp pieces of glass and bone attached to leather thongs was found in the ruins of Pompeii. However, three different sources depicting drawings of flagra found in the neighboring town of Herculaneum (buried by the same eruption of Mount Vesuvius that buried Pompeii) show multiple flagra, all without pieces of bone or glass attached. I have found no source, including Dr. Kubala's book, that mentions where pictures or descriptions of such flagra from Pompeii can be found. Dr. Kubala's book does not provide a reference supporting his claim.

Praying When the Pain Seems Too Great to Pray

In *Salvifici Doloris*, Saint John Paul speaks of suffering of the body and of the soul. In the Garden of Gethsemane, Jesus suffered intensely in his soul, so much so that blood leaked out of his skin. The Gospels give no indication of how Jesus suffered in his soul during his scourging; however, we do have an indication of how he suffered in his body. Perhaps because Jesus had given himself up to his Father's will in the garden and accepted the challenge of his Passion, he was now in a flow state in which every ounce of his being was willingly and lovingly given up for us, who did not deserve it. He was not distracted by anxiety or fear and was fully aware of the pain he was enduring.

In chapter 3, we learned how reframing a situation can help us to overcome fear and anxiety. In his encyclical letter *Spe Salvi* (Saved in Hope), Pope Benedict XVI reminds us of a divine aid — hope — to reframe our fears, even in the midst of our sufferings. "The one who has hope lives differently; the one who hopes has been granted the gift of a new life."[51] He also writes, "Here too we see as a distinguishing mark of Christians the fact that they have a future: it is not that they know the details of what awaits them, but they know in general terms that their life will not end in emptiness."

One way that Christians live differently is by seeing that suffering can lead to blessing and joy. We know, because of hope, that suffering is not the end and is not meaningless. We know this because Jesus showed it to us in his life and in his suffering.

Jesus prophesied not only his suffering and death (causing Saint Peter to try to save him from it) but also his resurrection. Clearly, his apostles understood neither Jesus' prophecy of his death nor his prophecy of his resurrection. Jesus had hope that he would rise again; and hope, among other things, is anticipated joy. Hebrews

12:2 tells us that Jesus endured the cross "for the joy that was set before him." But before he could get to the cross, he had to endure the scourging.

In the midst of our most agonizing pain, it can seem impossible to pray, except perhaps short aspirations such as "Thy will be done," "Help me, Lord," or simply the Divine Name, "Jesus." We do not know how Jesus endured the scourging so that he could reach the cross and accomplish his goal, but we do know that he did reach the cross. When something seemingly insurmountable stands between us and our goals, we can recall Jesus enduring the pain of his scourging to accomplish his goal — his offering of himself on the cross.

While fear is anticipated suffering, hope is anticipated joy. Jesus knew that his suffering was going to lead to joy; therefore he had hope. As Christians, we receive the theological virtue of hope at our baptism. The *Catechism of the Catholic Church* states, "Hope is the confident expectation of divine blessing and the beatific vision of God" (2090). With this virtue, "we desire the kingdom of heaven and eternal life as our happiness, placing our trust in Christ's promises and relying not on our own strength, but on the help of the grace of the Holy Spirit" (1817).

CHAPTER 6

Royal Treatment

Date: Good Friday, April 3, AD 33
Time: Late morning
Place: The praetorium — Herod's Palace near the Jaffa Gate, western side of the walled city of Old Jerusalem in the Tower of David complex

---

Gospel Narrative

And the soldiers led him away inside the palace (that is, the praetorium); and they called together the whole battalion. And they clothed him in a purple cloak, and plaiting a crown of thorns they put it on him. And they began to salute him, "Hail, King of the Jews!" And they struck his head with a reed, and spat upon him, and they knelt down in homage to him. And when they had mocked him, they stripped him of the purple cloak, and put his own clothes on him. And they led him out to crucify him. (Mark 15:16–20)

And the soldiers plaited a crown of thorns, and put it on his head, and clothed him in a purple robe; they came up to him, saying,

"Hail, King of the Jews!" and struck him with their hands. ... So Jesus came out, wearing the crown of thorns and the purple robe. Pilate said to them, "Here is the man!" ... They cried out, "Away with him, away with him, crucify him!" Pilate said to them, "Shall I crucify your King?" The chief priests answered, "We have no king but Caesar." Then he handed him over to them to be crucified. (John 19:2–3, 5, 15–16)

Jesus Is Condemned to Die

Late Friday morning, April 3, AD 33, at Herod's Palace (see the image on page 80 showing the location of Herod's Palace) on the west side of the walled city of Jerusalem, Pontius Pilate gave in to the demands of a crowd to release a murderer in place of Jesus. He released one who took innocent life, instead of the One who is the source of life. The murderer Barabbas (literally, *bar-abba*, "son of the father") was exchanged for Jesus Christ (the Son of the Father). We learn from Matthew and Mark that the soldiers received Jesus and carried him away from the outdoor public area into the palace for some extracurricular activities. Now that Jesus was condemned, the soldiers knew they had free rein to take advantage of their prisoner. And so they did.

Claims

The claims of other authors regarding Jesus' suffering during the royal mocking line up with the best evidence that I found:

> The Roman soldiers, amused that this weakened man had claimed to be a king, began to mock him by placing a robe on his shoulders, a crown of thorns on his head, and a wooden staff as a scepter in his right hand. Next, they spat on Jesus and struck him on the head with the wooden staff. Moreover, when the soldiers tore the robe from Jesus' back, they probably reopened the scourging wounds.[1]

It is generally admitted that they belong to a thorn-bearing tree which is common in Judea, the Zizyphus spina Christi. ... Its thorns are long and very sharp. The scalp bleeds very easily and very vigorously, and as this cap was driven against the head by blows with a stick, the wounds must have caused much loss of blood.[2]

Roman Soldiers Mock Jesus

On his way to Jerusalem, toward which he set his face "like flint" (Lk 9:51; Is 50:7), Jesus had predicted this mocking. "Behold, we are going up to Jerusalem; and the Son of man will be delivered to the chief priests and scribes, and they will condemn him to death, and deliver him to the Gentiles to be mocked and scourged and crucified, and he will be raised on the third day" (Mt 20:18–19). Since the crime Jesus was accused of was setting himself up as the "King of the Jews," the soldiers decided to play off the royal motif.

In Matthew, Mark, and John we see that Jesus' "royal treatment" included four trappings befitting a king:

1. A crown
2. A royal robe
3. A royal staff
4. Homage of his subjects

The Crown of Thorns

Matthew and Mark refer to what was placed on Jesus' head as a *stephanos*, a Greek word that often meant a wreath or garland awarded as a crown of victory to the winner of an athletic contest.[3] To fashion this *stephanos*, the soldiers had to twist together portions of a thorny plant. Holy Land botanists have suggested one plant as the most likely one used to make the crown of thorns, and it even contains the name of Our Lord: *Zizyphus spina-christi*, colloquially known as the Syrian Christ thorn.[4] This evergreen member of the buckthorn family grows wild in Israel, typically as a shrub 9 to 15 feet tall, although it can reach heights of over 60 feet with a trunk

Zizyphus spina-christi along roadside in Galilee. (Thomas W. McGovern)

This photo and next page: Close-up of spines of Syrian Christ thorn. (Thomas W. McGovern)

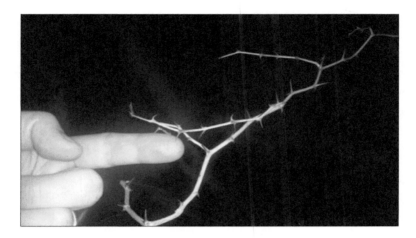

two feet in diameter.[5] It has been found at altitudes of up to 5,000 feet above sea level and is so drought resistant that it can survive on as little as 4 inches of rain annually.

Barbet suggests that such thorns would have been close at hand for the soldiers to use as kindling for a fire.[6] Dr. Zugibe writes about a discussion he had with Dr. Michael Evenari, a professor of botany at Hebrew University in Jerusalem, who believed that the Syrian Christ thorn likely grew in and around Jerusalem at the time of Christ.[7]

On a recent trip to Israel, our tour guide pointed out this plant along the highway at many locations. We stopped to inspect some, and with difficulty that involved skin piercing and bleeding for the guide and me, we were able to separate a small branch from a tall shrub. The thorns are incredibly sharp and measure 1 to 2 centimeters long. I have no doubt that with pressure, they could easily pass through hair and scalp skin. Because of the difficulty in handling the branches of this plant without inflicting wounds on oneself, I doubt that the soldiers made a tightly woven circlet out of this plant. Why would the soldiers take the time — and personal blood loss — to artistically fashion a circle from a thorny plant?

In the mid-fifth century, the former Roman soldier Saint Vincent of Lerins wrote, "They placed on [Jesus'] head a crown of thorns; it was, in fact, in the shape of a pileus, so that it touched and covered His head in every part."[8] A pileus was a Roman cap made of felt. It was used as a symbol of liberty by freed slaves or as a head covering beneath a soldier's helmet.

A relic of the crown of thorns was rescued from the April 2019 Notre Dame Cathedral fire in Paris. That crown consists of rushes wrapped into a wreath and tied with gold filament. The rushes are smooth, with no thorns. Historical data[9] and the reasoning of Dr. Barbet[10] suggest that these rushes were used to bind a cap of thorns (separated earlier in history from the rushes) to Christ's head; this was accomplished by wrapping the wreath of rushes around the cap of thorns along the nape of the neck at the base of the skull, across both temples, and onto the forehead. Without such a band, the thorns would easily have fallen off. The internal diameter of this thick circlet of rushes is 8.3 inches (21 centimeters), and its external diameter is

Pileus between two daggers, on the reverse of a denarius issued by Brutus to commemorate the assassination of Julius Caesar on the Ides of March. Saint Vincent of Lerins believed that the crown of thorns took the shape of a cap. (Courtesy of Goldberg Coins)

26 inches (66 centimeters).[11] According to one study, the current average head circumference for men is about 22.4 inches (57 centimeters), giving a diameter of 7.1 inches (18 centimeters).[12] This means that the crown of thorns venerated in Paris would slide over the head and onto the shoulders of nearly all men with just over a half inch to spare all around the head. However, if the relic in Paris was used to bind a thick plait of thorns against a man's head, the missing diameter (about a

half inch circumferentially) would have been occupied by a thick mass of thorns. These rushes would also have helped to press many thorns through the scalp skin of Jesus. We will see shortly how the crown of thorns was further used to torture Jesus.

From the Gospels, we cannot know for certain the shape of the crown of thorns, but as a former army soldier, I find it helpful to reflect on the near-universal way that soldiers typically perform unpleasant duties: in such a way as to cause the minimum amount of personal discomfort.

If one accepts the Shroud of Turin as the burial cloth of Christ bearing his crucified image, there is yet more to learn about the crown of thorns. The Shroud's image reflects a cap of thorns, for there are blood patterns suggesting both venous and arterial flows from multiple points on the scalp, not just in a ring around the head. There is a pattern on the left forehead near the midline that looks like a number three (on the photo negative) or a Greek epsilon (on the photo positive). This pattern suggests blood meandering down around muscle-induced furrows from the supratrochlear vein.

Dr. Barbet points out that the Shroud shows no marks on the top of the head, where a bandage would have been used to tie the jaw shut (by circling the head from top to temples and under the chin).[13] He points out that the blood flows stop abruptly at the back of the head, near the nape of the neck, where the band of rushes was likely located. One can easily see blood flows from near the top of the head, flowing down the back of the head and stopping abruptly.

The Royal Robe

Before placing a royal robe on Jesus, according to Matthew, the guards first stripped him. The tearing off of his tunic, dried to the mass of clotted blood, skin, and muscle on his chest and back, would have painfully opened the wounds from the Roman flagrum. The scarlet or purplish robe placed on Jesus was a chlamyda (Mt 27:28), a short cloak worn by military officers and soldiers, which had probably been dyed a red or purple color. This new robe then gradually dried to his back as the soldiers mocked and struck him.

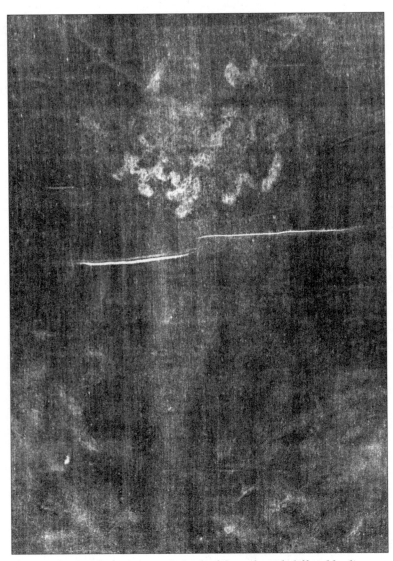

Shroud of Turin photo showing the back of the scalp with diffuse bleeding.

Shroud of Turin photo showing the front of the scalp with diffuse bleeding locations.

Arundo donax (a giant reed of Israel), pictured here when almost dried out and ready to use to make cane implements.

The Royal Staff

Matthew calls the royal staff, or scepter, that was given to Jesus a "reed." I had always pictured a reed as something like the wavy palm branch we carry into Mass on Palm Sunday. Now I have discovered why. One type of reed in the Bible (Hebrew, *gnome*) refers to a waterside bulrush used to make papyrus (see Is 58:5). In fact, these rushes were probably not unlike the rushes used to bind Jesus' crown to his head, as found in the relic in Notre Dame Cathedral.

The word used in the Gospels for "reed," however, is *kalamo*, referring to a "reed in its various appliances, such as a wand or staff."[14] The plant that most likely provided the reed was *Arundo donax*, the giant reed or Cyprus cane of Israel, an abundant waterside plant that grows over 30 feet tall in ideal conditions. This plant is more like bamboo than like a soft wavy plant, and it was commonly employed to manufacture walking sticks, measuring rods, fishing rods, and musical pipes. Think of a modern pool stick for thickness and weight. A staff made of this plant could inflict significant damage.

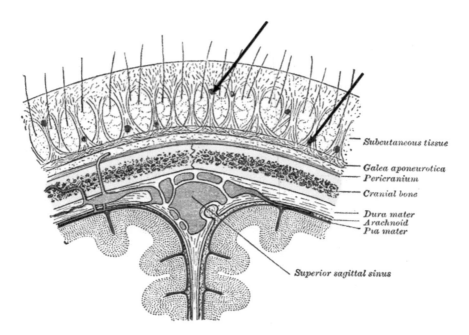

Labels on diagram:
- *Subcutaneous tissue*
- *Galea aponeurotica*
- *Pericranium*
- *Cranial bone*
- *Dura mater*
- *Arachnoid*
- *Pia mater*
- *Superior sagittal sinus*

Gray's Anatomy diagram of the scalp. The subcutaneous tissue is a fibrofatty layer that connects skin to the underlying aponeurosis (galea aponeurotica) of the occipitofrontalis muscle and provides a passageway for nerves and blood vessels. Blood vessels are attached to this fibrous connective tissue (arrows point to example red artery and blue vein attached to fibrous septae). If the vessels are cut, this attachment to the fibrous bands prevents vasospasm (vessel narrowing to stop blood loss), which could lead to profuse bleeding after injury.

Let the Homage Commence

After providing Jesus with the three physical attributes of his kingly power (crown, robe, and staff), his "subjects" used them to pay him a grisly antihomage. After letting Jesus hold his scepter in his hand, Matthew (27:30) and Mark (15:19) note, the soldiers struck his head with the reed. Of course, these evangelists want us to know that the solders used the reed to drive the thorns more deeply into the scalp of Jesus and enlarge the thorn-induced wounds, since the soldiers would not have wanted to cut themselves doing this with their hands.

I operate on the scalps of patients almost daily, and I am never disappointed by the ability of the scalp to provide a tremendous amount of blood through the smallest of incisions. Scalp bleeding does not stop easily because scalp skin is typically under significant tension. When there is a split in the scalp skin, it pulls open further than the original wound.

Furthermore, the anatomy of the scalp includes a thick layer of skin with dense fibers that connect to a thick band of tissue called the galea. The dense fibers have fatty tissue compartments (with skin above, galea below, and fibers to the sides) between them where nerves, arteries, and veins run. The scalp arteries are connected to these vertical dense fibers (fibrous septae) so that when the arteries are cut, they are prevented from spasm (clamping shut). In other words, the muscles of the arteries cannot tighten to close the cut and reduce the bleeding.[15]

Because of the structure of the scalp, it is difficult to compress the veins and arteries when they are cut. Additionally, unlike most of the veins of the body, many of the scalp veins have no valves to prevent loss of blood; this includes blood from the scalp and even the brain (which connects directly to the scalp through emissary veins that traverse the skull bone). Thus a visually significant amount of blood would have formed on Jesus' scalp and forehead, at least reaching the circlet of rushes affixing the crown. The significant blood loss from Jesus' scalp could also have contributed to what Pilate considered Jesus' rapid death on the cross.

John tells us that soldiers used their palms to strike Jesus' face while they spat on him, knelt before him, and gave him false homage by hailing him as "King of the Jews" (see Jn 19:2–3). When they tired of their sport or simply had to move on to Calvary, they stripped off his robe, freshly opening his clotted wounds, only to affix his own outer tunic yet again (Mt 27:31; Mk 15:20) — the same tunic for which soldiers would soon gamble. This makes the second of three times on Good Friday that a garment dried to the blood of Jesus' back would be removed.

Response to Claims

The research supports both of the claims laid out at the beginning of the chapter. First, a wooden staff was indeed used to beat Jesus about the head and body during a grisly royal homage, and a purple robe likely dried to clotted blood on his body, only to be forced off to reopen his wounds.

Second, the Syrian Christ thorn (*Zizyphus spina-christi*) is likely the plant that was used to make a cap of thorns for Our Savior. Its placement on Christ's scalp caused him to lose a significant amount of blood when coupled with the beating with the staff.

"Here Is the Man"

When Pilate cried out to the crowds, *"Ecce homo"* ("Here is the man," Jn 19:5), Jesus was wearing the purple robe, bleeding from the crown of thorns, and exhibiting bruises wherever skin was visible.[16] In such a state, Jesus could have looked attractive to no one, thus fulfilling Isaiah's prophecy of the Suffering Servant: "As many were astonished at him — his appearance was so marred, beyond human semblance, and his form beyond that of the sons of men" (Is 52:14). Isaiah adds, "He had no form or comeliness that we should look at him, and no beauty that we should desire him. He was despised and rejected by men; a man of sorrows, and acquainted with grief; and as one from whom men hide their faces he was despised, and we esteemed him not" (Is 53:2b–3).

What do we do in the presence of this kind of trauma to a fellow human being? We cringe in disgust internally (and sometimes externally) in the face of ugliness, pain, and injury. Is it any wonder that onlookers would see "no beauty" in him, "hide their faces" before him, and "despise and reject" him?

And yet in all this scourging and royal mocking, Jesus, unlike the two victims crucified with him, was innocent. Isaiah prophesied that the Messiah would be "like a lamb that is led to the slaughter" who "had done no violence" and who had "no deceit in his mouth" (Is 53:7, 9); he had transgressed neither in deed nor in word, and therefore he suffered unjustly.

it times, but oh, how we complain. We
on't we? Let's see what Saint John Paul
at the Suffering Servant — and this is
rist's Passion — takes those sufferings
iry way:

Christ suffers voluntarily and suffers innocently. With his suffering he accepts that question [What is the meaning of suffering?]. ... Christ, however, not only carries with himself the same question ... but he also carries the greatest possible answer to this question. ... Christ gives the answer to the question about suffering and the meaning of suffering not only by his teaching, that is by the Good News, but most of all by his own suffering, which is integrated with this teaching of the Good News in an organic and indissoluble way. ...

The words of that prayer of Christ in Gethsemane ["nevertheless not my will, but yours, be done," Lk 22:42] prove the truth of love through the truth of suffering. Christ's words confirm with all simplicity this human truth of suffering, to its very depths: Suffering is the undergoing of evil before which man shudders. He says: "Let it pass from me," just as Christ says in Gethsemane.[17]

Jesus not only suffers unjustly, for he is innocent, but he does so voluntarily, without complaining. And in doing so, he gives us a glimpse at the answer to that deep question, "What is the meaning of suffering?" For Christ, the meaning was "the joy set before him" (Heb 12:2), "that whoever believes in him may have eternal life" (Jn 3:15).

The Song of the Suffering Servant (Is 52:13—53:12) describes vividly how the Messiah will be unattractive, rejected, hated, grief-stricken, and sorrowful — and yet it is his unjust suffering that heals us of our unattractiveness, our rejection, our experience of hate, our grief, and our sorrow. And how often do we want to forget what Jesus said about our own unjust suffering: "A servant is not greater than his master. If they persecuted me, they will persecute you; if they kept my word, they will keep yours also" (Jn 15:20). Although this is part of the Good News (the Gospel), it certainly does not feel like good news. Yet we must follow in Jesus' footsteps.

Nobody wants to be mocked, and nobody likes to be mocked. Yet if we are mocked for being like Christ, no everlasting harm can come to us. "If God is for us, who is against us?" (Rom 8:31). We want to have not only the right friends but also the right enemies — and then through our own suffering, we can offer that up for the conversion of those enemies, that they might become friends of Christ. We must remember that even during his mocking, Christ was intending, planning, and carrying out the salvation of his mockers through his very mocking. What brilliant spiritual jujitsu: Jesus turns the suffering delivered by those soldiers into the very means of their salvation. This serves as yet another manifestation of my favorite Bible verse: "We know that in everything God works for good with those who love him, who are called according to his purpose" (Rom 8:28).

Our Savior can relate to us; he has experienced what we have, but even more so. We can never truthfully say, "God doesn't understand what I'm suffering." This very fact can disarm us and give us hope. When I am tempted to complain to God, all I need to do is try to speak my complaint while looking at a crucifix. What in the world do I have to complain about when the perfect man, who was God incarnate, was murdered by lawless men? The crucifix disarms me; the words I planned to use as a complaint fall away because they no longer have any power or meaning.

If Jesus could endure his mocking patiently, so can I. If he could love those who were mocking him, so can I. And if he could endure the cross for the hope of the joy set before him, so can I. For I can do all things in Christ who strengthens me (see Phil 4:13).

CHAPTER 7

The Way of the Cross

Date: Good Friday, April 3, AD 33
Time: Late morning
Place: The route from the praetorium (Herod's Palace) to Calvary through the Old City of Jerusalem

---

Gospel Narrative
And when they had mocked him, they stripped him of the robe, and put his own clothes on him, and led him away to crucify him. (Matthew 27:31)

So they took Jesus, and he went out, bearing his own cross, to the place called the place of a skull, which is called in Hebrew Golgotha. (John 19:17)

And they compelled a passer-by, Simon of Cyrene, who was coming in from the country, the father of Alexander and Rufus, to carry his cross. (Mark 15:21)

And there followed him a great multitude of the people, and of women who bewailed and lamented him. But Jesus turning to them said, "Daughters of Jerusalem, do not weep for me, but weep for yourselves and for your children. For behold, the days are coming when they will say, 'Blessed are the barren, and the wombs that never bore, and the breasts that never nursed!' Then they will begin to say to the mountains, 'Fall on us'; and to the hills, 'Cover us.' For if they do this when the wood is green, what will happen when it is dry?" (Luke 23:27–31)

And they offered him wine mingled with myrrh; but he did not take it. (Mark 15:23)

Saint Paul says that Christians should desire spiritual gifts (see 1 Cor 12), but he ends this chapter of his Letter to the Corinthians by saying that he will show us "a still more excellent way" than desiring spiritual gifts. That way is love (1 Cor 13). I think this is why Dr. Peter Kreeft says that the song "I Did It My Way" is "the national anthem of hell."

Jesus lived out that most excellent way of love by traveling the Way of the Cross in the fashion chosen for him, not by him. In the late morning of Good Friday, April 3, AD 33, Jesus carried his own cross from the palace of Herod and began the quarter-mile trek to Calvary. In this way, he lived out what he had prayed the night before to his Father: "Not my will, but yours be done" (Lk 22:42). We each have the opportunity in our own lives to live the Way of the Cross in a unique way. We can embrace it like Jesus, or we can run from it and live life "my way." For Christians, there are really only two ways: my way or the Way of the Cross.

On Fridays during Lent, Catholics traditionally commemorate the Way of the Cross in homes and parishes. The fourteen stations are so embedded in our consciousness that many Catholics are surprised to learn that five of the stations are not found in Scripture. Nowhere do the Gospels tell us that Jesus fell with the cross (stations 3, 7, and 9), that he met his mother on the way (station 4), or that Veronica wiped his face (station 6). This doesn't mean that these events did not happen; it only means that they are not in Scripture.

In fact, Matthew, Mark, and Luke don't even mention that Jesus carried his cross. Only the Gospel of John does (see 19:17); the Synoptics state merely that Simon of Cyrene was compelled to carry the cross behind Jesus.

As we continue this journey through the Passion, let us consider this question: What was the cross that Jesus carried?

Claims

Descriptions of crucifixion often suggest that there was one consistent way in which crucifixion was carried out. But the deeper I have studied, the more I have found variations. (These details are covered at length in the two appendices to this book.) While it is not possible to tell exactly how Jesus was crucified, I apply the evidence for the way I believe Jesus was most likely crucified, beginning with his painful walk to Calvary.

> The cross, according to the general rule, the regulation cross, if one may so express it, was made of two distinct pieces. ... The one, which was vertical, and was a permanent fixture, was the 'stipes crucis'; the other, which was movable and was fixed horizontally on the first, was the *patibulum*.[1]

> The *patibulum*, weighing 75 to 125 lb. (34 to 57 kg) was placed across the nape of the victim's neck and balanced along both shoulders.[2]

> At the site of execution, by law, the victim was given a bitter drink of wine mixed with myrrh (gall) as a mild analgesic.[3]

What Did Jesus Carry to Calvary?

John (19:17) tells us that Jesus carried his cross (*stauros*). The Synoptic Gospels tell us that Simon of Cyrene also carried a *stauros*. What
was a *stauros* (or *stauron*, the male accusative singular form often
found in the Gospels and ancient Greek writings)? Was it one piece
of wood, or were there two pieces of wood attached together? Was it
unbearably heavy or lighter than we anticipate based on the artwork
we have been conditioned by throughout our lives?

Ancient Greek, Carrying a *Stauros*

In the first century BC, the Greek writer Dionysius of Halicarnassus penned a history of Rome from its founding through the Punic
Wars, which ended in 146 BC. In a section about events in the fifth
century BC, he describes an act of torture involving a long piece of
wood: "Those who led the slave to the punishment, having stretched
out both his arms and tied them to a [beam of] wood [*xulo prosde-
santes*], which extended across his chest and shoulders as far as the
wrist, were following him lacerating his naked body with whips."[4]

Chariton was a Greek author who, sometime in the first century, wrote what is believed to be the world's oldest surviving novel.
In it, he describes a group of men being sent to execution carrying a
pole (*stauron*): "And this one, without even seeing them or listening
to their defense, at once ordered the sixteen cellmates to be suspended [*anastaurosai*]. They were brought out chained together by feet
and neck, and each of them carried the pole [*ton stauron ephere*]."[5]
In another section of his novel, Chariton describes a man executed
by suspension (in this case, crucifixion rather than impalement or
hanging, the other two types of suspension executions): "[Theron]
was suspended [*aneskolopisthe*] in front of Callirhoe's tomb, and
from his cross [*apo ton stauron*] he saw the sea."[6]

The Greek historian Plutarch (AD 46–120) writes in his *Moralia*: "Every criminal who goes to execution must carry his own cross
[*stauron*] on his back."[7]

From Dionysius and Chariton, we learn that one could both
carry a *stauron* and be suspended upon a *stauron*. From Plutarch,

we learn that carrying a *stauron* was normal for a criminal being led to execution.

Ancient Latin, Carrying a *Patibulum*

Plautus (Titus Maccius Plautus, 255–185 BC) was a Roman playwright who wrote the earliest intact Latin plays. Most of them are comedies that divulge the daily nature of slaves' lives and relationships. In one play, he writes: "I will give a talent to him who will be the first to run to the cross [*crucem*] for me; but on one condition, that twice the feet and twice the arms are fastened."[8]

In another play, Plautus paints a picture of what a man looked like on the way to the cross. Sceledrus is blocking a doorway with his arms stretched out, and Palestrio says to him: "I think that in that position you will immediately be moved outside the gate, with arms spread out, carrying a *patibulum*."[9] Later, in line 372, Sceledrus says that he knows that the crux will be his tomb.

Finally, this line is found in a fragment of one of Plautus' plays: "Let him **carry** a *patibulum* through the city; let him thereafter be attached to a **crux**."[10] This fragment of Plautus, written more than 200 years before Christ, is likely the earliest known reference to someone carrying his cross.

A first-century Roman law regulating the undertaking trade was found inscribed on ancient columns in Pozzuoli, Italy, near Naples. Here is an excerpt of what is known as the Lex Puteolana:

> Whoever will want to exact punishment on a male slave or female slave at private expense, as [the owner] who wants the [punishment] to be inflicted, [the contractor] exacts the punishment in this manner: if [the owner] wants [him] to lead the **patibulated** individual [individual carrying a *patibulum*] to the cross [*crucem*], the contractor will have to provide **wooden posts**, chains, and cords for the floggers and the floggers themselves. And anyone who will want to exact punishment will have to give four sesterces for each of the **workers who bring the *patibulum*** and for the floggers

and also for the executioner.[11]

From Plautus, we learn that a cross (crux or crucem) is not the same thing as a *patibulum* and that the *patibulum* is where the arms are stretched out. The condemned appears to carry his *patibulum* to a crux. The Lex Puteolana also describes a condemned person carrying a *patibulum* to a crux.

John Granger Cook recommends reading the Greek texts that describe Roman executions (including the Gospels) in light of the linguistic precision offered by the Latin texts.[12] The best word for rendering *patibulum* into Greek was *stauros*. When the Gospels describe Jesus or Simon carrying a *stauros*, based on Roman usage they mean carrying a *patibulum* (since no classical author ever claims a person carried a crux). Therefore, since it had a *patibulum*, we have a fairly good idea of the shape of the cross on which Jesus was crucified.

The most probable interpretation of the above texts is that the *patibulum* represents the horizontal part of the cross, which was carried on the shoulders of the condemned. The condemned was then nailed to the *patibulum* once he reached the crux (the upright post fixed in the ground). Then the *patibulum*, with the victim fastened to it, was attached to the crux. This agrees with Firmicus Maternus, a Christian apologist who lived in the early fourth century, during the reign of Constantine I. He writes, "Fastened to the , he is raised on a cross [**patibulo** *subfixus in* **crucem** *tollitur*]."[13]

Are *Stauros* and *Patibulum* the Same Thing?

Prior to the New Testament, *stauros* and crux could both mean either a "pole" or "some kind of cross." In fact, either word can refer to the whole or the part, an example of a figure of speech known as synecdoche, in which a part can stand for the whole ("fifty sail" meaning fifty ships), or the whole can stand for a part ("the Pentagon" referring to a group of individuals within the Pentagon). Using this figure of speech, the species can refer to the genus (as "cutthroat" to mean an assassin), or the genus to the species (as a "creature" to mean a man). Synecdoche can also mean using the name of the material for the thing made ("boards" for stage or "threads" for clothes).

Cook says it was easier for early Christian writers to stick with crux than to teach a new word, such as *patibulum*. Therefore, "a cross" can refer to the crossbeam (*patibulum*), the upright post (crux), or the two-part construction of a cross. At the same time, *patibulum* can occasionally refer to the two-part construction as well as the crossbeam (but not the upright post alone). In Latin, the upright post is sometimes called a stipes, although this term is also employed for a sharp pole used to execute by impaling from the anus, through the body, and out the mouth. This was not a penalty used by the Romans, but it was inflicted by the ancient Persians. Finally, *stauros* can refer to the crossbeam or the two-part construction, and sometimes even the upright post. Context is essential.

It is the use of synecdoche that explains how Jesus can carry a cross (made of one piece of wood) and hang on a cross (made of two pieces of wood).

In the early fifth century, the Roman writer Macrobius provided the Rosetta Stone–style key that reveals that the words *patibulum* (Latin) and *stauron* (Greek) were interchangeable: "It is called the dies instauricius, not (as some think) from the *patibulum* — that is, *stauron* in Greek — but from the act of making whole again, as Varro holds."[14] When the Evangelists had to translate a Latin item (the *patibulum*) into Greek (the original language of the Gospels), they used the word *stauros* or the form *stauron*.

The meaning of *patibulum* was extensively investigated by Paolo Gatti and Guy Serbat in 1975. Their findings are used in the *Thesaurus Linguae Latinae*, the preeminent dictionary of Latin used by classical Latinists today. The Thesaurus says that *patibulum* is derived from a word meaning "to stretch out." It refers to a "wooden beam" or "length of wood," especially that by which someone or something is stretched out or extended. In customary usage, a *patibulum* refers more precisely to a wooden beam to which an individual who is to be punished is attached with outstretched arms and, less precisely, to a horizontal beam attached to an upright beam. The word *patibulum* also refers to a bar by which doors are shut.[15]

Seneca the Younger, a first-century Roman philosopher, dramatist, and statesman, wrote in his *De Vita Beata* (On the Good Life) that an individual nailed to a cross would spit on spectators from his *patibulum*.[16] In the same passage, he refers to stipes as the upright and *crucibus* (crosses) as the two-part instrument of death. This demonstrates that prisoners were not removed from the *patibulum* prior to crucifixion.

> Whereas they themselves are struggling to tear themselves away from crosses [*crucibus*] into which each one of you is driving his own nail [*clauos*]. Yet men who are crucified [*supplicium*] hang from one single pole [*stipitibus*], but these who punish themselves are divided between as many crosses [*crucibus*] as they have lusts, but yet are given to evil speaking, and are so magnificent in their contempt of the vices of others that I should suppose that they had none of their own, were it not that some criminals when on the gibbet [*patibulum*] spit upon the spectators.

Cook believes that *stauros* refers to a "pole" or a "cross" based on the ancient evidence. Another fascinating reference he uses to support this is from the Greek satirist Lucian (AD 125–180), who wrote *A Trial in the Court of Vowels*. On trial in the below-quoted section is the letter tau (which is equivalent to our "T"):

> Men weep, and bewail their lot, and curse Cadmus with many curses for introducing Tau into the family of letters; they say it was his body that tyrants took for a model, his shape that they imitated, when they set up the erections on which men are crucified. Σταυρός [*stauros*] the vile engine is called, and it derives its vile name from him. Now, with all these crimes upon him, does he not deserve death, nay, many deaths? For my part I know none bad enough but that supplied by his own shape — that shape which he gave

to the gibbet [instrument of suspension] named σταυρός [*stauros*] after him by men.

Clearly, Lucian assumes that a *stauros* is shaped like our capital letter T.

Finally, writing in the fourth century, Saint Ambrose says that Jesus carried a *patibulum*: "Isaac carried the wood for himself, Christ carried the *patibulum* of the cross for himself."[17]

Current evidence reveals no ancient literary or illustrated depiction of a condemned man carrying an upright post or two-piece cross — only the horizontal beam. Therefore, John 19:17 should be interpreted to mean that Simon and Jesus carried a horizontal beam across their shoulders and that Jesus was then nailed to it and attached to the upright post (crux) after he had been fastened to the horizontal beam (*patibulum*).

What Size Was the *Stauros* Jesus Carried?

Nobody knows how big the crossbeam Jesus carried was. But that doesn't mean that authors have not suggested estimates. Unfortunately, there are a lot of ifs involved in these estimates. Dr. William Edwards et al. say that the crossbar weighed 75 to 125 pounds,[18] based on references to Dr. Barbet and the *Wycliffe Bible Encyclopedia* (1975). An examination of Barbet's book reveals that his only reference to the cross's weight comes when he dismisses a colleague who claimed that the cross had to be 9 feet tall. Barbet responds, "This would mean a weight of about 275 pounds!"[19]

The Roman basilica Santa Croce in Gerusalemme (Basilica of the Holy Cross in Jerusalem, so called because it was built on soil brought to Rome from Jerusalem) contains many purported relics of Jesus' crucifixion. One of them is said to be the *stauros* of the Good Thief, commonly called Dismas. While I can find no complete measurement, I have found a photograph of this length of wood with a portion of the titulus of Christ (or more likely a medieval copy of the original, based on radiocarbon dating between the tenth and twelfth centuries) next to it. The reported width of the titulus is 25 centimeters (almost

10 inches); thus, based on ratios, the length of the *stauros* is approximately 174 to 180 centimeters (approximately 6 feet), depending how much of the titulus is covered by its frame. I estimated similarly that the wood might be as thick as 6 centimeters (less than 2.5 inches) and as wide as 13 centimeters (5 inches).[20] These dimensions suggest a volume of 0.014 cubic meters (half a cubic foot).

Stauros (crossbar) of the good thief, seen on the left side of the case of relics in Santa Croce in Gerusalemme in Rome. (Thomas W. McGovern)

Relics of the True Cross have been discovered to be composed of European black pine (Pinus nigra), which has a dry weight of 475 kilograms per cubic meter. This means that the good thief's *stauros* would have possessed a mass of about 6.7 kilograms or a weight of about 15 pounds. Note that this is an educated guess and nothing more. This is about how much a 6-foot-long 2 by 6 board of Douglas fir weighs (at 2.5 pounds per foot), or 12 to 20 percent of the weight proposed in Dr. Edwards et al.'s article. If the cross was roughly square in cross-section to begin (a little larger than 5 by 5 inches), it would have weighed approximately 30 pounds.

The Way of the Cross

That Jesus carried only the horizontal piece of his cross is consistent with the Gospels. Even though numerous articles state with apparent certainty the size and weight of what Jesus carried, we really don't know how big it was. What we do know is that it was too heavy for him, in his tortured state of near shock, to carry 400 meters, or

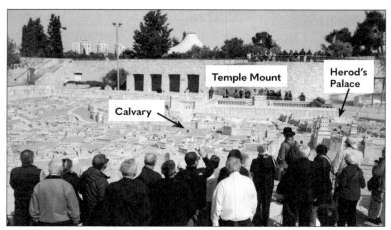

Path from Herod's Palace to Calvary (scale model). (Thomas W. McGovern)

once around a high school track. Based on his lack of food, water, and sleep; the tremendous pains he endured throughout his body; and his loss of blood, he had to be weak, disoriented, and breathing rapidly while exhibiting cool, clammy, pale skin. He likely experienced nausea and even vomiting and possessed a weak, thready pulse, and his eyes would have lacked luster and seemed to stare. Additionally, the longer one goes without sleep, the more intensely one experiences pain. Because Jesus had been awake at least thirty hours by the time of his crucifixion, his experience of pain would have been magnified compared to what it might have been if he had gotten to sleep the night before.[21]

We do not know whether the crossbeam was tied to Jesus' wrists or arms. It certainly could have been, and it would make sense from a pragmatic viewpoint. Because of his weakened state, it would have been easy for the beam to slip off his shoulders and the back of his neck, and this would only have further frustrated the soldiers. There are ancient references to crucifixion victims tied to the crossbeam while they carried it.[22] If Jesus' hands were tied to the crossbeam, he would not have been able to use his hands to break his falls to the ground, which would have increased his suffering and pain. With each fall, the crossbeam may also have forced the crown of thorns further into his scalp when his head struck the ground.

Every step that Jesus took magnified the constant pain of the nocturnal beatings, the scourging, and the royal mocking. Each movement of his head tore his scalp beneath the crown of thorns. Dehydration dried his tongue to the roof of his mouth. Each rapid, labored breath became more difficult with the increasing pain and excruciating thirst. Yet he had to carry a piece of wood strong enough to support him on Calvary. Because he was God and also possessed a human nature and a human body, we can be confident that Jesus wrung every last drop of life and effort out of his body, pushing himself to give the true — not figurative — 100 percent.

Evidence for the Way of the Cross on the Shroud of Turin

In *A Doctor at Calvary*, Dr. Barbet, referring to the Shroud of Turin, points out the presence of wounds on the face, back, and knees of the figure pictured on the Shroud. This could be due to Jesus' carrying of the cross to Golgotha (Calvary). Taking what we know from ancient literary sources — including the Gospels and Church Tradition — and Jerusalem geography — and adding information from the Shroud of Turin, we can put together a picture of what happened as Jesus carried his crossbeam.

We know from the Gospels and geography that Jesus

- walked from the "praetorium" of Pilate (Herod's Palace) to Golgotha — about 400 meters, or a quarter of a mile;
- initially bore the crossbeam himself; and
- needed Simon of Cyrene to help him carry his crossbeam part of the way.

We believe from Tradition that Jesus fell three times while carrying his crossbeam. This would be expected of a tortured, severely weakened man in a state of near shock (low blood volume) being forced to carry a beam about 6 feet long on his shoulders over a rough, undulating road littered with loose stones. Such a scenario explains why he needed Simon to carry the crossbeam part of the way to Calvary.

Let's look again at the Shroud of Turin. There are jagged marks on the knees (worse on the right than on the left). Smudge marks look worse on the right knee than on the left and are most pronounced on the knees. These jagged marks suggest excoriations — deep, linear, scratch-type marks — that could have been caused by a fall. There is the appearance of swelling around the knees that looks worse on the right knee.

On the back image of the Shroud, Dr. Barbet describes an excoriation of about 10 by 9 centimeters, which is a little higher up than a larger, 13.5-centimeter mark overlying the left shoulder blade. The smudge mark on the left is quite obvious and adjacent to the end of a vertical mark suggesting a ponytail of hair down the midline. The smudge on the right shoulder at its lowest aspect seems to match the upper limit of the left shoulder blade mark, while its superior aspect looks to extend nearly to the top of the shoulder. The Shroud image suggests to some physicians that the right shoulder was dislocated. If true, this shows why it was necessary for Simon to carry the crossbeam: With a dislocated shoulder, it would have been physically impossible for Jesus to carry something across both shoulders with a hand wrapped on top of each side. (I know this from personal experience; my right shoulder has been dislocated multiple times.)

Of the many marks seen on the face in the Shroud, note the swelling on the right malar cheek (cheekbone) compared to the left. This swelling could be due to Christ's beating at the home of Caiaphas, to the mocking by Roman soldiers when they struck him with a reed, or to a fall on the way to Calvary.

Given Jesus' weakened state due to blood loss and pain, it would be surprising if he did not fall. The Shroud supports this, showing abrasions in both knees. There are more and deeper abrasions on the right knee than on the left knee. So we can reconstruct a fall, or series of falls, to Jesus' right side with the crossbeam across his shoulders. While falling to the right, it would have been natural for him to turn his head to the left and place his right temple, zygomatic

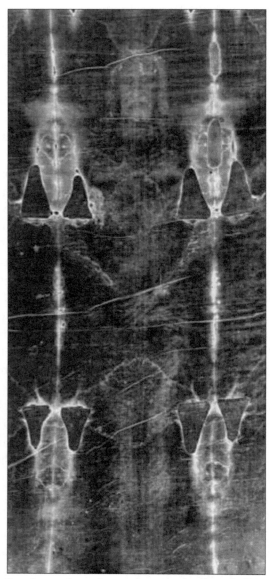

Smudge marks on knees of man in the Shroud of Turin. In this photo negative of the Shroud, we are looking at the man as if he were in front of us (left of photo is right side of man).

cheek, and lateral orbital rim onto the crossbeam and thus absorb some of the impact. Indeed, the Shroud shows more significant right than left infraorbital and periorbital swelling, a deep abrasion on the right infraorbital and malar cheek, and even a torn right upper eyelid.

It is interesting to note as well that Saint Padre Pio, the famous stigmatist, revealed to Karol Wojtyla in 1947 or 1948 that his most painful wound was in his right shoulder.[23] After Padre Pio died, his undershirt was found to possess a large bloodstain on the top of the right shoulder. If Padre Pio truly bore the wounds of Christ, then this shows us something of what Jesus endured on the Way of the Cross. A hard, rough crossbeam would have reopened his scourge wounds by rubbing back and forth across his shoulders and upper back while he carried it. With the added information of the Shroud and Saint Padre Pio's stigmata, we can imagine Jesus' focused stare, swollen face, halting steps, bleeding body, bloodstained knees and shoulders, and drooping right arm as he inched his way to Calvary, the Place of a Skull.

What Was Calvary?

Father Jerome Murphy O'Connor, an archaeologist, describes the setting of Jesus' crucifixion:

> The historical Way of the Cross started in the area of the modern Citadel, just inside the Jaffa Gate. From the palace Jesus would have been led across the upper forum into a street leading to the Gennath Gate, in the first (north) wall of Herodian Jerusalem.
>
> The centurion in charge of the execution party had selected an abandoned quarry just outside the gate as the place of execution. On the east side of the quarry, a rock projection called Golgotha somehow gave the impression of a skull (Mark 15:22). There the Roman soldiers raised the cross. In April the bed of the quarry was a sheen of green. After the winter rains, windblown seeds flourished in soil

deposited by a century of sandstorms. In the west wall of the quarry, an entrepreneur had cut a catacomb, in which tombs opened off a central passage. The disciples who took the body of Jesus from the cross used one of these tombs as a temporary measure. It was close, and the Sabbath was about to begin (John 19:40–42). That particular Friday was the Day of Preparation for Passover (John 19:31).[24]

Calvary was a hill outside the western wall of Jerusalem where limestone was quarried from the eighth to first centuries BC. Only eight or nine years after the crucifixion of Jesus, Herod Agrippa enlarged the walls of Jerusalem to encompass Calvary. Today, visitors to Jerusalem see numerous buildings constructed of stunning white limestone.

When quarry workers chiseled into strong limestone, the rock would be taken away for construction purposes. On the other hand, when workers found weak, crumbling limestone, they would leave it in place. The hill of Calvary was composed of the remaining, poor-quality limestone, and apparently it resembled a skull. After the quarry was abandoned, it was used for a number of family tombs and vegetable gardens. There was a fissure, or large crack, through the limestone in a hill or mound about 30 feet high that would have been high enough to display execution victims to people passing by.[25] An ancient Christian Tradition, dating back at least to Origen, who quoted an older Jewish tradition in the third century, proposed that the "skull" of Calvary is that of Adam, who was buried there.[26]

Jesus Reaches Calvary

When Jesus reached Calvary, he was offered wine mingled with myrrh, but he did not take it (see Mk 15:22–23). What is myrrh, and why did the soldiers offer Jesus wine mixed with myrrh immediately before crucifying him?

Numerous Bible commentaries and internet sites to this day report that wine and myrrh were offered to reduce Jesus' pain. For years, I parroted this during talks about the crucifixion. The argu-

Model of Jerusalem with Calvary just outside the wall. (Thomas W. McGovern)

White limestone buildings in Jerusalem (modern-day). (Thomas W. McGovern)

ment goes that myrrh, a plant resin found in the Middle East, had many medicinal properties, including pain relief — and this is true. However, the analgesic effects of myrrh are weak — so weak that wine alone offers as much pain relief as wine mixed with myrrh. Myrrh in very small amounts was a common preservative in wine, but Mark would not have mentioned the myrrh specifically if it were only present as a preservative.

On the other hand, when myrrh is dissolved in wine in larger amounts, the wine takes on a taste too bitter to drink; it becomes as thirst-quenching as gasoline — or vinegar.[27] We know that the executioners had no interest in relieving any of Jesus' suffering. Since he had endured significant fluid loss in the Garden of Gethsemane from sweating, suffered more voluminous blood loss from the scourging and crowning with thorns, and had nothing to drink since the Last Supper, he would have been insanely thirsty. Yet when he tasted the offered drink, Jesus recoiled in further torment (see Mt 27:34).

Saint Augustine has this to say about the wine mixed with myrrh: "And they gave him to drink wine mingled with gall. Mark says, mingled with myrrh. Matthew put gall to express bitterness, but wine mingled with myrrh is very bitter; though indeed it might be, that gall together with myrrh would make the most bitter."[28]

Finally, just before Jesus was crucified, his clothes were stripped from him (see Mk 15:24), reopening any bloody wounds that had dried to the cloth. He was then thrust down with his back on the rocky, dirty ground and nailed to the *patibulum*.

Response to Claims

The first claim is confirmed by the evidence — namely, that an upright post would have been fixed in the ground for crucifixion victims who carried the crossbar (*stauros* or *patibulum*) across their shoulders to the place of execution.

The second claim regarding the weight of the crossbar (75 to 125 pounds) cannot be confirmed by any evidence.

The final claim, that crucifixion victims were required to receive wine mixed with myrrh as a mild analgesic has no evidence to support it; as we have seen, wine mixed with myrrh would have increased the torture, not lessened it.

Jesus Didn't Go It Alone; Why Should We?

Sometimes in our own suffering, we reject help from others and think that we can handle it ourselves. However, Jesus showed us in his suffering that even he needed help to carry his cross. If he couldn't do it alone — without Simon — why should we expect ourselves to be any different?

Jesus knows what it's like to be lonely. Although he needed help carrying the cross, someone had to be forced to help him. Imagine how lonely it must have been for him to carry that cross along narrow, crowded streets with people hurling insults — or even worse, simply ignoring him, because the truth is that "the opposite of love is not hate, it's indifference."[29]

In our culture, which is growing increasingly lonely, it is important for us to remember that Jesus felt the pain of being alone. Feeling alone is a growing experience in the world, and the COVID-19 pandemic has highlighted this as vulnerable populations, particularly those over 65 years old and in nursing homes, have experienced significant restrictions on seeing others.

Even before COVID-19, nearly half of Americans reported sometimes or always feeling alone or isolated from others. One in five Americans report they rarely or never feel close to people. Only around half of Americans have meaningful in-person social interactions, such as having an extended conversation with a friend or spending quality time with family, on a daily basis. This epidemic of loneliness is perhaps at the root of increasing deaths by suicide, which are being called an epidemic of "deaths of despair."[30]

Compounding these deaths of despair are known increases in medical conditions due to loneliness. Both subjective loneliness and objective social isolation lead to increased coronary artery disease (29 percent), strokes (32 percent), dementia (50 percent), and diabetes (40 percent); as well as indeterminable amounts of increased smoking, hypertension, and obesity; decreased physical activity; and poorer sleep.[31]

Not only do lonely people experience worse physical health, they die from it. Objective isolation and subjective loneliness lead to a 26 to 32 percent increase in deaths compared to matched controls — with no significant difference in whether their isolation was subjective or objective.[32] This is a greater mortality risk than that of severe obesity. Furthermore, the risk of early mortality was greater for younger individuals, with a 57 percent increased risk for those under 65 years of age.

Loneliness is an intense form of suffering — both emotionally and physically — and it seems that it would be impossible to share loneliness, because the very nature of loneliness is not to share. However, Christ experienced a deep loneliness. When I walked and prayed the Way of the Cross with other pilgrims in Jerusalem, I noticed how little attention the crowds, the merchants, and the locals gave to us. It had to be much worse for Jesus, who later spoke from the cross about his sense of abandonment.

The faithful women who followed Jesus to Calvary to keep him company (see Lk 23:27) were beating their breasts, signifying that they were cut to the heart by the injustice of his execution. Their sorrow was rewarded with words of Jesus comforting them even while he was in agony (Lk 23:28–29). Surely those women must have wondered why he was suffering so much. John Paul II tells us that, like those women, we can only grasp the meaning of suffering to the extent that we are "capable of grasping the sublimity of divine love. … This answer has been given by God to man in the Cross of Jesus Christ."[33]

Just as Jesus comforted those women from within his loneliness, he wants to comfort us in our loneliness. He withholds his love from no one. When we are lonely, we can offer to keep him company as the faithful women did while he carried the cross. That may be as simple as holding a crucifix in our hands or lap and silently gazing at it. And in that companionship of loneliness, we can experience his love.

The Price of Love Is Suffering

In *Salvifici Doloris*, Saint John Paul revealed two startling facts about love: Suffering is both necessary for love and conquered by love. There can be no love without suffering. The great Russian author Fyodor Dostoevsky knew this instinctively, which is why he wrote, "I want to suffer so that I may love."[34] If we live out this radical idea that the price of love is suffering, we will be like the early Christians about whom the pagans said, "See how they love one another."[35]

The Gospel of John affirms that the greatest love (God's love) required the greatest suffering (the giving of God's Son to suffer and die): "For God so loved the world that he gave his only-begotten Son, that whoever believes in him should not perish but have eternal life" (3:16).

The love of God is the greatest love, and the suffering and death of God on the cross was the greatest suffering in history — and this love and suffering are mysteriously united. The salvation of man required the unjust suffering of God. The infinite love of God dying on the cross for man is a "salvific love";[36] God's love saves us from evil that we might have eternal life.

According to Saint John Paul, "Human suffering has reached its culmination in the Passion of Christ."[37] Not only does human suffering reach its culmination in Christ, it also enters a new dimension because it is linked to a love that draws out good by means of suffering. By his suffering that included his carrying the cross to Calvary, Christ draws out the supreme good of the redemption of the whole world. From the worst episode of suffering in history spring forth rivers of living waters. Only at the cross can we read the answer to the meaning of suffering to its very depths.

But we need to remember that those who do not follow Christ also suffer. No one escapes suffering. Buddhism addresses the inescapable aspect of suffering front and center in its philosophy. Like Christianity, it sees love and suffering as inextricably linked. But whereas the Church embraces love and suffering together, Buddhism throws out the baby with the bathwater; it seeks to eliminate suffering by eliminating love. Buddhism teaches that if we do not love anything (become attached to it), then we cannot suffer.

When Simon of Cyrene is mentioned by the Synoptics, he is compelled (*engareusan*) to carry the cross, just as someone might be forced unwillingly into military service. Simon almost certainly wanted nothing to do with the cross, yet it transformed his life and his family. How do we know? Mark tells us that Simon was the "father of Alexander and Rufus" (Mk 15:21), and in Romans 16:13, Paul says "Greet Rufus, eminent in the Lord, also his mother and mine." Why would Mark mention Simon's sons if they were not known to his audience? Simon's family members were transformed to become pillars of the early Christian Church. Carrying the cross with Jesus can transform us, too.

CHAPTER 8

The Crucifixion of Jesus

Date: Good Friday, April 3, AD 33
Time: Midday to midafternoon
Place: Rock of Calvary, in an old quarry just outside the city wall of Jerusalem (just north and west of the center of the walled city)[1]

Gospel Narrative

And it was the third hour, when they crucified him. (Mark 15:25)

When the soldiers had crucified Jesus they took his garments and made four parts, one for each soldier; also his tunic. But the tunic was without seam, woven from top to bottom; so they said to one another, "Let us not tear it, but cast lots for it to see whose it shall be." This was to fulfill the Scripture,

> "They parted my garments among them,
> and for my clothing they cast lots."

So the soldiers did this. (John 19:23–25a)

And over his head they put the charge against him, which read, "This is Jesus the King of the Jews." (Matthew 27:37)

And with him they crucified two robbers, one on his right and one on his left. And the Scripture was fulfilled which says, "He was reckoned with transgressors." (Mark 15:27–28)

With great difficulty — and with the assistance of Simon — Jesus and his crossbeam reached Calvary after traveling about a quarter of a mile. Jesus arrived in a severely weakened, tortured, and dehydrated state. His clothes were probably glued to his body by clotted blood. He was weak, stumbling, dizzy, short of breath, and likely sweating, thereby diminishing his already depleted body fluids. His suffering had not yet ended; it would now take the form of crucifixion.

Claims

Descriptions of the crucifixion of Christ often refer to the position of Jesus on the cross. Some also refer to other parts of the cross, such as a crude seat and a footrest. They often refer to difficulty breathing and his feet being nailed to the front of the cross. But are they accurate?

> Although the feet could be fixed to the sides of the stipes or to a wooden footrest (*suppedaneum*), they usually were nailed directly to the front of the stipes. To accomplish this, flexion of the knees may have been quite prominent, and the bent legs may have been rotated laterally.[2]

> The major pathophysiologic effect of crucifixion, beyond the excruciating pain, was a marked interference with normal respiration, particularly exhalation.[3]

What Happened to Jesus on Calvary?

In his magnum opus, *The Death of the Messiah*, Father Raymond Brown states clearly the frustration of all who seek to know more about the details of what happened to Jesus Christ on Calvary: "We now come to the centerpiece of passion, the crucifixion itself, more often portrayed in art than any other scene in history — with great variation in the shape and position of the crosses, in how Jesus is affixed to the cross, in how he is clothed, in his expressions of anguish, etc. Yet in all comparable literature, has so crucial a moment ever been phrased so briefly and uninformatively?"[4]

From the Gospels, we learn through direct statements and by inference that the following things happened on Calvary:

- Jesus was stripped of most, if not all, of his clothes.
- Simon finished carrying Jesus' crossbeam to Calvary.
- Jesus was attached to the crossbeam with nails.
- A sign was placed over Jesus' head listing his name and crime.
- Jesus was alive on the cross for about three hours.
- The place of crucifixion could easily be seen by many people.
- Jesus could see and speak from his cross.
- Jesus was able to cry out in a loud voice at the moment of his death.
- Pilate was surprised at the rapidity of Jesus' death.
- Jesus' legs were not broken, although the legs of the two men crucified beside him were broken to bring about a rapid death.
- After death, a spear pierced Jesus' side, from which blood and water flowed.

What can we add to this from what we know of Roman practice?

According to John Granger Cook, based on the available historical evidence of crucifixion, there was no set procedure common to all Roman crucifixions. However, by using multiple historical and fictional accounts of crucifixion, we can see elements present in various crucifixions even though no one description is valid for all crucifixions.[5] Cook borrows an analogy from the philosopher Wittgenstein, saying that there are "family resemblances" shared by different narratives: "And the strength of the thread does not reside in the fact that some one fibre runs through its whole length, but in the overlapping of many fibres."[6]

From his extensive research,[7] key points of which are listed in appendices at the end of this book, Cook concludes that

- public crucifixions were common horrors of daily life about which the evangelists did not need to write details; and
- Roman crucifixion practice varied; but
- crucifixion evidence in literature, archaeology, graffiti, inscriptions, and art demonstrates many overlapping features.

The two appendices at the end of this book detail the ancient evidence for crucifixion from literature, archaeology, graffiti, inscriptions, and art. Many conclusions that I draw regarding crucifixion are based on the contents of these two appendices. Readers who want more background on the statements I shall make on what we know about crucifixion should read the appendices before moving on. In order to keep our focus on the sufferings of Jesus and the spiritual benefits of meditating on those sufferings, I have not included all of that information in the main body of the text.

We know that crucifixion was a miserable and shameful death:

- Justin Martyr (c. 100–c. 165): "For they declare that our madness consists in this, that we give second place after the unchangeable and eternally existent God and creator of all things to a person who was crucified."[8]
- Arnobius (d. c. 330): "The gods are not inimical towards you because you worship the omnipotent god,

but because you worship a man who was born and who perished by the notorious punishment of the cross that is for the lowest persons [i.e., common people]. In addition you contend that he was a god and you believe he still exists and you worship him with daily supplications."[9]

We know that crucifixion was typically reserved for men and women slaves, Roman citizens of low social standing, enemy soldiers, and foreigners. However, there are examples of men of high social standing who were crucified, albeit against the custom of the day.

We know that crucifixion was often preceded by various forms of torture, including scourging, burning with or without pitch, and burning through the application of heated metal plates (*laminae*).

We know that crucifixions were typically performed outside the boundaries of a city in designated, public places where the maximum number of people could witness the event.

We know that the condemned walked to the place of crucifixion. Sometimes they were chained, and other times they carried their crossbeam (*patibulum*). If they carried their crossbeam, the upright stipes was already in place at the site where crucifixion would take place.

We know that *stauros*, used to describe what Jesus carried, was the preferred Greek word to render the Latin term *patibulum*, meaning the crossbeam.

We know that whether or not they carried the *patibulum*, victims were attached not to crosses laid on the ground but to standing crosses.

We know that victims could be attached by ropes and/or nails, as ancient Greek and Roman writings reveal:

- Pliny the Elder (c. AD 23–74): "So, too, in cases of quartan fever [modern malaria], they take a fragment of a nail from a cross, or else a piece of a halter/cord that has been used for crucifixion, and, after wrapping it in wool, attach it to the patient's neck; taking care, the moment he has recovered, to conceal it in some hole to which the light of the sun cannot penetrate."[10]

- Xenophon (c. 430–354 BC): "The Governor relying upon the Credit of these Letters, without further Enquiry into the Merits of the Cause, commanded him to be Crucified. … Those who received the Order, drew him to the Banks of Nile, and perceiving a Place where a craggy Rock projected over the River, they there erected the Cross, and fastened him thereto with cords [ropes] by binding his Hands and Feet, as is the Custom of Crucifixion in that Country [Egypt]."[11]

We know that at least three writers believed death normally occurred slowly, even due to starvation: Philo of Alexandria,[12] Bishop Eusebius of Caesarea Maritima,[13] and Saint Augustine.[14]

We know that crucifixion victims could be placed in different positions.[15]

We know that crucifixion victims were portrayed as completely without clothing, or "nude" in the Greek or Roman sense of still wearing a loincloth.

We know that crucifixion could be conducted by a public executioner/undertaker known as a *carnifex* or by a military authority such as a centurion or even a common soldier.

We know that the earliest images of crucifixion portray arms extended horizontally, not vertically, on the cross.

We know that the earliest images of crucifixion portray the victim's head at and above the level of the *patibulum* (whether or not the upright post extends above the *patibulum*).

We know that the earliest images of crucifixion and the archaeological evidence never depict one foot on top of the other foot. Most commonly, they show the knees bent outward with the outside of the heels next to the front of the upright post (stipes). It is less common to see early depictions with each foot to the side of the stipes.

We know that the earliest images of crucifixion portray hands or wrists attached by nails, fetters, or ropes. Also, in these images, the wrists — not the palms of the hands — appear to be attached.

Questions to Answer

With the above findings at our disposal, there are still seven un-answered questions I would like to explore. We will explore these questions in this and the following two chapters.

1. How were Jesus' hands fixed to the *patibulum*?
2. How were Jesus' feet fixed to the stipes?
3. What did Jesus' body look like on the cross?
4. Did Jesus have difficulty breathing on the cross?
5. What was the cause of Jesus' death?
6. Why would breaking the legs of crucifixion victims hasten their death?
7. What was the source of the blood and water when a spear pierced Jesus' side?

The first three questions will be explored in this chapter; questions 4 and 5 on the cause of Jesus' death will be explored in chapter 9; and the final two questions will be covered in chapter 10.

To further research these questions, we will now turn to literature published by physicians. Some of it is from peer-reviewed journals; some from articles published on the internet without prior peer review; and some from non-peer-reviewed books published by physicians, focusing on Barbet (1963), Zugibe (2005), and Kubala (2017).[16] With medical and scientific investigations, peer-reviewed sources carry the most weight, as other experts have examined them; yet these are not guaranteed to be accurate. Original sources, such as those quoted in the appendices of this book, are the most helpful for historical inquiries. This book is a hybrid historical-medical analysis. If published medical books and articles propose something contrary to original historical source material regarding various aspects of Jesus' Passion, then these various sources of evidence will have to be weighed to determine what most likely happened.

Finally, I will also turn to the Shroud of Turin for information, but to a much lesser extent. While we can never prove that it is the burial cloth of Christ, it is an ancient cloth depicting someone who appears to have been scourged, crowned with a multipointed, sharp cap, pierced through the right side of the chest, and crucified. Different readers will take evidence from the Shroud with various levels of credulity. In this book, it is not my purpose to convince you one way or the other regarding its authenticity. Even for those who believe it is definitely the burial cloth of Christ, there are more limitations than one might expect to the information it yields. None of my conclusions relies on evidence from the Shroud that I could not at least infer from other sources.

When attempting to answer each of these questions, we must realize that absolute certainty is not possible and that, in many cases, multiple explanations are consistent with our limited data. I liken this situation to an algebra problem in which there are more variables than there are equations demonstrating their relationships. For instance, if we are given the equation $2x + 2y = 10$ and asked to solve for x and y, there are an infinity of correct answers. If we are given two equations with three variables (x, y, and z) and asked to solve for x, y, and z, we still cannot do it. However, if we know that x $= 2$, then we can solve for y in the first case and y and z in the second.

Similarly, if we know that Jesus was nailed to the cross (versus being tied with ropes), we will be able to infer certain other things. Still, while we can come to some conclusions about what happened to Christ on Calvary, we will never know this side of heaven exactly what happened. So why should we bother with this investigation at all? Because to know Christ is to love Christ. Even if we can't know every detail with certainty, we can still know many things, and I believe it is worthwhile to try to determine what we can know about his suffering.

Finally, I will use a pragmatic argument in some discussions. I was in the military, and I know from experience what all soldiers through time have known: If there is an easier way to get a dull, repetitive task done, a soldier will find it. We will consider that maxim when we speculate on how a Roman soldier or carnifex would approach the grisly task of execution by crucifixion.

Question 1: How Were Jesus' Hands Fixed to the *Patibulum*, and What Suffering Did That Cause?

We know that nails held Jesus' hands to the cross because of his conversation with Thomas recorded in John 20:24–29. Both Jesus and Thomas use a Greek word derived from *cheri*, meaning "hand." The Greek word for palm is *palame*, and the Greek connotation for wrist is *karpos cherion*. So you can see that the Greek word for wrist is actually two words: the word for hand (*cherion*) combined with *karpos*, from which we get "carpals," or wrist bones. Therefore, the Greek word *cheri* includes both the palm of the hand and the wrist.

Where did the nails go through Jesus' hands? There is no way to know for sure. We have no archaeological evidence of a crucifixion nail in a bone or between the bones of a hand. The argument has been put forth that, since there is no strong tissue in the palms of the hands perpendicular to the metacarpals (the palm bones), nails through the palms would pull through the soft tissues of the hand.

As early as 1598, Archbishop Alfonso Paleotti of Bologna, Italy, viewed the Shroud of Turin and reportedly said that Jesus could not have been suspended by nails through his hands "because the nail would not have supported the weight of the body but, owing to this weight, the hand would have been torn, as has been proved by the experiments carried out by talented sculptors on corpses with a view to making a picture."[17]

Dr. Barbet reported nailing a freshly amputated arm through the palm with a nail 1 centimeter in diameter. After 10 minutes of attachment with an 88-pound weight, the wound lengthened. With a moderate shake of the arm, the wound lengthened so far that the palm split between two fingers, and the arm fell from the nail. Dr. Barbet therefore concluded that nails through the palms would not hold a live person on a cross, especially, he reasoned, since the weight pulling on each palm of a 176-pound man would be 88 pounds if the forearms were directly above him. If the arms were at any angle away from the body, the weight pulling on each arm would increase. If the arms were 25 degrees above horizontal (or 65 degrees below vertical as assumed by Barbet), each arm would bear a force of 209 pounds.

Unfortunately, Dr. Barbet's experiment has the following weaknesses:

- The formula for force used to determine the pull on each arm assumes that the feet are hanging freely.
- Only one arm was used for the experiment, and the experiment was not repeated.
- We don't know why the arm was amputated. There was some kind of disease or trauma requiring its amputation that almost certainly would have made it less strong than an arm that was not diseased or damaged. Gangrene was one common reason for amputation, and this implied reduced blood flow and gradual death of the tissue due to infection or significantly reduced blood flow.

In his book published in 2005, Dr. Zugibe describes how he performed experiments with men weighing 174 to 204 pounds while attached to a cross with leather wrist and foot gauntlets.[18] The feet were attached side by side with the soles against the upright post. He then measured the force on each wrist and found that, with the arms in the 25-degree position assumed in Dr. Barbet's experiment, force decreased to about one-third of the force of a free-hanging body with feet not attached. He found, in contrast to Dr. Barbet's experiment, that for a 176-pound man, the force per arm would be 69 pounds, or less than half of the man's body weight. That means the total force on the hands of the 176-pound man was less than 140 pounds if his feet were attached and his arms were at a 25-degree angle above horizontal. If the arms were completely horizontal, the force on the wrists would have been negligible, with virtually all the weight supported by the feet.

The horrific picture on page 162 was the result of Dr. Marie Louis Adolphe Donnadieu's response to another faculty member in Lyon, France, who stated that nails through Jesus' palms would not support him on a cross. Around 1900, he nailed a cadaver through one palm and published the photo in his book. He hoped this one "experiment" would end his colleague's continued arguments.

The earliest images we have of crucifixion (found on gemstones and graffiti) show attachment of the hands at the wrist. This makes sense, as there is a strong, perpendicular band of tissue (the flexor retinaculum, which forms the walls of the carpal tunnel) around the wrist bones, so it is more likely that the nails went through Jesus' wrists than through his palms.

Thinking like a first-century Roman soldier for a moment, if I had to drive a nail through the hand of a struggling man, I would find an area on the hand that would be easy to fix to a cross and would be least likely to come off, so I didn't have to repeat the job or risk reprimand from my superior for a job poorly done. Now, the Gospels tell us that Jesus had nail marks in his "hands" (which, as we saw above, could mean the palms or the wrists), so this eliminates the distal forearm as the location for the nails. A struggling man was much more likely to pull his hand off over the head of a nail through the palm (since only soft tissue would have to be pushed out of the way), while it would be virtually impossible to pull the wrist, along with its eight tightly packed bones, over the head of the nail. So if the Roman soldier(s) tasked with crucifixion did try to ensure the simplest, most secure job, they probably tried to put the nail through the middle of Jesus' wrist.

Dr. Barbet came to the same conclusion, but he based his conclusion on one visible wound on the back of the left wrist of the man depicted on the Shroud of Turin. Both Dr. Barbet and Bevilacqua et al.[19] drove nails through the wrists of cadavers to try to better understand how a crucifixion victim would be affixed to a cross.

In Dr. Barbet's study, he used a short, 2-inch (5-centimeter) nail 1 centimeter across to make it easier to see the location of the nail on X-rays. He placed the point of the nail at multiple sites around the middle of the bending fold in the wrist at the base of the palm where there is a depression between two tendons. (This depression is between the palmaris longus and flexor carpi radialis muscles that flex the wrist toward the forearm.) Then he pounded the nail through the tissue at those sites in "over a dozen freshly amputated forearms."[20] Each time he did this, the nail shifted at an angle so that the point of the nail moved toward the elbow and the head of the nail bent toward the fingertips. Thus, the nail exited the dorsal wrist (back of the wrist) closer to the elbow than it entered the wrist.

Dr. Barbet said it felt as if the nail were passing through a "funnel" as it went between the wrist bones. No bones were ever broken in these experiments. (Recall that Saint John reported in his Gospel that the Scripture

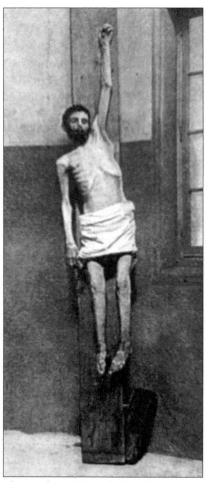

Photo of a cadaver held up by a nail through one palm. (Marie Louis Adolphe Donnadieu, 1904)

was fulfilled that "Not a bone of him shall be broken" [Jn 19:36].) The nail always passed through an anatomic space known as Destot's space, which is bounded by the lunate (semilunar), capitate (os magnum), triquetral (cuneiform), and hamate (uncinate) bones.

In the experiments of Bevilacqua et al., three right upper limbs

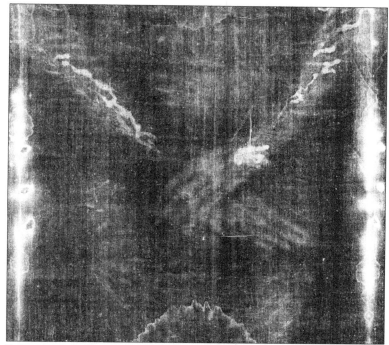

Exit wound of nail on the back (dorsum) of the left wrist on the Shroud of Turin image.

removed from cadavers (not fresh like those used by Dr. Barbet), were nailed in the space between the forearm and wrist bones and in two different locations of the wrist. One of the wrist locations was the one that Dr. Barbet used. The researchers viewed the locations of the wrist bones by X-ray while driving the nails through the wrist or the wrist/forearm junction.

When nailing between the wrist and forearm, Bevilacqua et al. placed the nail between the same two tendons that Dr. Barbet used, but closer to the elbow. When a nail was driven through this space, no bones were broken, the thumb was moved slightly closer to the side of the index finger, and there was minimal injury to the large median nerve. Nailing through an area toward the thumb side of the wrist caused no fractures and no nerve injury; the thumb was again partially moved toward the index finger. Nailing through an area more toward the little finger side of the wrist still caused no fractures; the nail found its way through Destot's space, injured the tendon of the flexor digitorum superficialis muscle, and damaged the ulnar nerve and artery.[21]

Contrarily, Dr. Barbet stated that as the nail traversed Destot's space, the thumb always bent sharply to face the palm when the nail went in. He also said that the trunk of the median nerve, not the ulnar nerve, was mostly transected each time and that there was a moderate release of venous blood. Bevilacqua et al. believe that Barbet confused the ulnar and median nerves, because the median nerve is on the opposite side of the wrist from the bones forming Destot's space. However, the median nerve is actually fairly close to the midline of the wrist, closer than the ulnar nerve in most instances.

Finally, in a study published in 2020, Stephen Bordes and several colleagues tried to recapitulate Barbet's experiments by pounding nails through the wrist and then dissecting the wrist to precisely follow the path of the nails. Each of five nails pounded through the middle of five cadaver wrists found their way through Destot's space without transecting an artery or a nerve. The ulnar nerve was far medial to each nail, while the median nerve was close to the nails but never touched. The authors believe that the median nerve may have been stretched mildly and pushed laterally as the nail took up space in the wrist and moved contents of the carpal tunnel toward the median nerve.[22]

Drs. Zugibe and Kubala have suggested that an acute injury of any nerve would lead to causalgia (now called complex regional pain syndrome). However, causalgia is a chronic inflammatory condition that typically does not appear until about three weeks after trauma, and no single injury will reliably cause it. In fact, only a small minority of injuries lead to it, and it is not yet known what predisposes an injury in one person to lead to causalgia while hundreds of others that are practically identical do not cause it. Given this evidence, I think it almost certain that a nail passing through Jesus' wrist and damaging a nerve would not have led to this type of intense pain; it

Destot's space
Right hand - palmar aspect

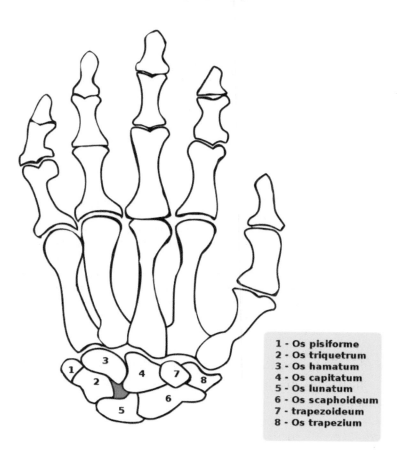

1 - Os pisiforme
2 - Os triquetrum
3 - Os hamatum
4 - Os capitatum
5 - Os lunatum
6 - Os scaphoideum
7 - trapezoideum
8 - Os trapezium

Destot's space in red, visualized as if looking at the palm of a right hand. The space is bounded by the hamate, capitate, triquetral, and lunate bones. This is the place where Dr. Barbet and others (Bevilacqua et al. [2014] and Bordes [2020]) discovered that a nail passes when pounded into the middle of a wrist.

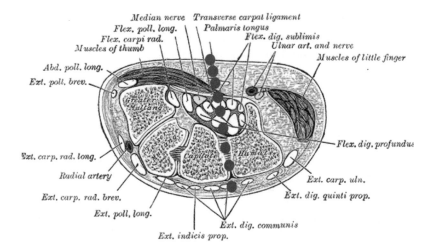

Transverse section through the left wrist. The palm is up, the back of the hand is down, the thumb is to the left, and the little finger side is to the right. Imagine you are looking from the forearm toward the hand. The two large arteries (in red — ulnar and radial) and two large nerves (in yellow — median and ulnar) would be missed by a nail passing through Destot's space in this section, between the capitate and hamate bones (see blue dotted line). Look at bones 3 and 4 in the figure on page 165 to find the space where the nail goes, just to the little-finger side of the midline. (Note that the figure on page 165 depicts a right hand and this figure depicts a left hand; thus the thumb and little finger sides are reversed).

would have led to a different type of pain called neuropathic pain, in which injury to a nerve causes a burning, searing, or ripping sensation.

Does the Shroud of Turin Help Us Here?

There is a blood flow on the Shroud of Turin that appears to emanate from the dorsal surface (back) of the left wrist. The point closest to the fingers appears to exit between the base of the middle and ring fingers.

The cross section of the wrist in the article by Dr. Edwards et al., seen in his figure 4,[23] shows the nail passing directly through the median nerve as it goes through a line parallel to the fingers be-

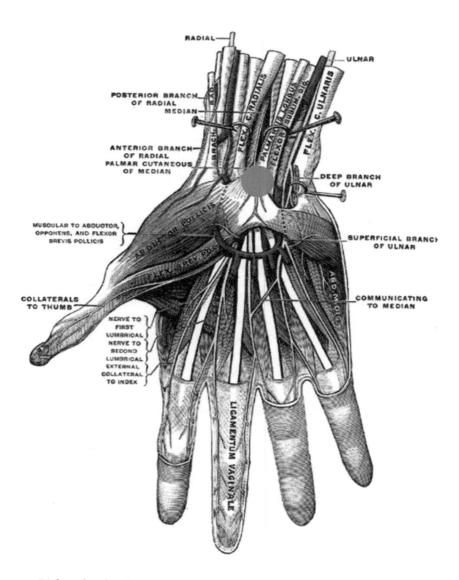

Right palm showing approximate location of nail that would pass through Destot's space when a nail is started through the palm side of the wrist from anywhere near the middle of the wrist. The yellow nerves and red arteries are not touched, but the nearby median nerve might be stretched toward the thumb.

tween the index and middle fingers. This area is closer to the thumb side of the wrist than to Destot's space, which would be more on a line between the middle and ring fingers. In the superficial wrist anatomy diagram in the same figure 4, the nail is pictured exactly in the middle of the wrist between the thumb side and the little finger side, so there is a discrepancy between the two drawings in figure 4. Dr. Edwards et al. believe that the median nerve and flexor pollicis longus tendons would have been transected, yet the diagram shows the nail passing through a wrist bone instead, farther toward the little finger side of the wrist, where it could pass between the bones forming Destot's space.

Many articles have been published debating exactly where the nail passed through the hand of Jesus and exactly what position Jesus' hand was in on the cross: Was it an "ulnar claw hand" or a "hand of benediction"? Was the thumb pulled? Which fingers were flexed, and which were extended? From the evidence I have seen, the nail most likely traversed Destot's space and was located a little closer to the little finger side of the wrist than the thumb side of the wrist.

The Shroud of Turin provides the only possible objective evidence, and it gives us far too little information to determine the path of the nail. Even if the Shroud did wrap Jesus' body, we only have one exit wound on which to base any conclusion. Without the entrance wound on the palmar side of the hand, we cannot know from the Shroud what structures the nail passed between or through.

What about Stigmata?

While stigmata are not historical evidence of Jesus' crucifixion, for those of us who believe that God sends this experience to certain individuals, the phenomenon certainly raises interesting questions. Those who have reportedly received the stigmata (the wounds of Christ) always bear the wounds in the palms of their hands. Saint Paul wrote, "I bear on my body the marks of Jesus" (Gal 6:17), leading some to speculate that he was the first stigmatist, but if he was, we don't know what his marks looked like. Indeed, he may have been referring figuratively to the many beatings he suffered for preaching the Gospel.

The first known stigmatist was Saint Francis of Assisi, whose stigmata included nails protruding from the skin. This may not be evidence of what Jesus suffered, however. By the thirteenth century, when Saint Francis lived, all known crucifixes depicted nail marks on the palms of Jesus' hands. So if God had given Francis the stigmata on his wrists, it would have been confusing not only to Francis but to those who witnessed his wounds.

In his book, Barbet quotes twentieth-century stigmatist Therese Neumann on this very subject. (I have not been able to independently corroborate this quote.) According to Barbet, Neumann said, "Do not think that Our Savior was nailed in the hands, where I have my stigmata. These marks only have a mystical meaning. Jesus must have been fixed more firmly on the cross."[24] Barbet says further that the appearance of the wounds and their precise location vary among different stigmatists.

Dr. Frederick Zugibe believed that he found a solution during an autopsy that both satisfied the stigmatists' experience and the evidence from the Shroud of Turin. He inserted a long needle through a self-defense stab wound in a cadaver. The needle entered the palm and exited through the wrist in the location depicted by the Shroud of Turin. This is not impossible, but it seems difficult to believe that this was standard practice when considering how a Roman soldier could achieve that angle without the nail slipping while keeping the hand in position.

I think Dr. Zugibe's finding says it all. The Roman executioners plying their trade were not at all concerned about the precise path of the nail through or between bones. They had a job to do and did it as efficiently as they could. They had large iron nails to drive through a wrist. They probably pulled the arms taut, for this allows less "give" when trying to pound something through relatively soft tissue (as compared to a block of wood), and then aimed at the center of the wrist so the nail was less likely to glance off. Whether a specific nerve was transected or specific bones were contacted is far less important than the fact that it hurt — excruciatingly.

I believe that, since the nail almost certainly passed through wrist bones or between the bones of the wrist and forearm, there would have been pain from the nail scraping against the bone. The bone is covered by a layer of dense, irregular connective tissue called the periosteum that has many sensory nerves that transmit pain impulses. Once the nails rested against bone (such as those in the wrist), intense, lancinating (lightninglike) pain, worsened by any movement of the body hanging on those nails, would wrack the victim until his death.

In the diagram of a cross-section through the wrist on page 166, I placed blue dots to demonstrate the approximate path of a nail through Destot's space, as described by Barbet (1963), Bevilacqua et al. (2014b), and Bordes (2020). From this diagram, you can see that the major blood vessels passing through the wrist and hand form an arch within the palm. The large radial (thumb-side) and ulnar (little-finger-side) arteries pass away from the middle of the wrist, where a large nail would have passed. Therefore, it is almost certain that there was no significant arterial blood loss from driving a nail through the palm or wrist. There would have been bleeding, as this happens when the skin is transected anywhere, but it would likely have been a slow, constant ooze from small veins.

If you look back at the photo negative of the hands from the Shroud of Turin, you will notice two flows of blood from the wrist wound. Dr. Barbet and Dr. Edwards et al. (and others) took this double flow to reflect two different positions of the body on the cross. While I will discuss this more in the section on question 4, I think there is a simpler explanation for the double flow.

The image shows the ulnar head (the large end of the ulna, the forearm bone on the little finger side of the wrist — arrow). This bump is elevated enough that blood would flow with gravity and separate to go around it. (Yes, wounds do bleed after death.)

How much damage occurred to either of the main nerves of the wrist (the median nerve or the ulnar nerve)? It depends on where the nail penetrated the wrist. It is virtually certain that the ulnar nerve

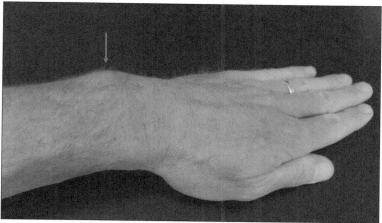

Ulnar head (blue arrow) likely responsible for different flows of blood from wrist wound of the man in the Shroud. (Thomas W. McGovern)

was not injured or transected. It is possible that the median nerve was partially damaged, especially if the nail went through an area away from Destot's space toward the thumb side of the wrist. It is unlikely that it was fully severed.

Question 2: How Were Jesus' Feet Fixed to the Stipes, and What Pain Did That Cause?

The Gospels do not tell us that nails were used to fix Jesus' feet to the cross. However, since nails were used to fix the hands, it is unlikely that another method, such as ropes, would have been used for the feet. This would be the case especially if a speedy execution was desired so as to get the victims off the crosses by sunset.

If we base the position of Jesus' feet on the earliest artistic representations of crucifixion found on graffiti and gemstones, then his feet would not have been placed on top of each other. Instead, they would have been side by side.

Archaeological evidence of one crucifixion suggests that the nail went sideways from lateral to medial (outside to inside) through the heel and into the cross (see appendix 2, "Jehohanan ben Hagkol"). Remains of another crucifixion victim, however, suggest that the knees would have been turned out to the sides to nail the heels from the front of the stipes from medial to lateral (see appendix 2, "Fifty Years Later, A Second Case"). Ancient images in graffiti and gemstones depict both possibilities. It is important to note that archaeological findings for both positions demonstrate that a nail can pass through the heel bone without breaking it ("not a bone of him shall be broken"). (For more detail on this, please see appendix 2.)

An internet search for "earliest religious crucifixion art" reveals that the vast majority of ancient depictions of crucifixion show the feet side by side. The earliest example I can find depicting overlapping feet on the cross is from the fourteenth century by Giotto, but Dr. Zugibe states that depictions of crucifixions showing one foot on top of the other appeared as early as the eleventh century.[25] According to the Encyclopedia Britannica website, the earliest image of Christ dead on the cross is from the ninth century.[26]

No ancient images show the feet adjacent to each other with toes pointed downward. Even so, Dr. Edwards et al.'s diagram portrays one possible location of a nail affixed through a foot with the sole flat against the front of the stipes.[27] While Dr. Edwards et al.'s depiction of the nail in the foot is plausible, it is unlikely given evidence from archaeology, ancient graffiti, and ancient gemstones. Because of the ancient evidence (described in detail in the appendices), I do not agree that one of Jesus' feet would have rested on the other. A soldier would likely have placed the spike in the middle of the foot just beyond the ankle bones. This would put it between the second and third metatarsals (the foot's version of the bones in the palm of the hand). As with the nail in the wrist, no large artery or vein would be severed, and there would be considerable pain from the periosteum of the metatarsals constantly weighing on the iron spike. No large nerve runs through this area, but branches of the medial and/ or lateral plantar nerves could have been transected.

Consider again our lowly Roman soldier. If the victim was struggling — and even if he wasn't — how in the world would the soldier force an iron spike up to one foot long first through one foot and then through the other while contorting the victim's knees and legs into position? Unless the sole of the first foot was placed tightly against the cross, there would be nothing solid against which to pound the spike through the foot. But if the spike went into the wood, the soldier would then have to pull it back out before placing the foot with the spike through it on top of the other foot and then pounding the spike through that one as well and into the stipes. From a practical viewpoint, this seems rather contrived and very difficult.

If I were that soldier, I would find it much easier to bend the knee and place the foot flat against the upright stipes and pound a spike through the dorsum (top) of the foot and into the wood. In fact, the feet could be first tied around the ankles before pounding in the nails. With the foot flattened against the cross, and no bones to impede the spike, it would be relatively easy to affix the feet with a large iron nail.

Regarding the Shroud of Turin, medical authors have commented that there is a very bloody imprint of the right sole and only a partial imprint of the left sole. They conclude based on this that the right foot rested against the stipes and the left foot rested on top of the right foot. Images of the Shroud of Turin show that the soles of both feet are nearly covered with blood, while only the top of the right foot reveals blood. It is not clear that these images strongly suggest, yet alone prove, that one foot rested on top of the other rather than next to the other.

Shroud researchers say that the position of rigor mortis (stiffening of a body after death) suggested by the Shroud image points to the knees being bent differently so that the left foot rested on the right. But what if one knee was bent more than the other when the body was on the cross, or one foot was not exactly at the same height as the other? Could that account for the differences seen on the Shroud? Additionally, if rigor mortis had begun, could the stiffening have been broken more on one side of the body than the other when the body was carried away and prepared for burial?

Also of note: Although it is pictured in some paintings from the Middle Ages on, there is no evidence in ancient literature or art of a foot support (*suppedaneum*) used to elevate the feet at an angle away from the cross.

Question 3: What Did Jesus' Body Look Like on the Cross?

You have likely seen innumerable crucifixes portraying Jesus in many different positions. The angle of the arms can range from nearly horizontal to nearly vertical. The feet might be portrayed side by side or one on top of the other, and in either case they might be flat against the stipes or angled on a foot-block of various inclinations so that the knees would not have to bend as much. In virtually all cases, Christ's back is pictured snug against the back of the cross.

Position of the Arms

Relying on graffiti, early gemstones, and literary descriptions of condemned men attached to a *patibulum* with their arms outstretched, I believe it is reasonable to assume that a crucifixion victim's arms were stretched horizontally along the *patibulum* and then nailed. Certainly some victims' arms were more taut than others' before nailing. Some authors[28] suggest that the shoulders were even purposely dislocated to pull the arms out farther, but I found no evidence of that in the ancient manuscripts.

No matter how tautly the arms were pulled away from the body and nailed, the body would sag. The only two ways to keep the arms at 90 degrees from the body would be to rest the feet in a standing position after attaching the hands to the cross, or to run a rope or fetter under the armpits and tie it to the *patibulum* to keep the body from sagging. When Dr. Zugibe did his experiments with men attached to a cross using wrist gauntlets, he stretched out their arms to their natural length and then let the volunteers sag. When the men were hanging by their wrists alone (that is, without their feet affixed to the cross), their arms formed a 65- to 75-degree angle from vertical (15 to 25 degrees above horizontal). Dr. Barbet proposed a 65-degree angle in his book, while in Dr. Zugibe's photos, his volunteers' arms appear to be at 75 degrees, or 15 degrees below horizontal.

Bevilacqua et al. also assumed that a crucifixion victim's arms were maximally stretched before being nailed, and that the arms would stretch no more than 2 centimeters each once the victim was put in an upright position. They additionally assumed that the arms were dislocated with ropes, referencing Archbishop Paleotti (1598) as a source.[29] There is no contemporary evidence to confirm such a dislocation procedure.

A 2-centimeter lengthening of an arm measuring 54 to 60 centimeters (about 2 feet) from shoulder joint to wrist allows an arm angle of 15 degrees above horizontal. To achieve an angle of 25 degrees above horizontal, each arm would have to stretch over 2 inches (5 centimeters). Based on the results of Dr. Zugibe's volunteers on the cross, as well as on an experiment performed by Dr. Barbet using a cadaver nailed to a cross with a 25-degree angle, it seems unreasonable to accept an arm angle of more than 15 degrees below horizontal. Dr. Barbet most likely believed it was a 25-degree angle based on the different angles of blood flow at the wrist on the Shroud of Turin.

Because we don't know how far up or down the stipes the feet were affixed and in what manner they were affixed, we really cannot know how close to horizontal the arms were. They may have been completely horizontal or slightly below horizontal.

Position of the Feet

Archaeological findings and early crucifixion graffiti, gemstones, and artwork show that Jesus' feet were not placed one on top of the other. However, we don't have information to determine whether it is more likely that his feet were nailed through each heel bone from inside to outside (to the front of the stipes with knees turned outward), through each heel bone from outside to inside (with the inside of the heels along the outside of the stipes), or through the tops of the feet side by side on the front of the stipes (this one has the least ancient evidence).

Body Position, Pain, and Movement on the Cross

Multiple authors writing about crucifixion state that experiments such as those performed by Barbet, Zugibe, and Ball (1989) are of limited value because they cannot recapitulate the conditions of an actual crucifixion.

I agree that these experiments have limited value, but I do not think that they have no value. On the contrary, I think these experiments can teach us something. For instance, if a healthy volunteer in an air-conditioned room who is strapped (instead of nailed) to a cross and knows he is not destined to die on it experiences certain types of discomfort, then I think it exceedingly likely that an actual crucifixion victim would have experienced that discomfort. Also, if a healthy volunteer is unable to perform a maneuver ascribed to crucifixion victims, then I think it exceedingly unlikely that an actual crucifixion victim would have been able to perform that maneuver.

Ball (1989) describes observing volunteers attached with leather wrist straps to metal hooks on the wood of a cross. He notes that the volunteers experienced more pain as the arms were stretched closer to horizontal. Because crucifixion was meant to inflict maximum pain, he therefore believes that the executioners would have kept the arms as close to horizontal as possible to increase the victims' suffering.

Once attached, Dr. Zugibe's volunteers complained of "marked cramping of the calf and thigh muscles with numbness of the feet after hanging for a short period of time. Twitching was commonly noted, and after 10 minutes, the limbs felt cool. Arching of the body to extend the legs was common during the suspension to relieve cramping of the leg muscles."[30]

Not only did Zugibe find that volunteers constantly shifted and assumed various positions to relieve strain and cramps in their shoulders, arms, legs, and knees, but they developed muscle twitching in their arms, chest, and thighs within 10 to 15 minutes. Numbness and tingling (*paresthesias*) in their hands, forearms, and arms ensued, and their chests appeared fixed so that their breathing came primarily from the action of the diaphragm. Perspiration drenched the volunteers within minutes, even though they were in a 70-degree air-conditioned room.

Zugibe's volunteers also noted severe pain in their hands and shoulders when they were hanging freely from their wrists alone. Once their feet were strapped to the cross, this intense pain subsided. As part of the volunteers' constant shifting to relieve cramping, they often arched their backs. During this time, the back of the head hit the *patibulum*. That means that in the same position, Jesus would have driven the crown of thorns more deeply into his scalp, reopening bleeding wounds.

Perhaps it is this constant shifting to which a character in one of Plautus's plays refers when he says that his master will change his name from Chrysalus (his name, meaning "Gold Dancer") to Crucisalus (meaning "Cross Dancer" or "Cross Struggler").[31]

For years, I found it odd that every crucifix and crucifixion scene I saw had Christ's back flat against the upright post of the cross. Zugibe noted that at rest, the volunteers sagged away from the cross; there was nothing to hold their backs against the upright post, so their backs always rested away from it. Therefore, the scourge wounds on Jesus' back would not have been constantly rubbing on the rough wood of the cross, as I had erroneously thought (and taught) for years.

I found two other sources that support Dr. Zugibe's finding. First, in the 1989 movie *Cyborg*, Jean-Claude Van Damme's character is crucified. In photos from the movie that show him on the cross, you can see that a metal ring attached to the upright was hooked to his waist to prevent him from sagging forward like an archery bow. And second, at some point between 1865 and 1868, a 25-year-old servant in Japan was executed by crucifixion for murdering his employer's son during the course of a robbery. He was affixed by tying instead of nailing, and his legs were spread apart, but a photograph that can be found on the internet shows how the body naturally sagged forward.

Dr. Zugibe asked his volunteers on the cross to push themselves up as if their lives depended on it; none were able to straighten their bodies, no matter how hard or how many times they tried.[32] This will be important to remember when we consider the hypothesis that crucifixion victims died of asphyxiation/suffocation. If a healthy individual could not push his body up higher by straightening his legs, it is extremely unlikely that an injured, exhausted person in severe pain, nailed through his hands and feet, would have had the strength to straighten from a sagging position.

The experience of hanging on the cross was itself painful. Zugibe's and Ball's volunteers complained of severe pulling on the shoulders, tight, cramping calves, and pain in the knees, feet, and wrists. Subjects felt rigid after 5 to 10 minutes and started breathing with short inspirations and long expirations, although none reported shortness of breath — even when they changed experimental positions so that they were sagging on the cross with their hands nearly above their heads. A few felt that their shoulders were being pulled out of their sockets. Although arms felt tight at the beginning of experiments, they felt flabby and flaccid after several minutes. Zugibe's volunteers' legs felt cold below the knees after 12 to 15 minutes, but this abated after they arched their bodies. Undoubtedly, such pain would be exacerbated in victims of crucifixion who had already endured horrifying tortures, including scourging.

Response to Claims

The first claim above is partially supported by the evidence. Archaeological evidence suggests that the feet of a crucifixion victim could be fixed to the sides of the stipes. However, there is no ancient evidence to suggest the use of a footrest (*suppedaneum*) and no ancient evidence (contemporary with the era when crucifixions were performed) suggesting that the feet were usually (or ever) nailed directly to the front of the stipes through the tops of the feet.

The second claim, that marked interference with normal respiration was a major effect of crucifixion, is not borne out by crucifixion reenactment experiments or by ancient literature. Never once is a victim said to be gasping for breath, but multiple times they are said to speak (and even spit) from the cross.

Jesus, Compassionate in His Suffering

John tells us in his Gospel that "standing by the cross of Jesus were his mother, and his mother's sister, Mary the wife of Clopas, and Mary Magdalene ... and the disciple whom he loved standing near" (Jn 19:25b–26).

Three Marys and John watched the excruciating torments of Good Friday. They knew how Jesus appeared on the cross. They witnessed the nails going through his hands and feet. They saw his body arching and struggling to relieve the pains of cramping.

Saint John Paul II wrote that Jesus endured this suffering "in love, so that man should not perish but have eternal life,"[33] and he names Jesus' mother as the most excellent disciple, who lived the Gospel of suffering throughout her life. At the Presentation in the Temple, Simeon prophesied not only that Christ would save us, but that a sword would pierce his mother's soul (see Lk 2:33–35). At the foot of the cross, Mary's soul was undoubtedly pierced by the prophesied sword. Suffering was an integral part of the life of the Holy Family, and Mary's experience of it culminated in accompanying her Son on Good Friday.

Despite the horrific pains of his Passion, Jesus demonstrated while it was going on how to be compassionate (note the word "passion" within "compassionate") to others. He did not use his own inestimable suffering as an excuse to ignore the sufferings of others. Jesus showed compassion toward his mother in four steps that we would do well to emulate in our lives, even when we are suffering:

- First, he noticed that she was suffering: "When Jesus saw his mother, and the disciple whom he loved standing near" (Jn 19:26a).
- Second, he was emotionally moved by her suffering. He allowed himself to identify with her suffering, with the sword piercing her soul.
- Third, he decided to do something about, to relieve her suffering over the impending earthly loss of her son.
- And finally, he acted on that decision to relieve her suffering by instructing her and John: "'Woman, behold, your son!' Then he said to the disciple, 'Behold, your

mother!' And from that hour the disciple took her to
his own home" (Jn 19:26b–27).

We will examine this four-step compassion paradigm more deeply
in chapter 11, in light of John Paul's direction in *Salvifici Doloris* on
how we are to respond to the suffering of others.

Exercising His Priesthood on the Cross

At the foot of the cross, Mary was a witness to Jesus' exercising of
his priesthood. What does this mean? According to the author of
the Letter to the Hebrews, Jesus "had to be made like his brethren in
every respect, so that he might become a merciful and faithful high
priest in the service of God, to make expiation for the sins of the
people" (Heb 2:17).

This is the essence of priesthood: offering sacrifice to God for
the salvation of others. Where did Jesus do this? On the cross. The
cross is where he exercised (and exercises, in the sacramental time
machine of the altar during Mass) his priesthood.

Because Christ lives in us and because Christ's suffering has
meaning, our suffering has meaning; and we can, like Christ, offer
the sacrifice of our own suffering on behalf of others. As Christians,
we were baptized as priest, prophet, and king to share in the sac-
rificial, teaching, and serving offices of Christ, who is the perfect
and complete priest, prophet, and king. In a way, a priest's role is
the reverse of a prophet's role. A prophet speaks to the people for
God, while a priest speaks to God for the people — precisely what
Christ did on the cross, both implicitly and explicitly ("Father, forgive them; for they know not what they do" [Lk 23:34]).

God has given all of the baptized, regardless of age, sex, or mar-
ital status, a priesthood to exercise because the essence of priesthood
is the offering of sacrifice to God on behalf of others. In the Mass,
the priest says, "Pray, brethren, that my sacrifice and yours may be
acceptable to God." The priest's sacrifice is that of Calvary, though in
an unbloody manner. Our sacrifice is our entire lives — our sufferings, burdens, aspirations, gratitude, and especially our entire wills.

The priest offers all that he can — Christ's suffering and death. We offer all that we can, united to the sacrifice of the priest.

Even on the cross, Christ has dominion over his actions and offers everything for us. He teaches us in this example of examples how we can do the same in the midst of our own suffering outside the Mass. Every time we willingly accept some form of suffering or perform a sacrifice, we can "offer it up" for an intention. Think of the great power and dignity God gives us: In our priesthood, we offer sacrifices to God for others. No difficulty, no trial, no discomfort need be wasted because we can offer it up to God as a sacrifice for the good of someone else or for an intention that we have.

In the beginning of *Salvifici Doloris*, Saint John Paul issues a spoiler (without even giving us a spoiler alert) regarding the meaning of human suffering. Although he mentions at least seven purposes of suffering throughout the document, he discloses in the very first paragraph the meaning of suffering, the answer to the question of why regarding human suffering: "'Now I rejoice in my sufferings for your sake'. The joy comes from the discovery of the meaning of suffering, and this discovery, even if it is most personally shared in by Paul of Tarsus who wrote these words, is at the same time valid for others. The Apostle shares his own discovery and rejoices in it because of all those whom it can help — just as it helped him — to understand the salvific meaning of suffering."[34]

Suffering means salvation; suffering means redemption. Salvation is the reason Paul rejoiced in his sufferings. As Paul exercised his priesthood, his sufferings (united to Christ) saved others. How many of us grasp this in our lives? We can influence eternity! What "superpower" can compare to that?

CHAPTER 9

The Death of Jesus

Date: Good Friday, April 3, AD 33
Time: Midafternoon ("about the ninth hour")
Place: Rock of Calvary

Gospel Narrative

And Jesus uttered a loud cry, and breathed his last. (Mark 15:37)

When God Died

In the midafternoon on April 3, AD 33, God died on a cross.

At the moment Jesus died, it had been about eighteen hours since he had eaten, drunk, or slept. During that time, he had lost sweat and blood through his agony in the Garden of Gethsemane, beatings in the pit beneath Caiaphas's house, bleeding from the crown of thorns, and bleeding (both internally and externally) from the scourging, as well as from lacerations received while falling under the cross. He experienced excruciating pain from all of this and from the crucifixion itself.

Following his arrest, almost everyone he encountered mocked him and hurled abuse at him. He knew his mother remained present with him, but on the cross, he felt abandoned by his Father ("My God, my God, why have you forsaken me?" [Mt 27:46]).

While we know that Jesus is God and man, our question here is, how did he die as a man? How did his body finally give out in death — the separation of the human soul from the human body? By exploring the next two of the seven questions introduced in the last chapter, we will gain more insight into what happened to Jesus' body to end his physical suffering. Here we will explore Jesus' breathing from the cross and the actual cause of his death (including why Pilate was surprised at the rapidity of his death).

Claim

This claim has been repeated in numerous places since Dr. Edwards et al. popularized Dr. Barbet's book:

> The major pathophysiologic effect of crucifixion was an interference with normal respirations. Accordingly, death resulted primarily from hypovolemic shock and exhaustion asphyxia.[1]

Question 4: Did Jesus Have Difficulty Breathing on the Cross?

This is a big question, for the theory that Jesus died by asphyxiation has been gaining traction for many years, especially since the publication of Dr. Edwards et al.'s article made it widely known. Today, many websites, books, sermons, homilies, and interviews state confidently that Jesus suffocated on the cross. I hope that the information below will demonstrate clearly why suffocation did not happen to crucifixion victims.

Origin of the Asphyxiation Theory

It was Dr. Barbet who first popularized the idea that crucifixion victims died of asphyxiation. He credits another Frenchman, Dr. A. A. LeBec, for coming up with the idea in 1925[2] and reasons as follows:

> The raised position of the arms, which were thus in the position for inspiration, would entail a relative immobility of the sides, and would thus greatly hinder breathing out; the crucified would have the sensation of progressive suffocation. … And "as oxygenation is not properly produced in lungs which are not working sufficiently, the additional burden of carbonic acid provides an excitation of the muscular fibers and, in consequence, a kind of tetanic condition of the whole body."[3]

Dr. Barbet used the evidence of Dr. R. W. Hynek,[4] a Czech physician who in the Austro-German army of World War I witnessed a punishment called *aufbinden* (German for "untie" — probably what victims screamed during the torture). Barbet reports that this form of torture "consists of hanging the condemned man by his two hands from a post. The tips of his two feet can scarcely touch the ground. The whole weight of his body, and this is the important thing, drags on his two hands which are fixed above him. After a certain time violent contractions of all the muscles are seen to appear, which end in a permanent state of contraction, of rigidity in the contraction of the muscles [cramps]."[5]

The tortured man would try to relieve the cramps by pulling himself up, as if doing a pull-up. Dr. Hynek reported that the large muscles of the body gradually became cramped, including the neck, upper limbs, lower limbs, chest, and abdominal muscles, also involving the muscles used for inspiration and expiration. Finally, the lungs filled with air that could not be expelled. "The victim, with his chest distended, is then seen to show all the symptoms of asphyxia. His face reddens, and then goes a violet color; a profuse sweat flows from his face and from the whole surface of the body. If one does not wish to kill the unfortunate man, he must then be cut down. This common punishment, says Hynek, might not last more than ten minutes."[6]

Dr. Barbet claims that crucifixion victims' bodies sagged on the cross and put more "drag" on the wrists, so that the victim experienced the same kind of respiratory compromise as in *aufbinden*. However, he provides no research or evidence to support that claim.

In their 1986 article "On the Physical Death of Jesus Christ," cardiac pathologist Dr. William Edwards of Mayo Clinic et al. quote Barbet (and two other, later authors), reiterating the belief that crucifixion victims died (at least partially) due to asphyxiation and that they had to push themselves up on the cross in order to exhale. He holds that in the "at rest" position of sagging down, their lungs would naturally expand and fill with air. If the asphyxiation — or suffocation — theory is true, this means the victim could not exhale (to stay alive) without pushing up with all weight on his feet, twisting around the nails in his wrists, and bringing his elbows into his sides to force the "bad air" out of his lungs.

For about twenty years, I uncritically accepted (and taught) this understanding of crucifixion.

Evidence against the Asphyxiation Theory

In their 2006 study, Matthew Maslen and Piers Mitchell state that reenactment experiments, including Zugibe's, should not be trusted since his "victims" were not scourged, did not carry a cross, were not nailed to a cross, did not experience dehydration, and did not endure the dreadful anxiety of imminent death. They find, therefore, that his experiments, and subsequent ones with similar volunteers, cannot be used to disprove the asphyxiation hypothesis. Perhaps Maslen and Mitchell are right, but let's look at the data.

First, we know from the last chapter that Zugibe's test subjects could not raise themselves onto their feet and straighten their legs once they had been on the cross for only a few minutes. How could we expect that true crucifixion victims in a weakened, tortured state, who normally lived on the cross for over a day (unless death was hastened), could perform a maneuver that a healthy, nontortured individual could not?

Second, in all the ancient literature regarding crucifixion, there is not a single reference to victims rising and falling on the cross or to victims having difficulty breathing, wheezing, or gasping for breath. Granted, absence of evidence is not evidence of absence. However, if asphyxiation were the common final pathway of death for crucifixion victims, it would be reasonable to expect at least one ancient author to mention it. Philo of Alexandria mentioned in the first century that death was prolonged, usually from starvation,[7] as did Eusebius of Caesarea in the early fourth century[8] and Saint Augustine in the early fifth century.[9] This does not fit the picture of the victim constantly rising up to gasp out breaths of stale air so he could inhale fresh air.

Third, crucifixion differs in two substantial ways from *aufbinden*: The hands of a crucified victim were not bound directly overhead, as in *aufbinden*, but held to the side, most likely at about 15 degrees above horizontal. Additionally, while all the weight of *aufbinden* victims was on the wrists, crucifixion victims' weight was distributed between the wrists and feet; in fact, Zugibe's experiments suggest that roughly twice as much weight was on the feet as the hands.

Fourth, we have other information (presented below) from Zugibe's experiments and from those of Ball reported in 2008.

Zugibe's Results

After being strapped to their crosses, the men in Zugibe's experiments could tolerate between 5 and 45 minutes of suspension before they requested release due to painful cramping of the shoulders, arms, and hands. No volunteer ever asked to be released from the cross due to trouble breathing; painful muscle cramps were always the reason. The volunteers' arms were at an angle of 15 to 25 degrees above horizontal. None experienced breathing difficulty either subjectively or objectively, even though after 10 to 20 minutes the subjects' chests felt rigid and their legs cramped. While they did not and could not push themselves up, they did arch their backs to relieve cramps, and when they did this their shoulders and scalps touched the cross. At no other time did their backs touch the cross. Even when subjects were tested without their feet attached to the cross (hanging from the wrists only), they experienced no difficulty breathing.[10]

While preparing to give talks early in my career, I would often raise my hands overhead to try to convince myself that this made breathing difficult. But I never succeeded in convincing myself and wondered why the diaphragm wouldn't continue the work of breathing regardless of what position the arms were in.

Ball's Results

Dr. David A. Ball disagrees with Zugibe and argues that his experiments could not rule out that asphyxiation played a role in death by crucifixion. He says that Zugibe let his subjects down due to muscular pain, but he believes that suffocation might have ensued if they had been required to stay on the cross longer. However, Dr. Ball admits that "I have watched many volunteers hang on the cross. They never seem to have any significant respiratory difficulty. More to the point, they never engage in the rhythmical up and down movement Dr. Barbet describes as essential for efficient respiration to occur."[11]

The longest any of Ball's volunteers could tolerate being on the cross was 31 minutes, with an average of 8 to 12 minutes. All had to be removed due to muscle cramps. The longest any of Zugibe's volunteers lasted was 45 minutes. Ball rightly wonders whether respiratory efficiency might be a function of time — that is, might difficulty breathing begin only after a longer period of time on the cross?

Ball placed his 18- to 35-year-old male volunteers on crosses in one of two positions: ten had their arms extended horizontally, and ten had their arms extended vertically. In both cases, the feet were supported. It made sense to test the two extreme arm positions possible for crucifixion; if there were a difference based on the angle of the arms, this experiment would be more likely to find it than Zugibe's experiments, where the arms were all 15 to 25 degrees from horizontal.

One of Ball's findings confirmed one of Zugibe's findings regarding pain: Volunteers with arms stretched horizontally could tolerate an average of 8.1 minutes on the cross, while those with arms vertically overhead could tolerate an average of 12.6 minutes on the cross before pain became unbearable. Since horizontal placement was more painful, it would be reasonable to assume that the Romans discovered this and were more likely to use this position (and this fits with the ancient images made during the times when crucifixions were performed).

While Ball states that he "measured volumes and pressures" and "gathered data without knowing what I would find," this breaks a cardinal tenet of research in which a specific hypothesis or multiple hypotheses are tested. When we collect many types of data without a hypothesis, chances are good that something will show a statistically significant difference, even if by chance. And Ball does not mention the different types of spirometry (breathing) data he collected; he reports only one of the variables, the forced inspiratory vital capacity (FIVC). This test, not commonly used by pulmonologists, measures the difference in volume between a maximal exhale and a maximal inhale. A pulmonologist explained to me that a reduction in FIVC can demonstrate a reduction in lung function due to neuromuscular fatigue (as the volunteers clearly experienced).

As for the FIVC results, those with arms vertical experienced a 7.0 percent reduction (4.89 to 4.55 liters) over 12.6 minutes, compared to a 2.3 percent reduction (4.81 to 4.70 liters) over 8.1 minutes for those with arms horizontal (historically the more likely crucifixion position). Because no statistical tests were applied and because it is not known whether the results for the volunteers with arms vertical would have been equivalent to those with arms horizontal at 8.1 minutes and only worsened over the following 4.5 minutes (to the tested average at 12.6 minutes), we don't know how comparable the data is. Ball asks a good question: Does increased time on the cross contribute to increased difficulty breathing? Unfortunately, his study design, statistical evaluation, and reporting do not allow us to draw any meaningful conclusions. His reported results neither confirm nor deny the possibility that asphyxiation played a role in the suffering and death caused by crucifixion.

A pulmonologist who reviewed Ball's article told me that if a victim's FIVC continued to decline as it had for the first 8 minutes, then breathing could be significantly compromised by 3 hours (the amount of time Christ was on the cross). He doubts someone could survive on the cross for 12 to 24 hours or more if FIVC continued to drop.

Zugibe's Data

Zugibe also measured FIVC. In his subjects, it decreased somewhat after 2 to 4 minutes and then remained constant. The blood lactate (acid) levels increased to 3.5 times normal after 15 minutes, and the ensuing acidosis (decreased pH) of the blood stimulated subjects to breathe more rapidly to exhale the acid (as carbon dioxide).

Zugibe also reported that a healthy level of oxygen remained in the blood at all times (97 to 99.5 percent). The respiratory quotient increased as expected (more carbon dioxide was breathed out over time due to increased muscle activity). Volunteers hyperventilated for the first 6 minutes, reached 2 to 3 times the normal respiratory rate, and stabilized at that rate. In poorly conditioned individuals, the heart rate jumped as high as 175 beats per minute (perhaps due to the adrenaline release of the fight-or-flight response).

Mödder's Data

An Austrian radiologist named Hermann Mödder suspended medical students by their wrists from a horizontal bar with their hands above their heads and spread 40 inches apart, simulating *aufbinden* except that the wrists were farther apart. With their legs dangling beneath them, all the students' weight was on their wrists.[12] Within minutes, the students became pale, and the amount of air they breathed in and out with each breath decreased by 70 percent (from 5.2 to 1.5 liters on average); only their diaphragms (and not their chest muscles) were moving air. When the students could lift their legs, they could breathe more deeply, but their thigh and leg muscles fatigued. Within 6 minutes, the students could tolerate no more and had to be released.

Unlike the students, Jesus would have had his feet attached to the cross (not hanging freely), and his arms were at a much lower angle. It seems that *aufbinden* would significantly affect breathing within several minutes, while studies simulating crucifixion did not find this effect.

Comments of Barbet's Friend

In an appendix to *A Doctor at Calvary*, Dr. Barbet printed the dissenting view of his respected friend the physician Dr. P. J. Smith: "Asphyxia, or respiratory failure as we prefer to call it, the author [Dr. Barbet] thinks was caused by the respiratory muscles becoming fixed in inspiration due to the falling forward of the trunk away from the vertical section of the Cross and the consequent inability to expire and so empty the lungs of carbon dioxide. This theory is not supported by some of the evidence set out in the book."[13]

Breathing on the Cross

Zugibe's and Ball's volunteers had no difficulty breathing while on the cross, although they remained on the cross only for a maximum of 45 minutes. Volunteers on the cross could not raise themselves up to bring their elbows closer to their sides and make it easier to exhale. No ancient writer mentions the up-and-down movements that Barbet's asphyxiation thesis requires. No ancient writer mentions crucifixion victims suffering from shortness of breath or difficulty breathing. The hypothesis for asphyxiation as a major cause of death in crucifixion has its origins in the observation of a torture distinct from crucifixion.

Based on the above information, it seems unlikely that asphyxiation played any role, let alone a major role, in death by crucifixion. However, there is the possibility that prolonged metabolic acidosis (acid in the bloodstream) could lead to an increased breathing rate as the victim worked to breathe off the acid as carbon dioxide. If this continued in a spiraling fashion, where the respiratory rate and volume could not exhale the excess acid in the blood, this could lead to death by asphyxiation. This would have been more likely if Jesus' hands had been fastened above his head instead of horizontally. The presence of a pleural effusion (blood or other fluid between the lungs and chest wall [see chapter 10]) would have made breathing much more difficult and less efficient and could have contributed to a more rapid death.

Conclusion Regarding the Asphyxiation Theory

Advocates of the asphyxiation theory state that the high tension on each arm of the crucifixion victim would restrict chest wall movement and put the diaphragm at a mechanical disadvantage by flattening and restricting its movement. The victim would have to pull up to facilitate paradoxical respiration — paradoxical because inspiration would be passive (instead of active) and expiration would be active (instead of passive). This decreased movement of the chest wall/rib cage could lead to trapping of air in the lungs and increased acid in the blood.

Critics of the asphyxiation theory point out that *aufbinden* differs significantly from crucifixion in at least three ways:

1. The hand position is overhead in *aufbinden* and to the sides in crucifixion.
2. The feet are dangling in *aufbinden* and supported in crucifixion.
3. Death is far more rapid in *aufbinden* (within an hour) than in crucifixion (often a day or more).

Also, I find it significant that none of Zugibe's volunteers was able to push himself up as required by the asphyxiation theory. In fact, if the asphyxiation theory were correct, the victims would have had to push themselves up thousands of times in order to live as long as ancient documents stated that they did.

I find the strongest evidence against the asphyxiation theory in Scripture itself: "Then Jesus, crying with a loud voice, said, 'Father, into your hands I commit my spirit!' And having said this he breathed his last" (Lk 23:46). As Ball (1989) points out, patients dying of an inability to get necessary oxygen to their cells (as in suffocation) slowly fall into unconsciousness and die quietly, without the energy or consciousness to yell out at the moment of death. In other words, one cannot cry out while dying of suffocation. Yet the Scriptures suggest that something happened suddenly so that Jesus could cry out at the moment of death. This is not the picture of death by exhaustion/asphyxiation. Whatever caused Jesus' death must explain what Luke describes.

Question 5: What Was the Cause of Jesus' Death? Why Was Pilate Surprised at the Rapidity of Jesus' Death? And How Can It Account for Jesus Crying Out in a Loud Voice at the Moment of Death?

Up to this point, we have examined how Jesus physically suffered during his Passion. Now we come to the question of what put an end to his physical suffering — the cause of death. Multiple hypotheses regarding the cause of his death have been expounded, and as we like to say in medicine, the more plausible hypotheses there are, the less certain we are about which one is correct.

In 2006, Matthew Maslen and Piers Mitchell cataloged from the medical literature at least ten potential causes of Jesus' death. In 2012, a thoughtful review by Joseph W. Bergeron considered others. Hypotheses identified include the following:

1. Fatal stab wound
2. Jesus didn't actually die on the cross
3. Voluntary surrender of life
4. Suspension trauma
5. Respiratory acidosis
6. Asphyxia (suffocation)
7. Syncope (fainting)
8. Heart failure
9. Pulmonary embolism
10. Cardiac rupture (the broken heart theory)

11. Hypovolemic shock
12. Trauma-induced coagulopathy
13. More than one of the above

I do not intend to present the details of all of these possibilities; rather, I will review the most popular theories. If we believe the Gospels that Jesus died at the ninth hour (3:00 p.m.) on Good Friday, then we can eliminate numbers 1 and 2 above. As God, Jesus did not have to die until he wanted to, so there is certainly an element of number 3 involved in his dying, but he most likely constrained himself to the natural ability of a human soul (which he possessed) to animate a human body.

Suspension trauma (number 4) refers to someone hung by a harness (as a parachutist who lands in a tree or a mountain climber stranded in a harness due to bad weather) and dying after a prolonged time in that position. The methods of suspension by harness versus suspension on the cross are so different that I will consider that option no further. Respiratory acidosis (number 5) occurs when the lungs cannot exhale carbon dioxide as fast as the body produces it. This is a result of number 6 (asphyxia), which was covered in the prior section.

Syncope (number 7) is the medical term for fainting, loss of consciousness usually due to decreased blood flow to the brain. With regard to crucifixion, syncope would occur secondary to heart failure (number 8), shock (number 11), asphyxia (number 6), or pulmonary embolism (number 9; a blood clot in the vessels of the lungs). There is no plausible reason to consider heart failure (number 8) as a primary cause of death, although it certainly follows when and if shock or asphyxia occurs. Because of the complex interplay of various organ systems of the body during trauma and blood loss, it is almost certain that multiple factors (number 13) led to Jesus' death; we will consider most seriously hypotheses 9 to 12 from the list above.

Whatever potential causes of death we consider, they must account for Jesus' ability to do three things described in the Gospels:

1. Speak lucidly seven times from the cross while clearly observing those around him
2. Cry out loudly at the moment of death
3. Die far more rapidly than Pilate expected him to die (In the course of his career, Pilate must have ordered multiple scourgings and crucifixions, yet he was surprised at how rapidly Jesus died.)

Pulmonary Embolism

A pulmonary embolism is a blood clot that usually travels from the leg veins, through the right side of the heart, and into the lungs, where it blocks the pulmonary arteries from bringing oxygenated blood to the lungs. Significant obstruction of blood flow leads to high pressure in the right side of the heart, difficulty breathing, chest pain, low blood pressure, and death if the blockage is severe enough.

Blood clot risk increases two to three times in airplane flights over 4 hours where people do not contract their leg muscles, but the overall risk is still tiny in any one individual unless the person has other risk factors. The hypothesis that Jesus died of a pulmonary embolism relies on the increased risk of hereditary thrombophilia (making it easier to form blood clots) in Jewish populations due to Factor V Leiden deficiency. But Jewish populations in the Holy Land now may not necessarily reflect those of 2,000 years ago.[14] Today, about 5 percent of Jewish populations possess the gene mutation for hereditary thrombophilia,[15] and of those who have this mutation, only 1 per 1,000 per year will develop a blood clot deep in the legs that can possibly travel to the lungs.[16]

Moreover, as demonstrated in crucifixion reenactments, the cramping was so severe that the volunteers regularly moved to try to relax cramped muscles; such movement of the legs would significantly reduce the chance of deep vein thrombosis associated with sitting without moving, as on a long airplane flight. The likelihood that Jesus experienced a pulmonary embolism seems vanishingly remote, and even more unlikely to be a cause of death in the majority of crucifixions.

Cardiac Rupture (the Broken Heart Theory)

Of all the theories for the cause of Jesus' death, this one is perhaps the most poetic: the idea that Jesus both literally and figuratively died of a broken heart. In print, the main proponent of this has been a Mississippi family physician, Dr. David Ball, although it was first proposed in 1847 by a Dr. Stroud. The most common cause of cardiac rupture is a myocardial infarction (death of heart muscle, commonly called a heart attack). When an area of the heart wall dies, it can break open, allowing blood to fill the sac (pericardium) surrounding the heart. This prevents the heart from beating (cardiac tamponade), and the victim dies.

Ball writes that Jesus probably fell with a 100-pound *patibulum* on his back (recall that I earlier estimated a more likely weight of 15 pounds) that was tied to his wrists so that he could not stretch out his arms to break his fall. Then the crushing force of both hitting the ground and having the *patibulum* strike his upper back caused a cardiac contusion that converted to a rupture of the heart wall during the stresses of crucifixion. As in the cardiac rupture scenario following a heart attack, death ensued by cardiac tamponade.

Bergeron points out that cardiac rupture due to myocardial infarction is usually rapid and that there is no reason to believe that Jesus had a heart attack.[17] In the scenario where chest trauma (such as scourging and falling with the *patibulum*) leads to cardiac rupture, there are usually multiple rib fractures and blunt force to the sternum (breastbone). Moreover, the patient is typically unconscious, and death is immediate.

Furthermore, college and professional football players regularly and repeatedly experience chest trauma more significant than falling forward under a 6-foot board and landing on pavement, and no case of cardiac rupture has been recorded among them.

It is extremely unlikely that Jesus could have continued walking to Calvary, even with Simon carrying the *patibulum*, with a nearly ruptured heart wall, and then could have been able to speak lucidly seven times from the cross without losing consciousness. A practicing cardiologist confirmed to me that he is not aware of a scenario in which a patient could not only survive trauma that would rupture the heart wall but also remain lucid and live for several hours before the heart ceased beating.

Broken Heart Syndrome (Takotsubo Cardiomyopathy)

My consultants in cardiology and pulmonology/critical care (Dr. David Kaminskas and Dr. Eustace Fernandes) recommended that I add the consideration of a condition known as "broken heart syndrome" or "takotsubo stress syndrome."[18] This condition, first described in Japan in 1990 (Sato et al.), refers to an emotionally broken heart, not a physically broken (or ruptured) heart.

While 90 percent of patients with this condition are women (mostly postmenopausal), 10 percent are men (although only 3 percent of patients are under 50 years of age). In this condition, a traumatic emotional or physical event leads to a syndrome that mimics a heart attack: chest pain, increased cardiac muscle enzymes in the bloodstream, and similar electrocardiogram (ECG) findings. It is thought that increased release of adrenaline (epinephrine and similar chemicals, as in the fight-or-flight response) narrows the small branches of the coronary arteries that supply the heart muscle. If these small arteries spasm for long enough, the heart muscle doesn't function, and heart failure and even fatal arrhythmia can ensue. It is highly unlikely that this played a role in Jesus' death, though it is not, strictly speaking, impossible.

Shock (Hypovolemic and Traumatic)

Shock is "a systemic disease that results from any process that impairs the systemic delivery of oxygen to the cells of the body OR that prevents its normal uptake and utilization."[19] In shock, the body's organs (brain, heart, lungs, liver, kidneys, etc.) do not receive enough oxygen to survive because there is not enough blood reaching them. Inadequate pumping of the heart muscle prevents sufficient blood from reaching the organs.

Oxygen is essential to produce energy in the body; 18 times more energy can be produced in the body with oxygen than without oxygen. In shock, the sympathetic (fight-or-flight) nervous system activates to narrow blood vessels, increase blood pressure and heart rate, and make the heart pump blood more effectively. However, even if blood pressure is normal, once cells begin to swell with fluid, they cannot get rid of waste carbon dioxide and absorb oxygen as well as before.

The primary proponents of shock as a major cause of Jesus' death are Dr. Zugibe and Dr. Edwards et al., but others mention it as playing a significant role. These others include Dr. Joseph Bergeron and Dr. P. J. Smith (Dr. Barbet's friend, who wrote in an appendix of *A Doctor at Calvary*: "I am of the opinion that there is overwhelming evidence that Christ died from heart failure due to extreme shock caused by exhaustion, pain and loss of blood"[20]).

In traumatic shock, the main cause of reduced blood volume is hemorrhage — internal and/or external bleeding. Significant blood loss leads to failure of multiple body systems, inability of the cardiovascular system to pump and deliver necessary blood to the organs, tissues starving for oxygen, inflammation and swelling of body tissues, and an increased risk of thinner blood, causing increased blood loss from small vessels throughout the body.

While Bergeron's article explains details of hormonal and metabolic responses to shock,[21] it is sufficient for our purposes here to state that contributing factors to Jesus' loss of blood and fluid volume included the following:

- no fluid intake since the Last Supper
- hematidrosis (small amount)
- normal insensible water loss from breath[22]
- sweating profusely during night beatings, scourging, carrying the cross, and while on the cross
- normal evaporation of water from the skin[23]
- external blood loss from the scalp due to the crown of thorns, multiple beatings, and especially the scourging
- internal blood loss (into the space around the lungs and soft tissues) from scourging and possibly from falling

There are four stages — or worsening degrees — of traumatic shock:

1. *Compensated traumatic shock.* Normal blood pressure, pulse, and heart rate can be maintained, and recovery is easy as long as fluids are replaced and injuries are treated.
2. *Decompensated traumatic shock (a.k.a. progressive shock).* This is a reversible, transitory stage when cellular damage and toxic effects begin. Without immediate treatment, irreversible shock and death will ensue no matter what treatment is given.
3. *Subacute irreversible shock.* Resuscitation restores normal vital signs, but too much cellular damage has occurred and patient dies anyway. (Since he was not resuscitated, Jesus never experienced this.)
4. *Acute irreversible shock.* Spiral of ongoing (triad) hemorrhage, acidosis, and coagulopathy leads to early death from massive blood loss.

During his Passion, Jesus entered stage 1, then stage 2, and possibly (and finally) stage 4. However, we know that he did not lapse into unconsciousness prior to death, which means that some acute event interrupted this cascade (perhaps during stage 2) to bring about sudden death after he cried out. Jesus was in a vertical position and remained coherent and lucid until something drastically tipped his health downward; this does not fit with asphyxiation or shock as the sudden cause of his death.

With shock, lack of oxygen in one organ can lead to a cascade of inflammatory events that leads to disease throughout all organs of the body. This poor organ function leads to death. (Inflammation is most simply defined as swelling, redness, heat, pain, and loss of function in an organ. Inflammation initially occurs as a protective event, but if the response is too strong, it can lead to death. Think of people whose airways swell and block their breathing after a bee sting or during an asthma attack.)

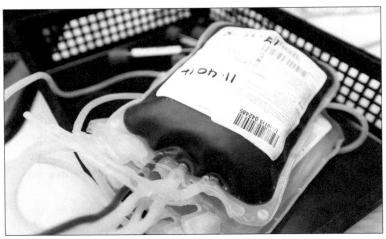

A pint of blood.

What Amount of Blood Loss Will Cause Shock Symptoms?

Based on estimates for the man represented in the Shroud of Turin, various researchers have suggested a height of 70 to 72 inches, with a weight of 170 to 180 pounds.[24] Since the nice round number of 80 kilograms is equivalent to 176 pounds, we will use that figure for Jesus' estimated weight. According to reference.medscape.com, an 80-kilogram man possesses 6 liters (12.7 pints) of blood. Think of blood filling three 2-liter bottles of pop.

According to the American College of Surgeons Advanced Trauma Life Support classification of blood loss,[25] a person can lose up to 15 percent of his blood volume without any symptoms. For a man Jesus' size, this would be just under 2 pints (units) (just under 1 liter) of blood. Once 15 percent of blood is lost, the pulse rises to 100 to 120 beats per minute, but the blood pressure remains normal. The respiratory rate increases to 20 to 30 breaths per minute, and urine output starts to fall. Patients become mildly anxious.

Once 30 percent (3.8 pints, 1.8 liters) of blood is lost, the pulse rises to 120 to 140 beats per minute, the blood pressure drops, and the respiratory rate climbs to 30 to 40 breaths per minute. Urine

Three 2-liter bottles.

output falls even more, and patients become anxious and confused. This assumes that the patient is lying down; it would be far worse for a patient in an upright position, as on a cross.

Once 40 percent (5.1 pints, 2.4 liters) of blood is lost, the pulse exceeds 140 beats per minute, the blood pressure drops further, and the respiratory rate remains over 35 breaths per minute. Patients are confused and lethargic and will typically die without fluid replacement. Therefore, if Jesus lost a little more than a 2-liter bottle volume of blood, death would be imminent due to shock.

Symptoms of Shock

Before becoming unconscious, patients develop a faint and rapid pulse, increased respiratory rate, cool and moist skin, and anxiety, followed by apathy and nausea.

At one point in the Gospel, Jesus says, "Hear me, all of you, and understand: there is nothing outside a man which by going into him can defile him; but the things which come out of a man are what defile him" (Mk 7:14–15). While he was speaking of food and drink, this statement could also describe traumatic hypovolemic shock. For it was the loss of blood and fluid from Jesus that "defiled him" or made him sick, and the lack of food and fluid entering him that contributed to his death.

Trauma-Induced Coagulopathy

Bergeron describes trauma-induced coagulopathy (TIC) as a common finding in trauma patients and suggests that it played a role in Jesus' death.[26] Immediately after severe trauma, the blood-clotting system becomes less efficient, meaning that the blood thins; this increases the blood loss caused by the trauma.

Two conditions are necessary for TIC to occur: shock due to blood loss and severe traumatic tissue injury that releases inflammatory and blood-thinning chemicals into the circulation.[27] Although there are many defects of the clotting system at this point, one key factor is that platelets, the cells that initiate clot formation in the blood, are present in normal numbers but do not stick to each other normally.

TIC is a relatively recently described entity that has likely always been present in patients with severe trauma and blood loss. Jesus may have developed the lethal triad that leads to rapid death: TIC, hypothermia (decreased body temperature), and acidosis (acid, low pH in the blood).

We know that Jesus had significant tissue injury from multiple beatings and the scourging. We know that he had probably lost a significant amount of blood from the scourging and crowning with thorns, which caused shock. We know that reduced breathing efficiency from shock and from splinting the chest due to pain can lead to acidosis (low blood pH). About 25 percent of trauma patients develop TIC, and it increases the risk of death fourfold. Finally, Jesus could have developed hypothermia due to shunting of blood away from his arms and legs, shock, blood loss, profuse sweating, and the environmental exposure of being naked (or nearly naked) in temperatures in the 50s or low 60s Fahrenheit. While this is not proof that Jesus developed the lethal triad mentioned above, if he did, it gives a possible explanation for why his death was more rapid than that of the average crucifixion victim. It certainly was not the final cause of death, or he would have rapidly bled internally and externally without a chance to cry out.

Multiple Contributing Causes

In their 1986 article, my medical school mentor, the cardiac pathologist Dr. William Edwards and his colleagues proposed the theory that asphyxiation plus shock plus cardiac arrhythmia caused Jesus' death. Dr. Edwards et al. proposed that exhaustion asphyxia was one of two primary contributors to Jesus' death and that his death came faster than expected because of an unusually harsh scourging. He concluded that the other primary contributor was likely hypovolemic shock. He believes that a stress-induced arrhythmia (irregular heartbeat that does not pump blood effectively to the body) was the terminal event leading to a sudden death; this scenario would have allowed Jesus to cry out at the moment of death.

I do not think that Dr. Edwards et al. added anything new (as of 1986) to the understanding of death by crucifixion. What he did better than anyone up to that time was to put together in a coherent way what many others had written about crucifixion for the prior fifty-plus years. He did this in a well-written article, in a widely circulated and respected medical journal, with stunning and memorable illustrations. Just do an image search on the internet for "Edwards" and "Physical Death of Jesus Christ" to see reproductions of many of the figures from that article. However, Dr. Edwards et al. may have relied too heavily and uncritically on the writings of Dr. Barbet, including his incomplete and sometimes misleading interpretation of ancient documents and too-heavy reliance on *aufbinden* as a way to explain suffering and death on the cross.

I completely agree with Dr. Edwards et al. that death from crucifixion had multiple contributing factors, and his hypothesis of a terminal arrhythmia brought on by shock and reduced oxygenation of tissues certainly would have allowed Jesus to cry out at the moment of death.

My friend Dr. David Kaminskas (cardiology) agrees with Dr. Edwards et al. that an arrhythmia is the terminal event that best matches the circumstances of crucifixion and the Gospel accounts. He says that ventricular fibrillation (V-fib or VF), when the ventricles quiver like a bag of worms, can be ruled out, since it causes an immediate loss of consciousness. He believes that ventricular tachycardia (V-tach or VT) is possible, because patients with VT can maintain consciousness for some time depending on the rate of the VT. Patients with VT commonly sense palpitations (strong, noticeable heartbeats) and light-headedness. It is reasonable that Jesus could have sensed the palpitations and light-headedness and had enough time and energy to cry out loudly, "Father, into your hands I commit my spirit" (Lk 23:46), and say, "It is finished" (Jn 19:30), before his heart stopped beating.

Conclusion Regarding the Cause of Death

From what I have read and studied in books and articles and learned from my colleagues, I believe that shock played the most significant role in Jesus' death, and that his death was more rapid than the average crucifixion victim because of a severe scourging that Pilate initially intended as his entire punishment (agreeing with Dr. Edwards et al.). Currently, there is insufficient evidence to conclude that difficulty breathing contributed to Jesus' death on the cross. Jesus was able to cry out loudly at the moment of death, which does not fit well with a patient dying from only traumatic, hemorrhagic shock, although two of my colleagues in critical care medicine and cardiology have told me that they have witnessed patients cry out just before dying of shock. (They also say that it is terrifying to witness!)

Dr. Kubala agrees that Jesus' death was primarily due to traumatic and hypovolemic shock that led to the heart stopping (cardiac arrest), but he believes that hyperkalemia (increased potassium in the blood) was the cause of the arrhythmia.[28] However, according to my friend and colleague Dr. Kaminskas, when the heart stops beating due to hyperkalemia, it does so without warning (in contrast with VT above) because of asystole (loss of electrical conduction signals in the heart); therefore, with hyperkalemia, Jesus would have had no physical warning sign that the end was near.

It makes sense to me that shock brought about an acute event such as an arrhythmia or other cause of cardiac arrest. As my friend and colleague Dr. Eustace Fernandes wrote to me, "It certainly makes sense that Jesus might have experienced hemorrhagic and hypovolemic shock, suffered some respiratory muscle fatigue, developed consumptive coagulopathy as a result of hemorrhage and entered the spiral of irreversible metabolic derangements resulting in terminal arrhythmia."[29]

I agree with the conclusion of Maslen and Mitchell that "at present, there is insufficient evidence to safely state exactly how people did die from crucifixion in Roman times."[30] I also agree with Barbet, who wrote, "But it is evident with what serene self-control, with what supreme dignity He dominated this Passion which was foreseen and willed by Himself. He died because He willed it, when He was able to say to Himself in a state of full consciousness: 'It is consummated.' My task is accomplished (John 19:30). He died in the way that He willed."[31]

Response to Claim
Dr. Edwards et al.'s claim is likely half right. Evidence strongly suggests that the major cause of death in Jesus' crucifixion was hypovolemic shock. However, as we discovered, there is virtually no evidence to support that exhaustion asphyxia (suffocation) played any role in his physical death.

Suffering Reveals the Man
Although it is clear now that Jesus would not have been suffocating while speaking his seven last words from the cross, he was in excruciating pain, particularly from unrelenting muscle cramps and the injuries of his beatings and scourging. And yet it was during this

immersion in agonizing torment that he said, "Father, forgive them; for they know not what they do" (Lk 23:34).

When I experience intense pain, these kinds of thoughts don't pass through my mind. Yet we are asked to do no less than Jesus. We become even more like Christ when we pray for those who make us suffer — when, like him, we say, "Father, forgive them, they don't know what they're doing." Our human suffering reveals our greatness. Suffering may make the man, but suffering more especially reveals the man and his spiritual maturity.

When to Ask Why?

In this chapter, we have gazed (in our imaginations) at the original crucifix and seen Jesus die. There can be no better place for us to ask why we suffer. When tempted to ask "Why?" about your suffering or that of someone you love, do it while gazing at Jesus on the cross. When Christ answers our "Why?" of suffering, he does not give reasons; he issues a call. He says, "Follow me! Come! Take part through your suffering in this work of saving the world, a salvation achieved through my suffering!"[32]

The more we take up our crosses and unite ourselves to Christ on his cross, the more Christ reveals to us the meaning of suffering. We find the answer to the meaning of suffering only in our response to Jesus' suffering, and in that, we can discover peace and even joy. When we're faced with suffering, the answer to "Why?" is not found intellectually; it is found experientially.

Knowing that suffering eventually triumphs in resurrection and redemption casts a new light on human suffering, so that we can "go forward through the thick darkness of humiliations, doubts, hopelessness and persecution."[33] As Saint Paul reminds us, "For as we share abundantly in Christ's sufferings, so through Christ we share abundantly in comfort too" (2 Cor 1:5).

Through participation in Christ's sufferings, the Christian discovers the reality of Christ's redemptive suffering for him. He also rediscovers his own sufferings and finds that they have a new meaning in the light of Christ's sufferings for him. Christ suffers in the

Christian; the Christian suffers in Christ. Christ lives in the one for whom he suffered; Christ and the Christian are united through the cross. Thus could Saint Paul say in all truthfulness, "I have been crucified with Christ; it is no longer I who live, but Christ who lives in me; and the life I now live in the flesh I live by faith in the Son of God, who loved me and gave himself for me" (Gal 2:20).

CHAPTER 10

Post-Crucifixion Events

Date: Good Friday, April 3, AD 33
Time: Late afternoon
Place: Rock of Calvary

Gospel Narrative

And there was darkness over the whole land until the ninth hour, while the sun's light failed; and the curtain of the temple was torn in two. (Luke 23:44b–45)

And the earth shook, and the rocks were split; the tombs also were opened, and many bodies of the saints who had fallen asleep were raised, and coming out of the tombs after his resurrection they went into the holy city and appeared to many. When the centurion and those who were with him, keeping watch over Jesus, saw the earthquake and what took place, they were filled with awe, and said, "Truly this was the Son of God!" (Matthew 27:51a–54)

Since it was the day of Preparation, in order to prevent the bodies from remaining on the cross on the sabbath (for that sabbath was a high day), the Jews asked Pilate that their legs might be broken, and that they might be taken away. So the soldiers came and broke the legs of the first, and of the other who had been crucified with him; but when they came to Jesus and saw that he was already dead, they did not break his legs. But one of the soldiers pierced his side with a spear, and at once there came out blood and water. He who saw it has borne witness — his testimony is true, and he knows that he tells the truth — that you also may believe. For these things took place that the Scripture might be fulfilled, "Not a bone of him shall be broken." And again another Scripture says, "They shall look on him whom they have pierced." (John 19:31–37)

After this Joseph of Arimathea, who was a disciple of Jesus, but secretly, for fear of the Jews, asked Pilate that he might take away the body of Jesus, and Pilate gave him leave. So he came and took away his body. Nicodemus also, who had at first come to him by night, came bringing a mixture of myrrh and aloes, about a hundred pounds' weight. They took the body of Jesus, and bound it in linen cloths with the spices, as is the burial custom of the Jews. Now in the place where he was crucified there was a garden, and in the garden a new tomb where no one had ever been laid. So because of the Jewish day of Preparation, as the tomb was close at hand, they laid Jesus there. (John 19:38–42)

It is finished. The sacrifice is made. God is dead.

Jesus has given all — 100 percent. He has no more to give. His human soul awaits the resurrection of his human body, which remains on the cross. And in accordance with Scripture, not a bone of him will be broken (see Jn 19:36).

But that will not be the case for those crucified next to him; one more torture awaits them since they did not die as quickly as Jesus. And even though Jesus died quickly (so much so that Pontius Pilate marveled at the rapidity of his demise), his body must endure one more injustice before being taken down from the cross.

Claim

The key claim here is that breaking the legs of crucifixion victims tied in to the asphyxiation theory discussed in the prior chapter:

> Breaking legs below knees would place burden of exhalation on shoulder and arm muscles alone and soon would result in exhaustion asphyxia.[1]

Question 6: Why Would Breaking the Legs of Crucifixion Victims Hasten Their Death?

Based on John 19:31–33, it is clear that the Jews believed that breaking the legs of the crucifixion victims would hasten their death so that their bodies could be taken away before the high sabbath began at sunset.

Ancient Sources on *Crurifragium* (Breaking the Legs)

In John Cook's tome *Crucifixion in the Mediterranean World*, he writes that besides John's mention of *crurifragium*, "a few texts include crucifixion and *crurifragium* in the same sentence but do not specifically say that crucified individuals' legs were broken."[2]

At least one ancient passage describes the use of *crurifragium* alone as a form of execution. A slave had decided to accuse his master, Apollonius, as a Christian before the authorities in Rome. "But the wretched man [the slave] brought the case at just the wrong time, for by an imperial decree those who informed on such matters were not allowed to live. His legs were at once broken, this sentence being passed on him by the judge Perennius."[3]

The online Wiktionary defines *crurifragium* as the "breaking of the lower leg bones as an ancient form of punishment or execution."[4] Anatomically, "leg" refers to the region between the knee and the ankle, although popularly people mean the entire lower extremity from hip to ankle. Each leg has two bones between the knees and ankles: the weight-bearing tibia (shinbone) and the non-weight-bearing fibula. Breaking the thighbones would be incredibly difficult because of how deeply they are buried beneath the thick muscles of the quadriceps; the tibia, however, lies just beneath the skin of the shin.

The Wiktionary definition fits the sense found in ancient passages, including the only one where the specific term *crurifragium* (rather than words meaning "to break the legs") is found in a play of Plautus in which two slaves are talking:

> What is it you're scared of?
>   Of setting traps for master and having it settle me.
> Why, if master knows I've blabbed to any living soul, the next second he'd change me from Syncerastus to Splinter-shanks [*ex Syncerasto Crurifragium*].[5]

"Splintershanks" is a creative way to translate "*crurifragium*" (broken legs) into English, as the bone would be splintered by multiple heavy blows. "Shanks" is a term referring to the legs, as in King Edward I of England's nickname of "Longshanks" due to his great height.

Sextus Aurelius Victor wrote in a single passage of his fourth-century Roman history about both breaking legs and crucifixion; they are mentioned together as two different penalties that Constantine the Great abolished: "Finally, Constantine received all his enemies with honor and protected them by allowing them to retain their properties, and was so conscious of his obligation that he was the first to abolish the long-established and utterly frightful punishment of crucifixion [*supplicium patibulorum*] and the breaking of legs [*cruribus suffringendis*]."[6]

According to John Cook, the following passage from Firmicus Maternus, a fourth-century contemporary of Constantine who became a Christian apologist, mentions both penalties without applying them to the same individual: "If Auriga is found on the descendant and attacked by malefic planets, the natives will be thrown from a chariot and suffer miserable death with a broken body; or, struck by a thunderbolt, they will be crushed to death; or they are crucified or their legs broken by public sentence [*in crucem, aut crura illis publica animadversione franguntur*]."[7]

In this instance, the absence of evidence of using *crurifragium* on crucifixion victims in ancient literature is not evidence of absence of the practice, since it is stated explicitly with regard to the two thieves crucified next to Jesus. Unfortunately, the ancient literature gives us no hints about why *crurifragium* led to a rapid death.

Some ancient passages refer to *crurifragium* alone:

> By the Lord, your legs shall be broken to splinters [*crura diffrengentur* = legs will be shattered], if you don't give that shameless rascal a blowing up.[8]
>
> ... fear lest in that place they shatter your legs or your own neck [*metuerem ne ibi diffregisset crura aut cervices sibi*].[9]

Medical Theories

Virtually every article about crucifixion posits one or more ideas for why breaking the legs of the crucified would hasten death. Four hypotheses have been proposed.

The most popular hypothesis coincides with the asphyxiation theory. If the victim needed to repeatedly raise and lower himself on the cross to inhale and exhale adequately, broken legs would put a stop to that immediately, and the victim would soon suffocate. Drs. Barbet and Edwards et al. are proponents of this hypothesis.

Second, various articles list fat embolisms from the bone marrow causing respiratory failure. Fat embolisms occur rarely, in 1 to 11 percent of long bone fractures (such as in the tibia, the main bone connecting the knee and ankle), and much less commonly lead to death. Fat that makes its way into the small vessels of the lungs initiates an inflammatory response that can become fatal within 24 hours, but this is hardly the immediate effect we are looking for with *crurifragium.* Dr. Zugibe states that fat embolisms from fractures are rarely found at autopsy.

Third, Zugibe suggests,[10] along with authors François Retief and Louise Cilliers,[11] that breaking the legs simply added to the downward spiral of traumatic shock already induced by scourging and crucifixion. However, considering that Romans used *crurifragium* alone as a capital penalty, there must be more to the effects of leg shattering. Ancient literature indicates not only breaking of legs, but shattering or splintering of the legs. Perhaps *crurifragium*, like scourging, could be inflicted with various levels of severity. The more times the legs are struck, the greater the likelihood of inducing sudden death.

A fourth hypothesis suggests that breaking the leg bones (tibias) leads to rapid and severe hemorrhage from the bone marrow. Both Zugibe and Retief deny this possibility. However, a peer-reviewed article in the emergency medicine literature states, "Untreated fractures of the lower limbs can lead to significant blood loss, which may be external and obvious, or covert. The estimated blood loss for a closed fracture of the femur is 1000–1500 ml and for a closed fracture of the tibia is 500–1000 ml. These figures can be doubled if the fracture is open. Fractures of the lower limb, particularly the femur, should be considered a potential cause of hypovolemic shock, especially if compound [open, exposed through the skin]."[12]

An orthopedic surgery colleague of mine with over thirty years of experience has corroborated significant blood loss in tibial fractures. This means that two open (bones protruding through the skin) tibial fractures can result in 2,000 to 4,000 milliliters (2 to 4 liters) of blood loss. Since a man's body contains only 6 liters of blood, it is easy to see why breaking the legs could lead to rapid death through shock.

Question 7: What Was the Source of the Blood and Water When a Spear Pierced Jesus' Side?

Yes, blood can flow from a corpse. I have witnessed this myself.

The Scriptures do not tell us which side of Jesus the spear penetrated. For the sake of discussion, I will refer to the right side for two reasons. First, the Shroud of Turin depicts a large clot of blood on the right side emanating from between the fifth and sixth ribs. If it is Jesus' burial cloth, then we definitely know which side the spear entered. Remember that in the picture shown here, the right side of the image depicts the right side of the body; this is because of how the linen shroud was laid on the body. If you look at the torso, you can see the dark, thick lines on the lower right-hand aspect. Researchers have found blood components here.

In the image above, you can see a fainter mark around the blood. This represents the watery serum that separated from the blood after it sat. In fact, this may be the very blood and water

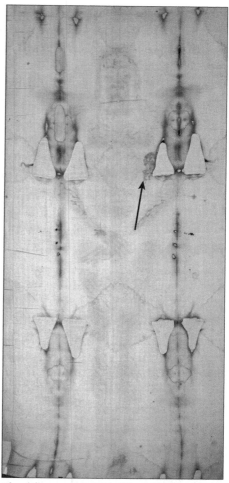

Blood flow on the right side of the chest on the Shroud of Turin image. Note: The image is reversed from normal viewing because when the Shroud was in contact with the body, the right side of the image would have been in contact with the right side of the body.

that Saint John witnessed coming from Christ's open side!

A second reason to consider the right side more likely is that if the blood came from a ventricle of the heart, the wall of the right ventricle (which pumps blood to the nearby lungs) is thinner than that of the left ventricle (which pumps blood to the rest of the body). If a spear perforated the right ventricle of the heart, it would be much more likely that its thinner muscle would be damaged enough that it could not seal the wound shut (either around the spear or after the spear was removed). This would allow blood to flow around the head of the spear more easily than the thicker left ventricle would.[13]

Various potential sources of the blood (representing the Eucharist) and water (representing baptism) have been posited. Forensic pathologists who have viewed the Shroud of Turin say that the blood pattern on the chest has the characteristics of a postmortem (after death) blood flow from a cavity (rather than from blood vessels), because there is no spattering of blood and the blood flows downward with gravity (assuming an upright position of the body).[14]

Barbet's Experiments

Dr. Barbet performed experiments to try to determine how blood and water would flow from a spear wound in the location depicted on the Shroud of Turin. He writes that the marks on the Shroud show that the point of entry is 4 inches below the nipple and just lateral to a vertical line through the nipple (at the superior aspect of the dark blood imprint). If you look at the figure of the heart and lung outlines superimposed on a chest, you can see that the heart lies behind the sternum (breastbone); about one-third of the heart is to the right of midline, and two-thirds is to the left.

About a pint of fluid in the pleural space causes the fluid level to rise above the diaphragm (purple line on chest diagram), which is above the junction between the fifth and sixth ribs. (See the figure above for relative location on the skin.) In one experiment, Dr. Barbet placed a metal plate on medical students at the point of spear entry indicated by the Shroud of Turin and found with X-rays that the proposed spear entrance wound was 3 inches (8 centimeters) from the right heart margin.

In a cadaver, he pushed a long needle through the presumed entrance point (while pulling back on the syringe), and just before

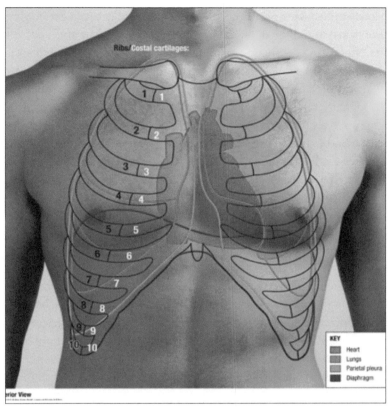

Surface anatomy correlation of locations of internal organs and diaphragm. (*Journal of Ayurveda and Integrated Medical Sciences*, 2 (3) May – June 2017. Used by permission.)

4 inches, he entered the right atrium and got liquid blood. No water entered the syringe when it passed through the pleural space or lung (but these cadavers did not have a pleural effusion). Next he pushed a large amputation knife through the path created by the long needle. When he withdrew the knife, blood continued to flow through the wound after withdrawal. He believed that only blood coming from the heart could create the quantity of staining seen on the Shroud.

When he tried to determine where the water came from, he very slowly pulled back on the needle in the pericardial sac (surrounding the heart) and drew out a "considerable quantity of serum."[15] When he "vigorously" pushed his amputation knife through the pericardium, blood came out with serum separating around the edges (the way you may have seen ketchup separate if it sits on a plate for a while). He thought that the blood came from the right atrium (smaller, superior chamber) and that the water was serum from the pericardial sac. Because Barbet had to use a fine needle very carefully and slowly to get the pericardial fluid out separately from the blood, I believe it is too contrived to consider that the harsh conditions of a vigorous Roman spear thrust would have allowed Saint John to see a small amount of clear serum as it came out of the Lord's side.

Zugibe's Comments

As a forensic pathologist and medical examiner with several decades of experience, Dr. Zugibe writes that pleural effusions are common within a few hours after severe beatings of the chest.[16] He believes that blood would have come from the right atrium when Jesus' side was pierced and that the fluid in the pericardial sac would have been too little to be noticeable, but would have mixed rapidly with the blood as the spear was withdrawn.

He says that pleural fluid would have come out with the initial spear thrust since the lung would have collapsed after the spear was removed, and air would have rushed in through the spear wound, preventing pleural fluid from escaping.

Bevilacqua et al.'s Comments

Italian researchers Matteo Bevilacqua and his coauthors believe that the blood and water both came from a hemothorax (blood in the pleural cavity between the lungs and inner lining of the chest wall).[17] The authors state that blunt chest trauma causes small blood vessels within the lungs to bleed slowly and at low pressure. Because of repetitive movements of the chest due to breathing and the beating of the heart, this blood stays liquid and does not clot. After death, the blood initially clots in the pleural space, but within a few hours, a

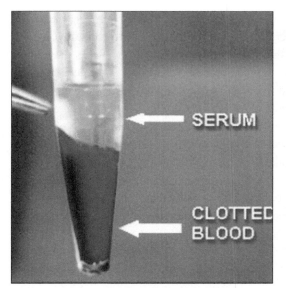

Separation of blood into serum (top) and clotted blood cells (bottom).

process called defibrination causes the blood cells to separate from the liquid serum. This would lead to a layering of blood cells beneath the clearer serum (see photo of test tube with blood).

What Is the Most Likely Explanation?

These are the two primary theories for the source of the blood and water that Saint John witnessed flowing from Jesus' side:

1. The blood came from the right side of the heart, and the water came from serous pericardial and pleural fluid (Barbet, Edwards et al.) or pleural fluid only (Zugibe, 2005).
2. The blood and water both came from a pleural effusion (Bevilacqua et al., 2014).

If Bevilacqua et al.'s theory is correct, then the red blood cells would have settled to the lowest portion of the pleural space, and they would likely have been present below the level of a spear entering at the space between the fifth and sixth ribs (if the Shroud of Turin accurately reveals the location of the wound). However, even without the Shroud as evidence, we would not expect the spear thrust to go through the abdomen (below the rib cage), since the goal of the spear thrust was immediate death. Therefore, I think it is reasonable to assume that the soldier was aiming for the heart.

Also, if the blood serum had separated from the blood cells, the red blood cells would be quite thick and would not flow out of a wound very easily, especially compared to liquid blood. Additionally, the pericardial space is much smaller than the pleural space, and any fluid in the pericardial space is much farther from the chest wall than is the fluid in the pleural space.

Therefore, I believe that the most likely explanation for the source of the blood and water Saint John saw would be blood from the right side of the heart (atrium or ventricle) and "water" (most likely clear exudate) from the pleural space.

Burial of Christ

While the bodies of crucifixion victims were not always buried,[18] the Lex Puteolana (see chapter 7 and appendix 2), which dates from the time of Augustus Caesar, does not provide for allowing bodies to rot on crosses.[19] It seems that bodies of most crucifixion victims at the time of Christ were buried, although the Lex allowed the option of denying burial at the discretion of a magistrate (government official).[20] In these cases, bodies were dragged with hooks through streets and were placed in little pits, where they rotted.

We know from the Gospels that Jesus was allowed a burial. We don't have any information on how Jesus — or other crucifixion victims — were physically removed from their crosses. We do not know whether Jesus was carried in his burial cloth. We do know that nails were removed from crucifixion victims and sometimes found their way into magical and medicinal uses.[21] Presumably, the same nails would have been used on multiple crucifixion victims.

A common type of tomb in the Middle East at the time of Christ

Tombs carved into the Rock of Calvary, about fifty feet from the site of the empty tomb in the Church of the Holy Sepulchre. These tombs are believed to have been carved in the first century. (Thomas W. McGovern)

was a kokh tomb. *Kokh* is a Hebrew word for a narrow shaft that a body could be placed in to decompose. Romans referred to these shafts as *loculi* (singular *loculus*).[22] After descending a few steps, one entered a low-ceilinged room that would have a bench where the body could be placed. The women were expecting to find Jesus' body on this raised bench so that they could anoint it for burial on Easter morning (see Mk 16:1).

Until Jesus' body could be anointed for burial, it was entirely wrapped in a shroud. If the Shroud of Turin is this burial cloth, Jesus was placed on one half of the long, narrow Shroud, and then the other half of the Shroud was wrapped over his head and onto his front so that its ends were beneath and atop his feet. From John's Gospel (see 20:5–7), we know that another cloth was used to wrap his head.

After anointing, a body would be placed in one of the shafts, where it would decompose for about a year. Once a body decomposed, the bones were placed in a special box called an ossuary.[23] We know that Jesus' body did not decompose.

Response to Claim
An attractive feature of the asphyxiation theory is that it seems to account for other aspects of Jesus' crucifixion: the rapid death, various angles of blood flow on the forearms of the image on the Shroud of Turin, and now, the rationale for breaking the legs of the men crucified on either side of Jesus. However, we will see that there is a simpler explanation for how breaking the legs leads to a swift demise.

Jesus' Suffering Unleashes Love
In the blood and water flowing from the side of Christ, the Church has seen the symbolism of the sacraments of the Eucharist and baptism by which Christ gives us eternal life — his own divine life. And this life is love, "for God is love" (1 Jn 4:8). The suffering of Christ released from his love for us, who are the very cause of his suffering.

In *Salvifici Doloris*, Saint John Paul points this out when he writes that suffering "is also present in order to unleash love in the human person, that unselfish gift of one's 'I' on behalf of other people, especially those who suffer. The world of human suffering unceasingly calls for, so to speak, another world: the world of human love."[24]

Again we see the intimate relationship between love and suffering. Not only is suffering the price of love, but suffering also calls for, even yearns for, love. At the foot of the cross, the three Marys and John responded in love by accompanying Jesus in his suffering. And amazingly, after Jesus died, his suffering unleashed love from Nicodemus, a pharisee, and Joseph of Arimathea, a wealthy member of the Sanhedrin, who had nothing earthly to gain — and everything to lose — by exercising one of the corporal works of mercy: burying the dead Jesus.

CHAPTER 11

Our Response to Suffering: Personal and Relational

There are other books about the physical sufferings of Jesus Christ and many books about the mystery of suffering. This book has aimed to form a synthesis accessible to the general reader by examining the definitive historical act of suffering that gives our suffering transcendent meaning. Throughout this book, I have also tried to provide an understanding of suffering that we can apply to our sufferings in light of Christ's sufferings.

In the last sentence before his conclusion to *Salvifici Doloris*, Saint John Paul writes, "At one and the same time Christ has taught man to do good by his suffering and to do good to those who suffer. In this double aspect he has completely revealed the meaning of suffering."[1] His very next sentence is, "This is the meaning of suffering, which is truly supernatural and at the same time human. It is supernatural because it is rooted in the divine mystery of the Redemption of the world, and it is likewise deeply human, because in it the person discovers himself, his own humanity, his own dignity, his own mission."[2] We discover who we are and what we are called to do through the experience of suffering.

This final chapter will explore how we can better discern and complete our own missions in life through the "double aspect" of doing good by our own suffering and seeking to do good to those who suffer. In his own suffering, Christ teaches that suffering helps man to "discover himself, his own humanity, his own dignity, his own mission." It is important to dwell on this, especially when we are asking what God's will is for our lives. In our suffering, we discover our mission.

Doing Good by Our Suffering

Perhaps we can achieve good by our suffering through understanding more clearly some key ideas that we have explored while following Christ's Passion. This mysterious verse of Saint Paul serves as a good point of departure: "Now I rejoice in my sufferings for your sake, and in my flesh I complete what is lacking in Christ's afflictions for the sake of his body, that is, the Church" (Col 1:24).

What does it mean to "complete what is lacking in Christ's afflictions for the sake of … the Church"?

First, as a result of the Passion and resurrection of Christ, man is now united with Christ through baptism: "Do you not know that all of us who have been baptized into Christ Jesus were baptized into his death?" (Rom 6:3).

Second, by receiving the Eucharist (and the other sacraments), we receive the creative power of Jesus' Sacrifice on the cross so that we are spiritually built up as members of Christ.

Third, nothing can be added to Christ's suffering for the sake of human redemption. His redemption of us is complete, inexhaustible, and infinite. But when Christ suffered, died, and rose from the dead, he did so only in his own body, the fruit of the womb of the Virgin Mary. Now that he is united to us, he wants to suffer too in each of our bodies — the members of his Mystical Body. When any person shares in Christ's sufferings, at any time in history or place in the world, "he in his own way completes the suffering through which Christ accomplished the Redemption of the world."[3]

Even though the redemption is complete, it is still being accomplished. "Yes, it seems to be part of the very essence of Christ's redemptive suffering that this suffering requires to be unceasingly completed."[4]

When a child is conceived, the DNA that determines the structure and function of that new person is complete; nothing more can be added to it. Yet the destiny and life of that child has yet to be lived out in space and time. In a similar way, the redemption was completed on the cross, and no man can add anything to its infinite value. Yet the redemption must be applied and lived out in all the members of Christ's Church throughout history and across the world.

The Church is completed through Christ suffering in his individual human members. A good answer to the question "Where was Jesus when [some terrible tragedy] occurred" is this: He was in those persons, suffering and dying with them.

The divine and human natures of Christ are united in suffering, and therefore suffering has special value in the eyes of the Church. The suffering of the Church's members completes the work of redemption in the Church, and this work of redemption will not come to a close until the end of time.

In the Light of Love: Fear and Suffering, Hope and Joy

The Passion of Our Lord necessarily touches on the deepest experiences of a human life. While no intellectual answer can fully satisfy the "Why?" of suffering, some headway can be made through examining the relationships between fear, suffering, hope, and joy in the light of love.

In chapter 5 (on the scourging), we discussed that hope is anticipated joy. As discussed in chapter 3 (on Jesus' agony in the garden), a negative corollary is that fear is anticipated suffering. Hope and fear are both anticipatory, but their objects diverge profoundly.

So how can we unite these divergent ideas? Through love.

We have learned that suffering is the price of love (at least this side of heaven). Saint Thomas Aquinas teaches us that each of the fruits of the Holy Spirit is the result of the fruit that comes before it in Saint Paul's listing in Galatians 5:22–23.[5] Thus, in the listing of love, joy, peace, patience, etc., joy follows love because it is the fruit of love. As Aquinas writes, "The necessary result of the love of charity is joy: because every lover rejoices at being united to the beloved."

Therefore, strangely enough, love requires suffering and yields the fruit of joy! Because Buddhists believe that the secret to eliminating suffering is eliminating desire (including love, which desires to be united with the beloved, a Buddhist might say "No love, no suffering." But we Christians believe "Know love, know suffering."

Saint Paul describes in his Letter to the Romans how hope is related to suffering and love: "More than that, we rejoice in our sufferings, knowing that suffering produces endurance, and endurance produces character, and character produces hope, and hope does not disappoint us, because God's love has been poured into our hearts through the Holy Spirit who has been given to us" (Rom 5:3–5).

We can rejoice in suffering because we know that it leads to hope fulfilled through the love of God that results in our experience of joy. Joy is the "punch line" to the parable of the talents that Jesus told during that original Holy Week. In fact, it was the next-to-last parable he told according to Matthew (followed only by the parable of the sheep and the goats describing the Final Judgment). In this penultimate parable, the master says, "Well done, good and faithful servant; you have been faithful over a little, I will set you over much; enter into the joy of your master" (Mt 25:23). According to the *Catechism of the Catholic Church*, the Church sees in this parable of the talents an image of "the glory of heaven [where] the blessed continue joyfully to fulfill God's will in relation to other men and to all creation" (1029). This joy is a foretaste of the everlasting joy that is fulfilled in the beatific vision, which is described as "entering into the joy of the Lord" (CCC 1720).

As human beings, we experience these emotions (fear and joy) and virtues (hope and love) as embodied beings. We discussed in chapter 3 (on the agony in the garden) that when channeled through an act of charity, adrenaline, a feature of both fear and anxiety, can be used to achieve flow — that joyful experience when we fully act in love with dominion over our work. Jesus channeled the adrenaline of fear in the Garden of Gethsemane — and perhaps at multiple points during his Passion — in an act of complete love by which he suffered and died for us. Remember why he "endured the cross": "for the joy that was set before him" (Heb 12:2). We receive that same adrenaline to help us transform our fears into joyful acts of love.

We do good by our suffering when we suffer in union with Christ, offering it for the salvation of others: "For, whoever suffers in union with Christ — just as the Apostle Paul bears his 'tribulations' in union with Christ — not only receives from Christ that strength already referred to but also 'completes' by his suffering 'what is lacking in Christ's afflictions'. This evangelical outlook especially highlights the truth concerning the creative character of suffering."[6]

Through the "creative character" of suffering, Christ gives us the dignity of causality as members of his Church. We can apply our sufferings, united to Christ, for the sake of our own redemption and the redemption of others. This is the origin of that ancient Catholic admonition "Offer it up." This is a greater superpower than any superhero possesses — greater than remarkable strength, otherworldly wisdom or intelligence, lightning speed, or control of time. We can influence the eternities of other people by offering up our sufferings for them. This is the deepest possible causality: influencing a life for eternity.

To do good by his suffering, "each man, in his suffering, can also become a sharer in the redemptive suffering of Christ."[7] This is the exalted mission each man discovers in his suffering, the mission to offer his own suffering for the redemption of others. And in this book, we have seen how our teacher and master has done just that. Since "a disciple is not above his teacher, nor a servant above his master; it is enough for the disciple to be like his teacher, and the servant like his master" (Mt 10:24–25). Since Jesus offered his sufferings for our redemption, we are to do the same: offer up our own sufferings for the redemption of others.

Doing Good to Those Who Suffer

If we only did good by our suffering, it would leave out a great scope of human endeavor lived in relationship with others. Saint John Paul II of course addresses this relational aspect of suffering. In *Salvifici Doloris*, he reflects deeply on the parable of the Good Samaritan through lens of the last of Jesus' parables, the sheep and the goats:

> To the just, who ask when they did all this to him, the Son of Man will respond: "Truly, I say to you, as you did it to one of the least of these my brethren, you did it to me" (Matthew 25:40). The opposite sentence will be imposed on those who have behaved differently: "As you did it not to one of the least of these, you did it not to me." ...
>
> The first and second parts of Christ's words about the Final Judgment unambiguously show how essential it is, for the eternal life of every individual, to "stop," as the Good Samaritan did, at the suffering of one's neighbor, to have "compassion" for that suffering, and to give some help.[8]

Here John Paul reveals his three-step plan for responding to those who suffer:

1. Stop.
2. Have compassion.
3. Give some help.

These three steps can be unpacked in light of the most current understanding of the science of compassion from the points of view of both doctors and of patients.[9] However, these steps apply to any person demonstrating compassion for another and must involve the whole person. Consider the example of Jesus providing for the needs of his mother, whom he saw suffering at the foot of the cross (in chapter 8).

John Paul and modern research help give us an idea of what compassion looks like for us. In fact, the admonition of John Paul to "do good to those who suffer" is found in the etymology of compassion, which derives from Latin words meaning "to suffer with" another. How do we "suffer with" another person? Compassion research suggests that for a receiver to experience compassion, four steps (or conditions) must be met.[10]

1. The first step is to notice with our observing mind that another person is suffering. This fits with John Paul's instruction to "stop" in front of the one who is suffering. We must pay attention with our senses to see the person who is suffering.

2. The second step is to be emotionally moved by the suffering. This ability to understand and share the feelings of another is referred to as empathy, in which one acknowledges and attempts to understand another's suffering through emotional resonance. We feel what they feel. This is a natural skill each human possesses, to a greater or lesser degree. We vary, however, in how we naturally respond to it. Empathy is a neutral skill; it is not, by itself, enough to assuage the suffering of another.

3. Step three requires invoking our will to desire the relief of the suffering. (John Paul's second step of "have compassion" includes both the emotional and willful aspects of the four steps of compassion being described here.) We make a decision to alleviate the suffering. And this fulfills one of the simplest definitions of love, as taught by Aquinas: "to will the good of the other."[11]

4. The final step is to act to relieve the suffering, which matches with John Paul's call to "give some help." Our compassion must culminate in some physical act, which can sometimes be as simple as holding a hand or sitting quietly with the one who is suffering. If we don't know what to do, we can ask the other person "What are you going through?" and really listen. And we can

also ask: "It seems that you are hurting, and I want to help, but I don't know how. What can I do for you?"

We Can Only Give Compassion If We Have Received Compassion

The suffering that we encounter in others is meant to release love from us. Enough raw material of suffering is present throughout the world to unleash an ocean of God's love, but that love is meant to come through us to others. This happens when we are compassionate. And where do we get this compassion to share? Saint Paul tells us, "Blessed be the God and Father of Our Lord Jesus Christ, the Father of mercies and God of all comfort, who comforts us in all our affliction, so that we may be able to comfort those who are in any affliction, with the comfort with which we ourselves are comforted by God" (2 Cor 1:3–4).

Only if we are comforted with love in our own afflictions will we have loving comfort (compassion) to give to others who need it. We can't give what we don't have. When we release love in the face of suffering, we contribute to transforming "the whole human civilization into a civilization of love."[12] In so doing, we advance the culture of life amidst a culture of death.

Christ suffered a gruesome death so that we might live forever. He showed us how to suffer. He gave meaning to suffering and offers us the profound gift of finding meaning in our own suffering. Because Christ lives in us, we can do good with our suffering by offering it up for others. And we can do good to those who suffer by showing compassion in loving action.

What Ancient Literature Reveals about Crucifixion

M ost works describing crucifixion state that it was commonly performed at the time of Christ, but they provide few references to support this statement. To get a sense of the reality of crucifixion in the few centuries before and after Christ, it is helpful to learn what the literature of that period tells us. Was crucifixion really common? Are there any detailed descriptions of it? Was there one typical way crucifixion was performed, or were there many different forms of this torture? Delving into the ancient literature provides key insights into how contemporaries of Christ in the Mediterranean world viewed this punishment.

When I decided to put together an online course and then write this book, I accepted a challenge laid out in a review article by Matthew W. Maslen and Piers D. Mitchell about the potential causes of death by crucifixion:

Analysis of the clinical literature [about crucifixion] suggests that there has been **suboptimal use of historical sources** in most publications. ... The vast majority of articles do not refer to texts in the original languages that describe the details of crucifixion, which are mostly in Latin and Greek. At best there is occasional reference to the few Roman period texts that have been published in English translation. However, most papers do not even discuss the translations of these texts, **but chose to quote previous publications by other medical authors for their historical information**. In some cases the result is a series of misquotes that bear limited resemblance to the actual surviving evidence.[1]

Because I agreed with Maslen and Mitchell's evaluation of crucifixion literature, I endeavored to learn as much as possible about the history of crucifixion before and during the time of the Roman Empire. To this end, I reviewed every ancient reference I could find related to crucifixion. Furthermore, I thoroughly read and studied two books: Gunnar Samuelsson's *Crucifixion in Antiquity* and John Granger Cook's *Crucifixion in the Mediterranean World*.

Samuelsson's book is his doctoral thesis, in which he takes a skeptical view of ancient evidence, primarily literary evidence, for crucifixion. He applies a stringent test to determine whether a passage definitely mentions crucifixion or might refer to another type of punishment. He practices a hermeneutic of exclusion: According to him, unless crucifixion is explicitly described in a passage, the passage should not be trusted as a source of information regarding crucifixion. On the other hand, Cook's book takes a more balanced approach that makes sense to me.

Suspension Punishments

According to both Samuelsson and Cook, some ancient Greek and Latin words that refer to crucifixion can also be used to refer to "suspension" punishments in general. The three types of suspension punishments in ancient Mediterranean cultures were crucifixion, impalement, and hanging. Hanging (as from a noose) was never practiced in the Roman Republic (509–27 BC) or the Roman Empire (27 BC–AD 395).[2] While the Persians and Carthaginians were known practitioners of impalement, the Greeks and Romans rarely used this form of punishment.

Cook believes that because impalement was rare in Roman society and because it was described in specific Latin terms that were not used to describe crucifixions, it is generally possible to determine when a literary passage refers to crucifixion rather than impalement. In his book, he assumes that ancient literature mentioning a form of suspension generally refers to crucifixion and that, in these cases, impalement and hanging can be excluded. Unlike Samuelsson, Cook practices a hermeneutic of inclusion, but he still excludes passages that are ambiguous regarding the penalty described. It is important to note here that Samuelsson and Cook do not practice opposite approaches; Samuelsson applies what I believe are unnecessarily stringent criteria and only accepts a small subset of descriptions of ancient suspension punishments as referring to crucifixion. Samuelsson does not accept any cases as crucifixion that Cook excludes, and Cook does not exclude any cases as crucifixion that Samuelsson accepts.

Cook describes his approach thus: "If an author indicates in a context of execution that a living individual was suspended by a Roman authority, then crucifixion is a justified inference (impalement is extremely rare textually)."[3] Cook critiques Samuelsson's approach, saying, "What is logically possible in this context is not historically probable."[4] I agree with Cook's view that "the frequency, dreariness, and brutality of the act itself did not encourage authors to expend a great deal of energy making narrative descriptions."[5]

Cook takes up the mantle of the late professor Martin Hengel, who asked Cook to update his small book *Crucifixion*, published in 1977. After a short time working on the project, Cook realized it would be necessary to write his own book, and his effort now provides us with the most complete history of crucifixion ever written.

Key Greek Terms

Certain words recur in ancient Greek texts that give us an indication that what we today call crucifixion is being described. The meaning of the words can be ambiguous at times.

- **stauros (σταυρος)**: n. pole or cross. Prior to the New Testament, this word could refer to a pole or a two-part cross shaped like the Greek letter *tau* (T). This is an example of synecdoche, a literary device in which the whole is used to describe the part, or the part the whole. *Stauros* was never used in reference to impalement or hanging a living person by a noose.
- **stauroo (σταυροω)**: v. crucify. This word was never used to refer to impalement.
- **anastauroo (αηασταυροω)**: v. suspend, crucify, impale. This word can refer to crucifixion or to the impalement of a head on the end of a post but never to the impalement of a living person.
- **skolops (σκοιοπς)**: n. stake, cross. This can refer to an impaling stake.
- **anaskolopiso (αηασκοιοπισω)**: v. impale, crucify
- **apotympanismos (ἀποτυμπανισμός)**: v. expose on a board, beam, or plank. In Phalerum, Greece, seventeen skeletons were found attached to boards by iron collars about the neck and staples at each hand and ankle. Dated to the seventh century BC, this method of exposure probably caused a slow death.

Key Latin Terms

The Romans used specific terms when referring to the implements of crucifixion, and it was these terms that Jesus' executioners would have used. When the Gospels were written, these terms were translated into Greek, and we will later see how that has led to confusion, particularly when the terms are then translated into English.

- **patibulum**: n. wooden beam or length of wood; from a verb meaning "to stretch out." It commonly referred to an instrument of punishment to which a person was attached with outstretched arms, but it could also mean a beam attached to an upright post. In some articles on crucifixion, the *patibulum* is equated with the furca, but this was a fork-shaped implement of torture used after crucifixion that was abolished in the Roman Empire.

- **crux, cruces**: n. either a vertical post or a cross of two members. The *Oxford Latin Dictionary* includes the following in its entry for crux:

  > a. Any wooden frame on which criminals were exposed to die, a cross (sometimes also, a stake for impaling). b. In various phrases denoting crucifixion or impalement.

  There were many shapes of crosses. Crux never refers to a part of a structure; it always refers to the entire structure — whether it is a single upright post or a two-part construction. When the crux is a two-part structure, the upright portion is called a stipes and the crossbar is called the *patibulum*.
- **crucifago**: v. attach to a cross, crucify. John Granger Cook is aware of no instances where crucifago refers to an impalement.
- **stipes, stipites**: n. a stake or the vertical beam of a cross used in crucifixion. However, Seneca the Younger, a Roman contemporary of Jesus, uses the term cruces (crosses) to mean entities separate from stipites.[6] In Seneca's passage, stipes refers to the long, pointed pole used to impale an individual from the anus, through the body, and out the mouth.

Crucifixions in Greek Texts

There are many passages in ancient Greek and Latin literature that refer to what we today would call "crucifixion"; I have chosen what I believe to be the most illustrative for the purposes of this book. Those who desire a comprehensive review of the subject are referred to Cook's updated 2019 edition of *Crucifixion in the Mediterranean World*.

Before the Time of Christ

Although Jesus was crucified by Romans, references to crucifixion appear in Greek texts centuries before they appear in Roman texts. Herodotus (c. 485–424 BC) records the two oldest accounts of crucifixion. Because of his reports of the wars between the Greeks and Persians (499–449), the Persians are often credited with (or blamed for) inventing crucifixion. However, the first passage below describes a crucifixion by the Persians, and the second describes a crucifixion by the Greeks. Therefore, I see no reason from Herodotus to ascribe the origin of crucifixion to only one of these two groups. Both Cook and Samuelsson believe the following texts to describe crucifixions.

Herodotus (Fifth Century BC)

In 480 BC, Herodotus described the crucifixion of Sandoces, a Persian military captain who served under the Persian king Darius (reigned 522–486). Interestingly, Sandoces survives, because he is taken down before he dies.

> Being one of the royal judges, king Darius had seized [Sandoces] some time before and suspended [*anastaurose*] [him], according to the following accusation: Sandoces had given an unjust judgment for a bribe. When he had been suspended [*anakremasthentos*], Darius found that the good deeds done to the royal house by him outnumbered the offenses. Darius perceived this and understood that he had acted with more haste than wisdom, and released [Sandoces]. Thus, in this way [he] escaped destruction at the hands of king Darius and was still alive.[7]

The second passage describes how the Greeks crucified a Persian governor in 479 BC.

> But Xanthippus the general was unmoved by this promise, for the people of Elaeus desired that Artayctes should be put to death in revenge for Protesilaus, and the general himself was so inclined. So they carried Artayctes away to the headland where Xerxes had bridged the strait (or, by another story, to the hill above the town of Madytus), and there nailed him to boards and hanged him. As for his son, they stoned him to death before his father's eyes.[8]

Persian Impalement

While we know that Persians practiced impalement (forcibly driving a sharp, greased pole through the anus and out through the chest or mouth), there is no instance of a Greek verb form of *stauroo* or *anastauroo* used to describe impalement.

Some of the punishments mentioned in the Septuagint (the Greek translation of the Hebrew Scriptures), such as the execution of Haman (see Esther 7:9–10), are thought to refer to crucifixions. Haman tried to have all the Jews of the Persian Empire killed during the reign of Artaxerxes (486–465 BC), but the Jewish queen Esther interceded before the king, who spared the Jews and executed Haman on the tall pole meant for a Jew named Mordecai. According to John Granger Cook, it is most likely that the death of Haman was crucifixion,[9] although the Hebrew text seems ambiguous and impalement is still a possibility.[10]

Plato (c. 429–347 BC)

This famous passage from Plato's *Republic* has been seen as a secular "prophecy" of Christ's crucifixion: "What they will say is this: that such being his disposition the just man will have to endure the lash, the rack, chains, the branding-iron in his eyes, and finally, after every extremity of suffering, he will be ἀνασχολοπισθῆναι (*apotympanismos* — impaled/transfixed/exposed/crucified], and so will learn his lesson that not to be, but to seem, just is what we ought to desire."[11]

In his *Introduction to Christianity*, then-Cardinal Joseph Ratzinger (the future Pope Benedict XVI) reflects on this passage of Plato, using a translation that refers to this event as crucifixion.[12] However, there are many different translations of this passage. According to Cook, Plato most likely refers to exposition and less likely to being "transfixed."[13] Other translations, such as that at the Perseus Digital Library, translate the word as "'crucified' ... or strictly 'impaled.'"

Diodorus Siculus (First Century BC)

Greek historian Diodorus Siculus completed his *Library of History* in 30 BC. In this work, he mentions that the Carthaginians crucified [*anastauroo*] some of their prisoners in their war with Syracuse (402–399 BC) around the time of Socrates's death. From the eighth to the third century BC, Carthage (modern Tunis, Tunisia) was the capital of an empire that encompassed the northern coast of Africa, the southern coast of modern Spain, and portions of Sicily and Sardinia. Sometimes the Carthaginians are blamed for introducing crucifixion to the Romans, but other scholars believe that the Romans imposed their own practices on the Carthaginians. It is not unreasonable to believe that the Carthaginians (like the Greeks or Persians) may have developed crucifixion as an evolution of impalement.

Greek Contemporaries of Christ

Philo of Alexandria (First Century)

Philo Judaeus (a.k.a. Philo of Alexandria) writes that crucifixion led to death by starvation: "For death follows the scarcity of food; and the one who did wrong in these matters appropriately dies by being suspended, suffering the same evil that he arranged [for others], because he suspended and tortured the starved man with hunger."[14]

Flavius Josephus (First Century)

The Jewish historian Flavius Josephus (born 37) ended up working for and adopting the customs of the Roman emperors of his time.

For Josephus, *stauros* used with a verb means "crucifixion."[15] Although in his translation of the writings of the Hebrew Scriptures he calls many scenes crucifixions (as in his translation of Genesis 40:19, 1 Samuel 31:10, and Esther 2:23 and 7:9–10), he is most likely reading back into history the customs of his time. According to Cook, there is no reliable evidence in the Hebrew Scriptures of what the Romans would have called crucifixion.

Josephus writes of the evil Seleucid king Antiochus IV (Epiphanes), who reigned from 175 to 164 BC and persecuted the Jews: "Indeed, they [some Jews] were whipped, their bodies were mutilated, and while still alive and breathing, they were crucified, while their wives and the sons whom they had circumcised despite the king's wishes were strangled, the children being made to hang from the necks of their crucified parents."[16]

Josephus also writes of another evil king over Judea, Alexander Jannaeus (reigned 103–76 BC), who persecuted the Jews immediately after the Judean Civil War, around 88 BC: "And when he had shut up the most powerful of them in the city Bethome, he besieged them therein; and when he had taken the city, and gotten the men into his power, he brought them to Jerusalem, and did one of the most barbarous actions in the world to them; for as he was feasting with his concubines, in the sight of all the city, he ordered about eight hundred of them to be crucified; and while they were living, he ordered the throats of their children and wives to be cut before their eyes."[17]

Josephus states that during the Jewish wars, some Idumeans (their enemies to the south and reputed descendants of Jacob's brother Esau) did not bury the corpses of those killed in Jerusalem, but that this was not the practice of the Jews: "They actually went so far in their impiety as to cast out the corpses without burial, although the Jews are so careful about funeral rites that even malefactors who have been sentenced to crucifixion are taken down and buried before sunset."[18] This confirms what the Gospels relate, that the Jews wanted to bury the bodies of Jesus and the men crucified with him.

In his work *The Wars of the Jews*, Josephus describes crucifixion in a way that can be translated "the most pitiable of deaths": "He ordered a pole [*stauros*] to be erected as if he would suspend [*kremon*] Eleazar instantly. A deep pain fell upon those that had seen this from the citadel and they wailed vehemently crying that the calamity was not endurable. Whereupon Eleazar therefore begged them not to let him undergo the most pitiable of deaths and to provide their own safety by yielding to the power and fortune of the Romans, since everyone already had been subdued."[19] However, the phrase is translated by many Greek scholars as "a most miserable death."

After the Time of Christ

Plutarch (before 50–after 120)
The Greek historian and biographer Plutarch distinguishes clearly between impalement and crucifixion: "But will you nail him to a cross [*stauros*] or impale him on a stake [*skolops*]? And what does Theodorus care whether he rots above ground or beneath? Among the Scythians such is the manner of happy burial."[20]

Plutarch also gives us the image of the condemned man carrying the cross (crossbar): "And as every malefactor who suffers in his body **bears his own cross** to the place of his execution, so are all the various torments of various wicked actions prepared by wickedness herself."[21]

Plutarch suggests that the Romans learned about crucifixion from the Carthaginians during the Punic Wars. He also described the execution of a native guide who led Hannibal, the Carthaginian general during the Second Punic War, astray from his destination in 217 BC, before the Battle of Ager Falernus in the Campania region of Italy.[22]

Artemidorus (Second Century)
Artemidorus was a professional interpreter of dreams from Ephesus (modern Turkey). In one passage, he describes a cross as having multiple posts and nails. "Being crucified [in a dream] [*staroustai*] is a good thing for all sailors. For a cross [*stauros*] is made from posts and nails like a ship, and its mast is like a cross [*stauro*]."[23] Notice the

synecdoche here, for *stauros* is first mentioned being made of multiple posts and then said to be singular like a ship's mast.

Cassius Dio (c. 164–after 229)

Lucius Cassius Dio was a Roman consul who wrote in Greek. Although he wrote over 400 years after the fact, he claimed that during the Punic Wars, Carthaginians crucified losing generals. This first example he claims happened during the First Punic War in 251 BC: "Such was the victory of Metellus; but Hasdrubal, the Carthaginian leader, though he got safely away on this occasion, was later summoned by the Carthaginians at home and crucified."[24] This one would have been in that same war, in 241 BC: "Hanno [the Great] escaped and hastened at once to Carthage. But the Carthaginians, seized with wrath and fear, crucified him."[25]

Greco-Roman authors believed that the Carthaginians used the Roman form of crucifixion, but historians debate whether the Carthaginians did this or not.

Crucifixions in Latin Texts

Plautus (Wrote 205–184 BC)

Plautus was a Roman playwright who wrote the oldest surviving full-length comedies in Latin. His plays delved deeply and intimately into the lives of slaves and how they viewed the world, and he frequently alluded to crucifixion. He often used the term crux in curses and jokes among slaves; for example, the Latin phrase "*I in crucem*" (Go to the cross) was slave slang for "Go to hell."[26]

In his play *Miles Gloriosus* (The Braggart Warrior), we learn that crucifixion was viewed by slaves as a common end:

> SCELEDRUS: "Forbear to threaten me: I know that the cross [*crucem*] will prove my tomb; there are laid my forefathers, my father, grandfather, great-grandfather, great-great-grandfather."[27]

If the cross itself was viewed as a tomb, this supports the belief that some crucifixion victims' bodies were not buried. Earlier in the same scene, Plautus tells us that those sentenced to die carry the cross with arms outstretched — and that those who are crucified die outside the city walls:

> PALAESTRIO: "I think that **in that self-same position** you [Sceledrus] will have to die **outside the gates**, when, with **hands outstretched**, you will be carrying your **cross [*patibulum*]**.[28]

Regarding "in that self-same position":

> Sceledrus is standing before the door with both arms stretched out to keep Philocomasium from coming out "without his knowing. Palaestrio tells him that when he comes to be fastened on the cross for his negligence, he will have to assume that attitude. The gate here alluded to is supposed to have been the Esquiline, or Metian gate at Rome, a place near which was devoted to the punishment of slaves. Athens and other Greek cities had 'the gate of Charon,' through which malefactors passed to punishment."[29]

In Plautus's play *Mostellaria* (The Haunted House), we learn that nails are associated with the cross: "I'll give a talent to the first man to run to the cross [*crucem*] — but on these terms: that his feet and arms are double-nailed. When this is done, let him demand cash paid on the spot."[30]

In the play *Bacchides*, the slave Chrysalus fears crucifixion: "I think, by Hercules, that when he [the master] returns he will change my name and will make it at once 'Cross jumper [Crucisalus]' instead of 'chrysalus' [gold dancer]."[31] John Cook comments that "presumably dancing or struggling on a cross was fatal."[32] This word *crucisalus* has also been translated "cross-struggler." It is a play on words where the slave says, in essence, "Turn me from Chrysalus to Crossalus."

Marcus Tullius Cicero (106–143 BC)

The Roman philosopher, politician, and orator Cicero demonstrates in his writings that scourging and fire were used as precrucifixion punishments: "the lash [**verbera**], the fire [**ignes**], and that final state in the punishment of the condemned and the intimidation of the rest, the torments of crucifixion."[33] He sees crucifixion as appropriate for slaves but not Roman citizens[34] and finds the slow, agonizing death caused by crucifixion the "worst extreme of the tortures inflicted upon slaves."[35]

Cicero reports that crosses were set up on Campus Martius, a flood plain for the Tiber River just north of the Capitoline Hill and outside the Servian Wall of the city of Rome.[36] This site for crucifixion is confirmed by Livy, who describes the crucifixion of twenty-five slaves there in 217 BC.[37]

We learn from Cicero — as we did from Herodotus — that one could be pulled down from a cross alive: "Why did you send such a letter to him? That he was erecting that cross for himself, from which you had already pulled him down before?"[38]

Cicero reports that the bodies of those executed in Rome were exposed for wild beasts, but that money could be paid to allow them to be buried: "Many and terrible sufferings have been invented for parents and relations; many — still death is the last of all. It shall not be. Is there any further advance that cruelty can make? One shall be found — for, when their children have been executed and slain, their bodies shall be exposed to wild beasts. If this is a miserable thing for a parent to endure, let him pay money for leave to bury him."[39]

Cicero is perhaps the only source (other than the evangelist John) who mentions crucifixion together with the breaking of legs, although in an indirect way. Following a passage from his *Phillipics* (13.27), where Cicero wrote that "it is quite impossible for him to die unless his legs are broken. They are broken, and still he lives," a commentator's footnote says that "legs are broken" refers to "being crucified as a slave."[40]

Gaius Maecenas (d. 8 BC)

Gaius was a poet and friend of Augustus Caesar (Octavian). A fragment of his poetry, found in the writings of Seneca, mentions crucifixion. In the fragment, he suggests that to sit on a cross meant to sit on a sharp object. Perhaps this is a reference to that part of a cross called a *sedile*, a crude, curved seat (we will return to this idea when we review ancient graffiti in appendix 2).

Gauius writes:

> Fashion me with a palsied hand,
> weak of foot and a cripple.
> Build upon me a crook-backed hump.
> Shake my teeth till they rattle.
> All is well if my life remains.
> Save, oh save it, I pray you,
> though I sit on the piercing [or sharp] cross.[41]

Livy (Titus Livius) (59 BC–AD 17)

Livy wrote a monumental history of Rome covering the eighth century BC through his own time. Although he was writing over 200 years after the Punic Wars (264–146 BC) began, he attributes the Romans' knowledge of crucifixion to the Carthaginians. The Roman practice of crucifixion appears to have emerged during the Second Punic War (218–201 BC), so Livy's report is plausible if not credible, according to John Granger Cook (2014). Livy reported the crucifixion of Hannibal, son of Gisgo (not the Hannibal with elephants), by his own Carthaginian soldiers after their defeat in the First Punic War: "Hannibal, general of the Carthaginians, when the fleet that he commanded had been defeated, was crucified [*in crucem sublatus est*] by his soldiers."[42]

Livy also tells of the famous, elephant-warring Hannibal, who crucified a local guide who misled his army (also mentioned by Plutarch in a reference above) during the Second Punic War: "Did he perceive at last how the man had blundered, and that Casinum lay far off in another direction. Whereupon he scourged the guide, and to terrify the others, crucified him."[43]

Later Livy tells of scourging and crucifixion after a slave revolt in Etruria: "On this occasion many were slaughtered, many were captured; others who had been the leaders of the conspiracy he scourged and attached to cruces, while he returned others to their masters."[44]

Seneca the Younger (Lucius Annaeus Seneca) (c. 4 BC–AD 65)

Seneca, a Roman Stoic philosopher and statesman, includes a reference to people on cruces and further notes that those individuals spat on their spectators from their patibula [*ex patibulo suo spectatores conspuerent*]. In other words, the cruces had horizontal bars that were integral parts from which they could spit upon those watching them.

> ... whereas they themselves are struggling to tear themselves away from crosses [*crucibus*] into which each one of you is driving his own nail [*clauos*]. Yet men who are crucified hang from one single pole [*stipitibus*], but these who punish themselves are divided between as many crosses as they have lusts, but yet are given to evil speaking, and are so magnificent in their contempt of the vices of others that I should suppose that they had none of their own, were it not that some criminals when on the gibbet [*patibulum*] spit upon the spectators.[45]

In this passage, we see more clearly that the stipes and the *patibulum* are components of the crux (cross). Another passage from Seneca's *Dialogues* is also enlightening:

> Nails [clavi] pierce [his] skin [*figunt cutem clavi*] and wherever he rests [his] wearied body, he presses upon a wound, [his] eyes are open in unbroken sleeplessness. But the greater [his] torment is, the greater [his] glory will be. ... Al-

though he drugs himself with unmixed wine and diverts [his] anxious mind and deceives [it] with a thousand pleasures, he will [no more] fall to sleep on [his] pillow than that other on [his] cross [cruce].[46]

In this passage, Seneca tells us that

- nails are used in crucifixion;
- the victim has wounds all over his body (perhaps a reference to prior scourging); and
- wine will not reduce his pain.

Now we come to the only Latin passage that Gunnar Samuelsson (2011), based on his skeptical criteria, believes unequivocally refers to crucifixion. In this passage, we see that Seneca was aware of a variety of punishment forms and a spectrum of crux punishments:

I see crosses [*cruces*] there, not indeed of a single kind but different constructions by different people. Some had suspended their victims with the head toward the ground, others had driven stipes [*stipitem*] through the private parts of the victims, others had spread out their arms on a *patibulum*. I see cords, I see scourges [*verbera*], and for each limb and joint there is an engine of torture.[47]

Even Samuelsson agrees that the Latin word crux is an execution device, probably wooden, onto which a victim was suspended to be executed. He further sees that Seneca uses the word stipes to refer to a pointed stake used for impaling. A *patibulum* means a crossbeam onto which a victim was attached with outstretched arms, and nails were used during the crucifixion. If even the most skeptical, or rigorous, of researchers into the history of crucifixion believes that Seneca is talking about crucifixion in this passage, it is likely that other passages with similar terminology are referring to the same reality of crucifixion.

In another dialogue, Seneca tells us that crucifixion victims' arms were stretched out: "another to have his limbs stretched upon the cross [*alium in cruce membra diffindere*]."[48] In yet another dialogue, Seneca paints the picture of a scene of crucifixion with fires and drag-hooks:

> To the end that no one may be deceived into supposing that at any time, in any place, it will be profitable, the unbridled and frenzied madness of anger must be exposed, and there must be restored to it the trappings that are its very own — the torture horse, the cord, the jail, the cross [*cruce*], and fires [*ignes*] encircling living bodies implanted in the ground, the drag-hook that seizes even corpses [*cadauera*], and the different kinds of chains and the different kinds of punishment, the rending of limbs, the branding of foreheads, the dens of frightful beasts.[49]

Valerius Maximus (Reign of Tiberius Caesar, 14–37)
Valerius Maximus was a Latin writer who left behind historical anecdotes. One of them that mentions crucifixion alludes to bodies being left on the cross to rot after death instead of being buried: "This cross is a frightful thing for officials (clothed in purple), as for my cross, it makes no difference whether I rot in the ground or in the air."[50]

Pseudo-Quintilian (First Century)
Quintilian (AD 35–100) was a Roman rhetorician from what is now Spain. One of his students, known only as Pseudo-Quintilian, wrote a set of controversies from fictional law cases that is known as the *Minor Declamations*. In this work, we learn that crucifixion was meant to be a public spectacle to deter future crimes: "When we crucify criminals the most frequented roads are chosen, where the greatest number of people can look and be seized by this fear. For every punishment has less to do with the offense than with the example."[51]

We also learn that placards (*tituli*) were placed atop the cross, at least in some instances. In a longer section about the crucifixion of a slave, we have this excerpt: "It is prescribed in the will. ... The cross [crux] was written. Why? What had he done? ... Finally comes a description of the punishment under the appropriate placard [*titulo*]."[52]

In one of Pseudo-Quintilian's *Major Declamations*, we learn that once a crucified victim's body had been pierced, the body could be taken away for burial; we also see that the word carnifex refers to the executioner: "Crosses [*cruces*] are cut down, the executioner [*carnifex*] does not prevent those who have been struck/pierced [*percussos*] from being buried."[53]

Tacitus (56–118)

Publius Cornelius Tacitus was a historian and senator of the Roman Empire whose two main works, the *Annals* and the *Histories*, cover the years AD 14–70. He is a non-Christian source for the execution of Jesus. He writes:

> But neither human efforts, nor generosity of the first man or the appeasing of god could banish the malicious belief that the conflagration was ordered. Therefore, to get rid of the rumors Nero substituted as guilty and inflicted the most outrageous punishments upon those stigmatized by their shameful acts, the multitude called Christians. During the reign of Tiberius the founder of the name, Christus, was subjected to an execution [*supplicio adfectus erat*] by Pontius Pilate.[54]

Apuleius of Madaurus (b. c. 125)

Apuleius wrote a novel, the *Metamorphoses* (a.k.a. The Golden Ass) about a man, Lucius, who is transformed into an ass after becoming too interested in learning about the mysteries of witchcraft. There are multiple passages referring to crucifixion, ending with this sentence: "She will endure the torment of the *patibulum* when the dogs and vultures drag out her innermost organs."[55] Being crucified is equated with the torment of the *patibulum*. This confirms that *patibulum* can be used in synecdoche, or a "part for the whole" usage — that is, *patibulum* can refer both to the horizontal member of a cross and to the entire two-part structure of a cross.[56]

Juvenal (Second Century)

Decimus Iunius Iuvenalis (Juvenal), a second-century Roman satirist, teaches us two things about crucifixion. First, the cross — that is, the *patibulum* — was placed on the slave. Second, masters had the right of life or death over a slave without the need to prove an infraction deserving of death.

Juvenal writes, "Place the cross on the slave [*pone crucem seruo*]. For what crime does the slave deserve punishment? Which witness is present? Who accused him? Listen to the evidence; no hesitation concerning the death of a person is long. Mad man, is a slave a person? He has done nothing, so be it: this is what I want, so do I judge, let my will be the reason."[57] Juvenal also describes the fate of the unburied victim of crucifixion: "The vulture hurries from the beast of burden and from dogs and from what is left on crosses to its young and brings them part of the cadaver."[58]

Firmicus Maternus (Fourth Century)

Firmicus was a Roman writer and later convert to Christianity. In one of his pre-Christian works, written at the time of Constantine the Great's death in the spring of 337, he mentions crucifixion and states that a condemned man is first fixed to a *patibulum* and then lifted onto a cross: "For the person caught in those crimes, because of the severe sentence of the one who inflicts punishment, while fixed to the *patibulum* will be lifted to the cross [*sententia patibulo subfixus in crucem tollitur*]."[59]

Saint Augustine of Hippo (360–430)

Saint Augustine comments on use of nails in Roman crucifixions: "For the crucified, hanging on the tree, nailed to the wood, were killed by a slow lingering death. To be crucified was not merely to be put to death; for the victim lived long on the cross, not because longer life was chosen, but because death itself was stretched out that the pain might not be too quickly ended."[60]

Historical Crucifixions

In the second edition of his magnum opus, John Granger Cook (2019) includes a chapter in which he catalogs all known Roman crucifixions of antiquity. Reviewing some of these will give us a better sense of the Roman practice. He points out that only about twenty names of crucified individuals are known among the many thousands who perished by crucifixion.

Cook does not believe there is enough evidence to write an accurate history of crucifixion — that is, we do not know with a high degree of certainty where crucifixion originated or where the Romans learned it. In fact, the Romans may have developed it on their own. We do know that the Romans and Carthaginians were practicing it during the Punic Wars of the third and second centuries BC and that the Persians and Greeks were practicing it over 300 years before that.

217 BC

Twenty-five slaves were crucified on the Campus Martius, a field outside the walls of the city of Rome. This shows that victims were cast out of the community.[61]

201 BC

The Roman general Scipio Africanus punished Roman soldiers who had deserted to the Carthaginian army. They "suffered the punishment of a slave."[62]

196 BC

A slave revolt was put down by the praetor Manius Acilius Glabrio: "After scourging others who were leaders of the conspiracy he affixed them to crosses, and others he returned to their masters."[63]

(We see here that scourging could precede crucifixion or be the entire, nonfatal punishment, just as Luke tells us in his Gospel.)

71 BC

Crucifixion of 6,000 slaves in Spartacus's army: "They divided themselves in four parts, and continued to fight until they all perished except 6000, who were captured and crucified [*ekremasthesan*] along the whole road from Capua to Rome."[64]

71 BC

A Roman citizen, Gavius, was crucified even though he claimed to be a Roman citizen before the Roman magistrate of Sicily named Verres. Cicero wrote *Against Verres* to expose the wicked rule of this Roman governor.[65] Per Lactantius in his *Divine Institutes*, Gavius was crucified "against all laws."[66]

36 BC

Fugitive slaves were crucified in Sextus Pompeius's army: "Caesar kept his nerve, discharged 20,000 soldiers, restored 30,000 slaves to their masters, and crucified another 6,000 whose masters could not be found."[67]

22 BC

There is an example of a titulus on a slave prior to crucifixion: "[Caepio's father] ... in the case of the second slave, who had deserted his son, led him through the midst of the Forum with an inscription [*grammaton*] making known the reason why he was to be put to death, and afterwards crucified him."[68]

4 BC

After the death of Herod the Great, there was an insurrection in Syria. The governor of Syria, Quintilius Varus, crucified 2,000 of the guiltiest insurrectionists.[69]

AD 9

General Quintilius Varus (same as above) lost three Roman legions when he was ambushed by Germanic tribes led by Arminius in the Teutoburg Forest. Varus took his own life after this battle, and Arminius crucified many of Varus's defeated soldiers: "They pointed out too the raised ground from which Arminius had harangued his army, the number of gibbets [*patibula*] for the captives, the pits for the living, and how in his exultation he insulted the standards and eagles."[70]

28

Roman soldiers tasked with collecting taxes from the Frisians (in the area of the current coastal Netherlands and Germany bordering the southeast corner of the North Sea) were crucified by Germanic tribesmen.[71]

33

Jesus Christ and two brigands were crucified: "At this time lived Jesus, a wise man. ... And when Pilate, at the suggestion of the first men among us, had condemned him to the cross [*stauro*], those who first loved him did not give up their love."[72]

38

Philo of Alexandria confirms the Gospel accounts that bodies were removed from crosses before a great holiday: "I have known cases when on the eve of a holiday of this kind, people who have been crucified have been taken down and their bodies delivered to their kinsfolk, because it was thought well to give them burial and allow them ordinary rites."[73]

64

Many Christians in Rome were crucified under Nero after the great fire, "fixed to crosses and made flammable, on the dwindling of daylight they were burned for use as nocturnal illumination."[74]

64

Saint Peter was martyred by being crucified upside down to fulfill the prophecy of Jesus: "But when you are old, you will stretch out your hands, and another will fasten your belt for you and carry you where you do not wish to go" (Jn 21:18).

Tertullian records: "And if a heretic wishes his confidence to rest upon a public record, the archives of the empire will speak, as would the stones of Jerusalem. We read the lives of the Caesars: At Rome Nero was the first who stained with blood the rising faith. Then is Peter girt by another, when he is made fast to the cross. Then does Paul obtain a birth suited to Roman citizenship, when in Rome he springs to life again ennobled by martyrdom."[75]

In his *Church History*, Eusebius writes: "Peter appears to have preached in Pontus, Galatia, Bithynia, Cappadocia, and Asia to the Jews of the dispersion. And at last, having come to Rome, he was crucified head-downwards; for he had requested that he might suffer in this way. ... These facts are related by Origen in the third volume of his Commentary on Genesis."[76]

66

Procurator Gessius Florus (one of Pontius Pilate's successors) crucified individuals in an unruly crowd who insulted him after he had pillaged the Temple treasury. This passage describes the oddity of crucifying Romans of high rank:

> Florus ... had them first scourged and then crucified. The total number of that day's victims, including women and children, for even infancy received no quarter, amounted to about 3600. The calamity was aggravated by the unprecedented character of the Romans' cruelty. For Florus ventured that day to do what none had ever done before, namely, to scourge before his tribunal and nail to the cross men of equestrian rank, men who, if Jews by birth, were at least invested with that Roman dignity.[77]

70 (April/May)

During the Siege of Jerusalem, the Roman general Titus caught Roman deserters and other poor people desperate for food. Josephus records that he crucified over 500 people daily:

> The famine made them bold [enough] for the excursions and it remained [for them, if] being unseen, to be taken by the enemy. And when caught they defended themselves out of necessity, and after a fight it seemed too late to beg for mercy. So they were first scourged, and then tormented with all sorts of tortures, before they died, and were then crucified [*anestaurounto*] before the wall of the city. This miserable procedure made Titus greatly to pity them, while they caught every day five hundred Jews; nay, some days they caught more. ... So the soldiers, out of the wrath and hatred they bore the Jews, nailed those they caught, one after one way, and another after another, to the crosses, by way of jest, when their multitude was so great, that room was wanting for the crosses [*staurois*], and crosses [*stauroi*] wanting for the bodies.[78]

70 (after Jerusalem Captured)

A crucified friend of Josephus survived crucifixion at Tekoa (south of Jerusalem): "On my return [to Tekoa, I] saw many prisoners who had been crucified, and recognized three of my acquaintances among them, I was cut to the heart and came and told Titus with tears what I had seen. He gave orders immediately that they should be taken down and receive the most careful treatment. Two of them died in the physicians' hands; the third survived."[79]

305–313

Eusebius relates in his *Church History* the suffering of martyrs in Egypt: "Others again were crucified, some as malefactors usually are, and some, even more brutally, were nailed in the opposite manner, head down-wards, and kept alive until they should perish of hunger on the gibbet [mast/cross]."[80]

February 16, 310, is the date of the last known crucifixion in the Roman Empire. The victim was a Christian slave named Theodulus who lived in Palestine: "[Theodulus] had saluted a certain martyr with a kiss. So he was brought before his master, whom he infuriated to anger more than did the others, and received the same martyrdom as the Savior in His Passion; for he was delivered to the cross."[81]

Post-313: Crucifixion Abolished in Roman Empire

According to fourth-century Roman historian and politician Aurelius Victor, "Finally, Constantine received all his enemies with honor and protected them by allowing them to retain their properties, and was so conscious of his obligation that he was the first to abolish the long-established and utterly frightful punishment of crucifixion and the breaking of legs. Consequently he was regarded as a founder or as a god."[82]

Reasons for Crucifixion

According to John Granger Cook, there were many juridical reasons for crucifixion. Often, however, crucifixion was carried out at the whim of the mighty over the weak. Some of the reasons for crucifixion in ancient Rome included the following:

- aiding the seduction of a Roman matron
- arson (such as the Christians blamed under Nero)
- brute, coercive power
- disobedience of slaves (crucifixion is referred to as "the punishment for slaves")
- murder committed by a slave
- piracy
- poisoning a ward
- political disagreement
- rebellion
- sacrificing children
- slaves informing against their masters

- slave revolts
- spying for rebellious slaves
- various crimes of soldiers, such as disobedience

Parts of the Cross

The Greek word *stauros* could refer to either the horizontal bar or the entire two-part, T-shaped structure.

The Latin word *patibulum* could refer to the crossbar alone or occasionally to the entire structure.

The Latin word crux could refer to only the vertical post of a T-shaped cross or to the entire structure.

The Latin word stipes could refer to the vertical post of a T-shaped cross or to a sharp-ended pole used for impalement.

There could be a sharp-ended seat on a cross.

In literature written at the time crucifixion was performed, there is no report of a footrest (*suppedaneum*) used in crucifixion.

Crucifixion Practice: A How-To Manual

There are no detailed descriptions of the practice of crucifixion in antiquity. We get hints about aspects of crucifixion by piecing together information from multiple sources. Here are some things we do know:

- Victims were regularly whipped, scourged, or lashed before crucifixion.
- Crucifixion victims were sometimes burned with fire before execution.
- The crossbeam was typically carried on the back (across the shoulders) to the place of crucifixion, and often the victim was scourged while he carried it.
- There is no report of any condemned man carrying a two-part cross on the way to crucifixion.
- In Rome, victims were crucified outside the city walls.
- Crucifixions were performed in locations where the greatest number of people would witness them (such

as busy roads or intersections near cities), in order to instill fear.

- Nails were typically used to affix people to crosses. In Colossians 2:14b, Saint Paul writes, "This he set aside, nailing it to the cross."
- A victim was first fixed (nailed) to a crossbar (*patibulum*) before being lifted onto the cross (*crucem*).
- Crucifixion victims could be placed in a variety of positions; even if there was a standard position, multiple positions could be used. Peter and Egyptian Christian martyrs were crucified upside-down.
- A placard (*titulus*) was sometimes placed atop a cross after it was carried in front of the victim while he walked to the cross.
- When victims died on a cross, their arms were stretched out.
- Victims had wounds all over their bodies while they hung on a cross, and these wounds increased in pain from pressure and movement while they hung on the cross.
- The bodies of crucifixion victims were sometimes left to rot on the cross and sometimes allowed to be buried.
- Sometimes the bodies of victims were dragged away from the crosses using a drag-hook.
- Sometimes wild animals would eat the remains of crucifixion victims while they were attached to the cross.

The Nature of Suffering on a Cross

Crucifixion victims could see out from the cross and spit on spectators.

There is no evidence of victims moving up and down on the cross (as hypothesized by Dr. Barbet and others who promote asphyxiation as the cause of death). At least one reference implies that movement on the cross led to a more rapid death.

Crucifixion did not cause immediate death but instead caused a slow and lingering death from which one could be rescued if taken off the cross soon enough.

At least two writers (Philo of Alexandria and Eusebius) state that the crucified died of starvation.

APPENDIX 2

What Archaeology, Graffiti, Epigraphy, and Art Reveal about Crucifixion

In appendix 1, we covered the history of crucifixion as found in various forms of literature. In this appendix, we will consider the earliest nonliterary evidence for crucifixion. Let's start with some definitions so that we can better understand the research we will review to give us insight into the crucifixion practices most likely used on Our Lord.

- **Archaeology** is the study of human history (and prehistory) through the excavation of sites and the analysis of artifacts and physical remains such as skeletons.
- **Graffiti** are writings or drawings scribbled, scratched, or drawn illicitly on a wall or other surface in a public space.
- **Epigraphy** is the study and interpretation of ancient inscriptions.
- **Art**, in this instance, refers to the expression of human

creative skill and imagination in a visual form, such as painting, drawing, or sculpture, producing works to be appreciated for their beauty or emotional power.

Archaeology

Jehohanan ben Hagkol

Archaeological findings related to crucifixion are meager. Until April 2018, only one example of a probably crucified man had been found. In 1968, three first-century burial caves were discovered during an archaeological dig at Giv'at ha-Mivtar (about two miles due north of the Church of the Holy Sepulchre in Jerusalem.) Fifteen limestone ossuaries (ceremonial boxes to hold bony remains) containing the remains of thirty-five individuals were found. Five of the individuals died violently: in childbirth, by a mace blow, from an arrow wound, through burning, and by crucifixion. The bones

The James Ossuary, from the first century. The ossuary was on display at the Royal Ontario Museum from November 15, 2002 to January 5, 2003.

were "found in an exceptional, but ephemeral, state of freshness."[1]

The bones of the probably crucified individual suggest a 24- to 28-year-old man 66 inches (167 centimeters) tall, who was healthy until the time of his death during the reign of either Claudius (AD 41–54) or Nero (54 to 68). His name, found engraved on the ossuary lid, was Jehohanan (Hebrew form of John), son of Hagkol. Two articles detail the findings — Haas (1970) and Zias and Sekeles (1985). Zias and Sekeles's later article concludes that Haas made multiple errors in his appraisal of the bones, but there are arguments that the 1985 article is also wrong in its interpretation of findings.

The remains reveal four key findings:

1. An 4.5-inch (11.5-centimeter) bent, rusty, square, iron nail penetrated the right calcaneus (heel bone) from lateral to medial (outside to inside). Presumably, the nail hit a knot in the wood and was bent, thus preventing its removal and reuse on another crucifixion victim.

Reconstruction of a nail found pounded through the right heel bone from outside to inside (heel bone and nail from the ossuary of Jehohanan), discovered in Jerusalem in 1968. (Courtesy of the Israel Museum. Photographer: Ilan Shtulman)

Reconstruction showing how the nail went through olive wood before penetrating the heel bone and then into the wood of the cross (European black pine). (Joe Zias)

Left heel bone of Jehohanan showing the path of the nail. This is the side where the nail was removed. (Israel Exploration Society)

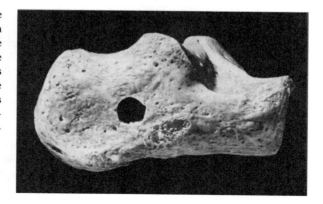

2. A 2-cm thick piece of olive wood was found between the head of the nail and the bone. This probably made it impossible for Jehohanan to pull his foot off over the nail.

3. There was a dent on the inner portion of the radius (forearm bone from elbow to wrist on the thumb side), suggesting that a nail may have been used between the two bones of the forearm near the wrist.

4. Broken leg bones (tibias and fibulas) suggesting violent fractures.

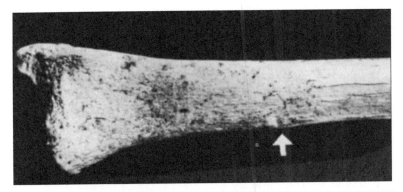

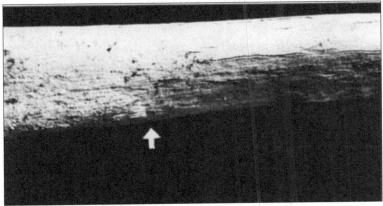

Plates 22a and 22b from Haas (1970), showing dent in distal forearm bone (radius) that may be due to a nail placed between the two forearm bones when victim was crucified. (Israel Exploration Society)

A Rebuttal of Zias and Sekeles

Zias and Sekeles published their late-1985 article on Jehohanan after Dr. Haas had died and could no longer defend his work. Among other things, Zias and Sekeles deny that the dent found on the inner portion of the radius (finding number 3) has anything to do with crucifixion, arguing that similar findings can be seen on other old bones; however, they provide no other examples or references to support their statement. They also state that broken leg bones (finding number 4) are common in ancient bones found in ossuaries — though again, they provide no other examples or references.

In 1986, *Biblical Archaeology Review* printed a letter by Dr. Eugenia Nitowski, a skilled American archaeologist with experience examining bones of the same era as Jehohanan's, challenging the 1985 article. She wrote that such scratches on the right radius (forearm bone) would be expected if the bones had been found loose in a tomb, but they would be unexpected if found protected from wear and tear in an ossuary. She says that the type of dent shown would have been made when the bone was fresh because fresh bone is pliable. Dry bone is not pliable, so when a bone is dry, a scratch can form but not a depressed dent. After viewing the photographs from the articles by Haas and by Zias and Sekeles, I do not think that Dr. Nitowski's argument can be easily discredited, and it is certainly possible that crucifixion victims could have been fixed to the cross with nails through the distal forearm near the wrist.

As far as the fractures in the leg bones, Zias and Sekeles argue that the breaks are at different angles in the tibias and fibulas and therefore could not be due to trauma. However, if multiple blows were struck, then multiple angles of fractures would be expected. Again, I do not think that their argument should be accepted in this case, for I find it hard to believe that bones preserved in an ossuary would spontaneously fragment.

Take-Home Points from Jehohanan

What do we know with certainty from the findings of Jehohanan?

A male in his twenties, buried in the first century in Jerusalem, had a nail driven through his right heel bone from outside to inside. His bones, preserved in a limestone ossuary, include a depressed dent on his right forearm and fractures of his leg bones.

What can we infer from these findings?

1. Jehohanan was crucified while his legs straddled the upright stipes of the cross. This finding contradicts virtually all religious pictorial representations of the crucifixion.
2. Nails may have been driven through his distal forearms between the radius and ulna near the wrist to affix his upper extremities to the cross.
3. His leg bones may have been violently fractured while he was attached to the cross.

Fifty Years Later, a Second Case Reported

Doubling the number of known skeletal remains of crucifixion victims, Italian researchers first reported the discovery of the remains of a probably crucified man in northeast Italy online in 2018 (in print in 2019).[2] This unnamed victim was male, 30 to 34 years old, and of short stature (62 inches).

A work crew that was laying a methane pipeline in the Po Valley in 2006–2007 found the adult skeleton buried alone directly in the ground, in an isolated grave, and without any other artifacts from his life. These circumstances strongly suggest a deviant burial of an individual who was an outcast from society, possibly a slave or captive who was thought to live an "execrable existence."[3] The bones, in rather poor condition, were found as if the individual had been laid on his back with arms and hands held stiffly at the sides and legs together and straight.

The most notable part of this finding was a full-thickness round hole, about 1 inch (24 millimeters) long, through the right heel bone (calcaneus). While the location of the hole is similar to that in Jehohanan, the direction is the opposite. The greater diameter (9 millimeters) is on the medial aspect (inside) of the heel, suggesting that a round nail went through the heel bone from inside to outside. The smaller diameter is 6 millimeters — the diameter of a pencil eraser. As no healing of the bone occurred within the hole, it is nearly certain that the wound was inflicted at the time of death. However, according to John Granger Cook,[4] some researchers believe the hole in this heel bone could have been caused by tree roots.

Based on the hole in the heel bone of the skeleton found in the Po Valley, Gualdi-Russo et al. propose two potential positions in which such an individual could have been crucified. The right hip could have been rotated outward with the knee to the side so that the outside of the right heel would rest against the front surface of the upright post of the cross. A nail could then have been driven through the right heel bone and into the cross. The left knee would then have been placed atop the right knee, and the left heel would have been nailed to the cross from outside to inside. I find this hard to picture, and I suspect a soldier would have found it even more difficult to accomplish. The second position would require the same treatment of the right lower extremity as above, but the left knee and heel would have been turned outward to mirror the right knee and heel. This would have been easier to accomplish, and as you will see below, Roman Empire–era images depict crucified men in such a position.

Remember these drawings when we discuss ancient graffiti.

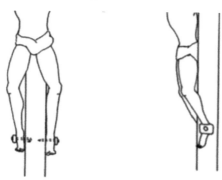

Positions of fixing the feet suggested by archaeological finding in Jerusalem, 1968. (Israel Exploration Society)

Why Is There So Little Archaeological Evidence?

Although there is literary evidence that crucifixion was common, why do we have so little archaeological evidence of crucifixion? First, we have to consider what we would accept as evidence of crucifixion. Even finding a body attached to a cross without further clues would only tell us that the body was attached to a cross — it would not necessarily tell us when it was attached (before or after death). At two sites in Greece (Phalerum and Delos), skeletons have been found attached to boards by fetters or nails; these people were allowed to die through starvation, dehydration, and exposure to the elements.[5] Although no such intact remains of crucifixion victims have been found, some historians believe that this Greek punishment of exposure was a predecessor of crucifixion.

The main problem is that it is very difficult to tell from the remains whether a person was crucified. If no nails were used in crucifixion, there would be no archaeologic evidence that a particular individual was crucified. Wood and rope decay, and they have other uses, so these things were not likely buried with crucifixion victims. Even if nails were used in particular crucifixions and later found with bones, that still would not be convincing evidence, since there is no way to see where the nails were fixed in the body. (It is unlikely that nails usually went through bones instead of between bones. If they did not bend, as Jehohanan's seems to have done, they were presumably removed and reused. They were also scavenged by the superstitious to use in various healing remedies.)

Graffiti

The Pompeii Graffito

In the Stabian Baths on the Via dell'Abbondanza in Pompeii, a (misspelled) graffito reads "IN CRVCE FIGARUS" (Figaris was probably intended as the final word). Here, crucifixion is used as an obscenity: "Nail yourself to a cross" or "May you be fixed on a cross." Because Pompeii was covered in volcanic ash in AD 79, this graffito must have been inscribed before then.[6]

The Alkimilla Graffito in Pozzuoli

About 7 miles west of Naples, in Pozzuoli, Italy (ancient Puteoli) eight ancient tabernae (inns or shops) were excavated in 1959. One of the tabernae boasted many fascinating graffiti, both images and words, written in Greek and Latin. One graffito, which dates from between AD 98 and 138, appears to depict a crucified woman named Alkimilla. This graffito depicts a cross 16 inches (40 centimeters) tall with a *patibulum* 10 inches (26 centimeters) long and a victim 14 inches (35 centimeters) tall.[7] This is likely the earliest known pictorial representation of crucifixion.

Full Alkimilla Graffito.

This image is thought to depict a crucifixion from the back, with the victim's head turned to the right. Above the left shoulder one can barely make out "ALKIMILLA." This is a woman's name, and the graffito artist may have been portraying an actual crucifixion (more likely) or possibly showing his contempt for someone named Alkimilla.[8]

What do we learn about crucifixion from the Alkimilla graffito?

1. The cross is shaped like a capital letter tau (T) and not like a plus sign (+).
2. The arms are spread mostly horizontally, and the wrists are attached to the cross a little higher than the level of the shoulders.
3. The feet are attached at the heels to the front of the sti-

Close-up of the Alkimilla Graffito.

pes with the knees bent outward, just as the archaeological finding from the Po Valley of Italy (Gualdi-Russo et al. 2019) suggests. I am aware of no depiction of
Christ crucified with his legs in this position.

4. The figure is viewed from behind, not from the front.
5. The body appears to be naked, and the curved marks
   could represent either scourge marks or merely the
   curved shape of the body.
6. The method of fixing the arms and feet is unclear.
7. The head is at and above the level of the *patibulum*.
8. A crude seat (*cornu* or *sedile*) is shown beneath the
   right buttock and thigh. Such a seat is not mentioned
   by ancient Greek and Roman writers, although it is
   mentioned by Church Fathers a century or more after
   the time of Christ:

   • Justin Martyr (AD 100–165): "And the
     part which is fixed in the center, on
     which are suspended those who are
     crucified, also stands out like a horn."[9]

- Tertullian (160–220): "But the entire cross is imputed to us, with its transverse part and with its projecting seat [sedilis excessu]."[10]
- Irenaeus of Lyon (130–202): "The very form of the cross, too, has five extremities, two in length, two in breadth, and one in the middle, on which [last] the person rests who is fixed by the nails."[11]

The Alexamenos Graffito on the Palatine Hill

In 1857, a building called the Domus Gelotiana was unearthed near the Circus Maximus on the Palatine Hill of Rome. While originally part of Caligula's (ruled AD 37–41) Imperial Palace, it became a school for imperial servant boys or slaves. Later, it was used as a prison for slaves, then as a barracks for foreign soldiers, after that as a meeting place for administrative officials, and finally as an infirmary for Circus Maximus participants injured during spectacles. In other words, any one of a wide variety of servile or foreign individuals could have produced the graffiti found there.[12]

One graffito found on a plaster wall there illustrates crucifixion and was likely inscribed between the late first and early third centuries. This section of the structure is thought to have been added during the reign of Emperor Septimus Severus (193–211). The figure on the cross has been described as an "ass-headed hominid" (head of an ass, body of a man).

Beneath the crucified figure is an inscription that reads "ALEXAMENOS SEBETE THEON." This Greek phrase can be translated as "Alexamenos worships [his] god." The graffito is thought to mock a Christian slave named Alexamenos, who is pictured to the left; he wears an informal tunic while, with an upraised left arm, he hails the ass-headed figure. He appears to be blowing a ceremonial kiss or raising his hand in prayer.

The ass-headed figure is thought to represent Jesus. He wears a

LEFT: The Alexamenos Graffito. RIGHT: The Alexamenos Graffito. Vector tracing from Ancient Rome in the Light of Recent Discoveries (1898) by Rodolfo Lanciani.

tunic like a commoner or provincial, unlike male Roman gods who would be depicted at least partially clothed in a toga. The tunic suggests that Alexamenos's god is no god at all.

Tertullian (writing in 197) tells us the origin of using an ass's head to depict Christ:

> In this matter we are (said to be) guilty not merely of forsaking the religion of the community, but of introducing a monstrous superstition; for some among you have dreamed that our god is an ass's head — an absurdity which Cornelius Tacitus first suggested. In the fourth book of his histories. ... He relates how the Jewish people, hard-pressed for water and wandering abroad in desolate places, were delivered by following the lead of a herd of wild asses thought to be in search of water after feeding. For this reason the likeness of this animal is worshiped by the Jew.[13]

The Alexamenos graffito is now located in the Palatine Museum in

Rome. Although blasphemous, it is the earliest known pictorial representation of the crucifixion of Christ. What can we learn from this graffito (seen in an archaeological tracing)?

1. The cross is T-shaped, as in the Alkimilla graffito.
2. The arms are spread horizontally.
3. The feet are to the side of the cross, and the figure appears to be standing with feet turned out (as when the knees are bent outward).
4. The figure is seen from behind, like the figure in the Alkimilla graffito.
5. While a tunic appears to be worn, the body is naked from the buttocks down.
6. The method of affixing the arms and legs is unclear.
7. The head is above the level of the *patibulum*.

Inscriptions

Pompeii Advertisement

On August 24, AD 79, the eruption of Mount Vesuvius rapidly covered the town of Pompeii with a pyroclastic flow of rock, ash, and hot gas. In 1958, Matteo Della Corte published his discovery of an advertisement found painted on the walls between the entrances to tombs 30 and 31 outside the Porta Nucerina in Pompeii. When I visited this site in early 2018, the painting had deteriorated significantly, so I am not able to provide a photograph of it. It has since been placed behind protective plexiglass.[14]

On the ancient advertisement, the top row letters read "CVMIS GLP XX" and between the two X's, CVMIS seems to appear again — at least the "CVM" is clear. "CVMIS" is a form of the city name Cumae (V was used for U in Latin). "GLP" probably stands for gladiatorial pairs[15] and "XX" for 20. The smaller words translate as "At Cumae, 20 gladiatorial pairs and their substitutes will fight on 1 October, 5 October, 6 October, and 7 October. There will be *cruciarii* [individuals to be crucified], a fight with wild beasts and the velarium [awning] will be used [over the arena]."[16]

Cumae and Pompeii are located just east of Naples and Pozzuoli (ancient Puteoli), where the Alkimilla graffito was found and where the next important inscription, the Lex Puteolana, was found. Cuma (Cumae) is near Pozzuoli, just west of Naples, Mount Vesuvius, and Pompeii.

Lex Puteolana (Law of Puteoli)

A law regulating crucifixion that dates from the time of Augustus Caesar (27 BC–AD 14) was found in Puteoli (modern Pozzuoli), Italy, just west of Naples within the Campania region. The inscription, with the heading "On the Public Undertaking Concession," was found in three parts between August 1955 and January 1957 in the public forum of ancient Puteoli. Remember, an undertaker is one who prepares dead bodies for burial. By this law, the undertaker also had the responsibility of producing the dead bodies, as undertaker and executioner were one and the same person.

The inscription, thought to date to the time of emperor Nero (54–68), was found on three columns, which have been separated by lines in the text below: column 1 (lines 3–7), column 2 (lines 8–10), and column 3 (lines 11–14). Lines 3–7 mention requirements of the workers, while lines 8–14 mention details related to the act of crucifixion. The Latin includes many abbreviations, which have led to disagreements regarding the precise translation.

On the Public Undertaking Concession (or Public Funeral Service)

3–7. The laborers assumed for carrying out that task [burying the corpses] must not have their domicile within the tower where the woods of Libitina now are; they must not wash themselves from the first hour of the night; must not enter into the city unless it is to carry away a dead person or to prepare [the corpse] or to carry out a punishment. If one of them must come into the city, every time that he comes in or has to remain there, he will wear a colored cap on his head, furthermore no one of them is to be more than 50 years old nor younger than 20; must not be ulcerous, cross-eyed, maimed, lame, blind, branded with marks. The contractor shall not have less than 32 assistants.[17]

8–10. Whoever will want to exact punishment on a male slave or female slave at private expense, as he [the owner] who wants the [punishment] to be inflicted, he [the contractor] exacts the punishment in this manner: if he wants [him] to lead the patibulated individual to the cross [vertical beam], the contractor will have to provide wooden posts, chains, and cords for the floggers [verberatores] and the floggers themselves. And anyone who will want to exact punishment will have to give four sesterces for each of the **workers who bring the *patibulum*** and for the floggers and also for the executioner [***carnifex***].[18]

11–14. Whenever a magistrate exacts punishment at public expense, so shall he decree; and whenever it will have been ordered to be ready to carry out the punishment, the contractor will have gratis to set up crosses [cruces], and will have gratis to provide **nails**, pitch, wax, candles, and those things which are essential for such matters. Also if he will be commended to drag [the cadaver] out with a hook, he must drag the cadaver itself out, his workers dressed in red, with a bell ringing, to a place where many cadavers will be.[19]

What does the Lex Puteolana reveal to us about crucifixion?

1. The condemned was "patibulated" on his way to the cross. This means the victim's arms were stretched out along a *patibulum* as he was brought to a waiting cross (presumably the upright stipes).
2. The condemned individual was scourged while attached to the *patibulum* (and possibly before), and scourging preceded death on a cross.

3. The upright stipes had already been set in place by the executioner. (This agrees with Plautus and Firmicus Maternus — see appendix 1.)

4. The text strongly suggests that the *patibulum* was not removed from the condemned criminal before crucifixion.

5. Chains may have been attached to individuals before crucifixion.

6. An individual attached to a *patibulum* normally died on a cross soon after donning the *patibulum*.

7. Pitch and wax were used for torture before crucifixion. (This agrees with Cicero, *Against Verres*, written c. 70 BC, which discusses the torture of Gavius with fire and hot metal plates before crucifixion.)

8. Nails were likely used for crucifixion.

9. There appears to be no provision for allowing bodies to rot on the cross.

Artwork: Gemstones

Pereire Gem

This 3.0 by 2.5 by 0.58 centimeter engraved red and green bloodstone now resides in the British Museum, Department of Prehistory and Europe, which obtained it from the collection of Roger Pereire of Paris. The stone probably originated in the Eastern Mediterranean (perhaps Syria) in the second or third century, and it may be the earliest surviving image of Christ crucified. Its rival is the Alexamenos graffito described earlier.[20]

What do we learn about crucifixion from this image?

1. The cross is tau (T)-shaped.

2. The arms are limp, horizontal, and attached at the wrists, apparently by something like straps.

3. The legs are on the side of the stipes with the knees bent

This gem, believed to date from the second or third century, shows a crucified man. (Magical gem, intaglio, Mediterranean. Source: The British Museum)

    out (again, as the Po Valley heel bone hole suggests), and the feet do not touch each other.

4.   The figure is depicted from the front, in contrast to the figures in the two graffiti (Alkimilla and Alexamenos).

5.   Jesus is naked.

6.   The method of fixing the legs is unclear.

7.   The head is at and above the level of the *patibulum*.

8.   Jesus is portrayed alive with long hair and a beard, and

his head is turned to his right.

The remaining portions of the obverse and the entire reverse are covered with Greek inscriptions of mainly magical names. Some of the inscriptions are Christian, including "Son, Father, Jesus Christ" and "Emmanuel." While the Church condemned such amulets, some Christians continued to use them. Alternatively, a pagan magician may have used this gem as a symbol of great power. Even non-Christians recognized that there was power in Jesus' name, and they tried to imitate what Peter had done, as described in the Book of Acts: "Then Peter, filled with the Holy Spirit, said to them, 'Rulers of the people and elders, if we are being examined today concerning a good deed done to a cripple, by what means this man has been healed, be it known to you all, and to all the people of Israel, that by the name of Jesus Christ of Nazareth, whom you crucified, whom God raised from the dead, by him this man is standing before you well'" (Acts 4:8–10). Also in Acts, we read that the Jewish sons of the high priest Sceva tried to use Jesus' name to expel demons (see 19:13–17).

The early Christian apologist Origen wrote in *Against Celsus,* "The name of Jesus is so powerful against the demons that sometimes it is effective even when pronounced by bad men."[21]

Constanza Carnelian

Carnelian is a semiprecious stone consisting of an orange or orange-red variety of chalcedony. The Constanza carnelian, measuring 1.35 by 1.05 centimeters, was found in Constanza, Romania. The gem dates to the mid-fourth century and likely originated in Syria.[22] It now resides in the British Museum with the Pereire bloodstone. In the image, you can see a hint of the handle on the reverse side; this carnelian served as a personal seal for use on melted wax.

The image depicts Christ alive and upright on a cross while the twelve apostles receive him in ceremonial adoration. "ICHTHYS" is engraved above Jesus' head, a Greek acrostic for "Jesus Christ, Son of God, Savior."

What do we learn about Christ's crucifixion from this gem?

1. The cross is tau (T)-shaped.
2. The arms are limp, horizontal, and attached at the wrists.
3. The legs are on the side of the stipes, the feet do not touch each other, and the figure appears to be standing.
4. Jesus is naked.
5. The method of fixing the legs is unclear, but the wrists seem to be attached by straps.
6. The heels appear to straddle the upright post.
7. The head is above the level of the *patibulum*.
8. Jesus is portrayed alive, and his head is turned to his right.

Unnamed Gem, Plaster Cast

A plaster cast was made from a gem that once resided in the collection of the German Archaeological Institute in Rome. It is thought to have originated in Syria in the fourth century.[23]

On this gem, Jesus is portrayed naked with his hands outstretched rigidly. A halo surrounds his head. Twelve individuals (the apostles?) stand beneath him, in contrast to the reality we know from the Gospels, which state that only John was present. Jesus is depicted as alive and triumphant, not dead and defeated. The gem contains an unconventional spelling of Jesus Christ in Greek. A lamb stands below Jesus, who appears to stand on a column.

Artwork: General Principles

Early in the research for this book, I thought that I would be able to learn a great deal about crucifixion from artwork contemporary with Christ and the Christians of the first few centuries after Christ. Only after an exhaustive search did I realize that, while early Christians emphasized the importance of what Jesus did for us by dying on the cross, they studiously avoided any visual depictions of the crucifixion for nearly four centuries after the event.

Tension between Word and Image

In the early centuries of the Church, both under an anti-Christian emperor and even for a century under a Christian emperor, the Christian community felt and maintained a tension between the text of their Scriptures and the images they produced, between their wisdom and their iconography. As a result, art historians and theologians have long puzzled over the rarity of depictions of crucifixion in early Christian art.

Not only is there no evidence of religious images of crucifixion before the fifth century, there is no evidence for Christian artwork before the early third century. For instance, Saint Clement of Alexandria in the late second century published a catalog of images suitable for Christian seal rings; the cross is not one of them:

> And let our seals be either a dove, or a fish, or a ship scudding before the wind, or a musical lyre, which Polycrates used, or a ship's anchor (as seen from engraving in Domitilla catacombs), which Seleucus got engraved as a device; and if there be one fishing, he will remember the apostle, and the children drawn out of the water. For we are not to delineate the faces of idols, we who are prohibited to cleave to them; nor a sword, nor a bow, following as we do, peace; nor drinking-cups, being temperate.[24]

The early Church historian Bishop Eusebius of Caesarea Maritima (263–339) wrote *Martyrs of Palestine* in the early fourth century. In this work, he explains that the deeds of the martyrs are known by word of mouth and not in artwork:

> THOSE Holy Martyrs of God, who loved our Savior and Lord Jesus Christ, and God supreme and sovereign of all ... let us also be partakers with them, and begin to describe those conflicts of theirs against sin, which are at all times published abroad by the mouth of those believers who were acquainted with them. Nor, indeed, have their praises been noted by

monuments of stone, nor by statues variegated with painting
and colors and resemblances of earthly things without life,
but by the word of truth spoken before God: the deed also
which is seen by our eyes bearing witness.[25]

Church Fathers and Christian writers of the second and third centuries (Justin Martyr, Hippolytus, Clement of Alexandria, Origen,
Tertullian, Irenaeus) teach us about the theological and practical
concerns of early Christians. Careful interpretation of their works
demonstrates that they were not hostile to the visual arts.

Crucifixion Not Portrayed by Romans

Writing a century before Christ, Cicero tells his Roman readers that
they should not give any attention to the cross of crucifixion: "The
very word 'cross' should be far removed not only from the person
of a Roman citizen but his thoughts, his eyes, and his ears. For it is
not only the actual occurrence of these things but the very mention
of them that is unworthy of a Roman citizen and a free man."[26] No
doubt, the general Roman disgust at crucifixion provided a deep
source of embarrassment and shame for Christians at the circumstances of Jesus' death.

Even Romans did not depict crucifixion publicly, such as on
their triumphal arches. While crucifixion was frequent and widespread, "the cultured literary world wanted to have nothing to do
with it, and as a rule kept quiet about it."[27]

Earliest Christian Images

Around 200, Christian images began to appear. The earliest paintings and drawings focused on salvation, deliverance from death,
and the hope of the resurrection to new life.[28]

The most significant early Christian images are found on the
walls of the catacombs of Rome. The earliest catacomb images include Abraham about to sacrifice Isaac, Jonah and the whale, three
men in the fiery furnace, Susannah, and Daniel in the lion's den.
Each illustrates a protagonist, portrayed in jubilation, transcend-

ing death through divine deliverance. None shows the suffering of Christ. The catacomb images dating from between 200 and 250 also show Noah praying in the ark, the adoration of the Magi, Jonah and the great fish, and Moses striking the rock for water in the desert — a prototypical image of baptism.[29]

A glass bowl from the fourth century found in Podgoritza, Montenegro, includes the prayerful inscription, "Deliver, Lord, his soul, just as you delivered … Elijah, Noah, Isaac, Daniel, Susannah, Peter, and Paul." The crucifixion did not fit in this narrative, because it did not depict jubilation.[30]

Outside the catacombs, the earliest painted images are found in the oldest Christian church ever found. In Dura Europos, Syria, a house church was found that dates to the 240s.[31] A baptistery in this house church includes images of the miracles of Christ, the resurrection, the Good Shepherd, Jesus with the woman at the well, and the women at the tomb on Easter morning. There are no images of Christ suffering.

Earliest Christian Images of Christ's Passion (Excluding the Crucifixion)

The New Testament Scriptures preach Christ crucified, for Saint Paul wrote in the first century, "But far be it from me to glory except in the cross of Our Lord Jesus Christ, by which the world has been crucified to me, and I to the world" (Gal 6:14). However, the earliest creeds did not mention the crucifixion. Even the Nicene Creed — written in 325 during the reign of the emperor Constantine, who made the Christian Chi-Rho his imperial insignia — states only that "[Jesus] because of us men and because of our salvation came down, and became incarnate, and became man, and suffered, and rose again on the third day."[32]

Compare this to the Nicene-Constantinopolitan Creed (completed fifty-six years later in 381) that we now recite at Mass: "For our sake he was crucified under Pontius Pilate, he suffered death and was buried, and rose again on the third day in accordance with the Scriptures. He ascended into heaven and is seated at the right hand of the Father."

Perhaps, therefore, it is more than coincidental that images of the Passion begin to appear about the time of the new creed. From 340 to 370, there are increasing numbers of individual scenes of the Passion presented apart from a narrative (a group of pictures or images telling a story).

The earliest depiction of the Passion in art is on the Brescia Lipsanotheca, a late fourth-century reliquary casket found in northern Italy.[33] The casket measures 22 centimeters (8.5 inches) high, 32 centimeters (12.5 inches) wide, and 25 centimeters (10 inches) deep. Carved ivory images mounted on a walnut wood frame depict images of the evolving Christian art of the time, including many scenes from the Old and New Testaments. There are multiple scenes of Christ's Passion — such as Jesus' betrayal and arrest in the Garden

Early Christian artwork from catacombs showing images of deliverance from death. In this image we see the three youths in the fiery furnace as related in the Book of Daniel.

of Gethsemane, Jesus before Annas and Caiaphas, Peter's denial of Christ, and Pilate washing his hands as he condemns Christ — but no crucifixion scene.

The Mosaics in Ravenna (500)

In the basilica church of Sant'Apollinare Nuovo, built in Ravenna under the Arian emperor Theodoric, one can view a mosaic in the nave that was likely made around 500. This shows Judas betraying Jesus, Pilate washing his hands, Christ led to Calvary, and the women at the tomb with an angel on Easter morning. But the crucifixion itself is not portrayed, possibly because of a continuing reluctance to depict Christ at the most human moment of his life. The mosaics were extensively modified after 561, when orthodox Christians confiscated this Arian property and rededicated the church to Saint Martin.

As we will see, Christian iconographers next found a way to depict the crucifixion that countered the shame and embarrassment attached to the punishment. Christ would be shown as triumphant over death. He would be depicted alive while transcending the moment of his execution. Yet while this served a worthy religious purpose, it does nothing to advance our understanding of crucifixion.

Artwork: Paintings

The Arieti Tomb (Pre-Christian)

The earliest painting that appears to portray a standing man with a *patibulum* attached was found by the archaeologist Antonio Arieti in 1875 in a tomb on the Esquiline Hill of Rome.[34] Although this tomb was destroyed during the construction of a modern building, five fragments of the original paintings survive. Watercolor paintings of the tomb made in 1875 show a procession that includes six lictors before four horses. The lictors carry bacilla (staffs of office) and fasces (composed of virgae and an axe). An eyewitness of the original image described it as "a tortured man, hanging naked by the arms." This image has been dated between 200 and 44 BC.[35]

The bearded man's wrist is attached to a horizontal bar by fetters. No vertical cross member is seen. This patibulated bearded man appears to be standing on the ground and probably depicts one element in the triumphal procession of a Roman praetor (a Roman magistrate below the level of consul). This painting provides us one of the oldest depictions (if not the oldest) of an element of crucifixion (the *patibulum*, or transverse bar) in existence.

Rabbula Gospels (586)

There are no images of crucifixion in the catacombs of Rome or on Roman sarcophagi. The first image of Jesus' crucifixion in an illuminated manuscript did not appear until the late sixth century in the Rabbula Gospels, which were completed in 586 in the monastery of Saint John of Zagba, in what is now Syria.[36]

This painting was produced over 500 years after the crucifixion of Christ and over 250 years after the last crucifixions in the Roman Empire. It is unlikely that it can teach us anything reliable about how the Romans performed crucifixion. However, it does show arms spread horizontally, heads above the patibula, and feet side by side. Differences include a stipes rising above the *patibulum* and clothes on the victims.

Artwork: Carvings

Santa Sabina Church Doors (Oldest Public Image of Christ's Crucifixion)

The earliest extant public image of Christ's crucifixion appears on the upper left panel of the early fifth-century wooden doors of the Basilica of Santa Sabina on the Aventine Hill in Rome. Construction of the church likely took place during the pontificate of Pope Celestine I (422–433).[37] As mentioned earlier, there is no evidence for Christian art before the third century and no evidence for a public representation of the crucifixion of Christ before the Santa Sabina doors. Even so, the image is placed up high where it is very difficult to see.

Main doors of Santa Sabina Church on the Aventine Hill in Rome. The doors date from between 420 and 430, with the crucifixion scene depicted in the upper left-hand corner.

The three male figures wear loincloths and appear upright and vigorously alive. Each of the three crosses is rudimentarily portrayed, yet an upright post can be seen extending above the head of each thief; the bottom of the upright (or perhaps the suggestion of a foot support, or *suppedaneum*) can be seen between the feet of each victim; the *patibulum* is seen behind the hands and forearms of each. Nails are visible in the palms of the hands, and each figure

Close-up of the crucifixion scene depicted on the doors of Santa Sabina. Note the similarities to the image on page 290.

is pictured standing with feet side by side. The arms are spread wide in the orans posture of prayer.

This image in fact can easily be mistaken for the image of the three youths in the Book of Daniel found on a fresco in the Velatio Chamber of the Saint Priscilla Catacombs in Rome. Among Christians of the fourth century, the image of Shadrach, Meshach, and Abednego in the fiery furnace (described in Daniel 3) was popular for use on sarcophagi and in the catacombs, as it represented hope in the resurrection. Art historians believe that this image served as the prototype for the carving on the Santa Sabina doors.[38]

Why was the orans position of prayer used in the portrayal of crucifixion?

Tertullian writes in the third century that Christians saw a parallel between crucifixion and orans prayer:

Although Israel wash daily over his whole body, yet he is never clean. At least, his hands are always unclean, for they are covered over for ever with the blood of the prophets and of the Lord himself; and therefore, inheriting the guilt of their fathers, they do not dare even to raise them to the Lord, lest some Isaiah should cry aloud, lest Christ should be filled with horror. We, however, do not merely raise them, but also spread them out, and we make our confession to Christ, while we represent the Lord's Passion and likewise pray.[39]

Both the Velatio Chamber image and the Santa Sabina image include three male figures standing and facing forward, hands held in orans position, within a torture motif based on a biblical text, and depicted as triumphing over suffering. In accord with the early Christian reluctance to portray Christ suffering in artwork, it should not be surprising that this earliest known image of the crucifixion of Christ is ambiguous regarding details of the practice of crucifixion.

Maskell Passion Ivories

The Maskell Passion Ivories, now located in the British Museum's Department of Prehistory and Europe, date from 420 to 430, the same period as the Santa Sabina doors. They provide the earliest surviving visual representation of Christ's crucifixion, in which Jesus is pictured on a cross as part of a pictorial narration of his arrest, death, and resurrection.[40] Four ivory panels almost exactly 4 by 3 inches (9.8 by 7.5 centimeters) were originally mounted on the sides of a square casket with a hinged lid. The four panels contain a total of seven scenes:

1. Pilate washing his hands
2. Jesus carrying his own cross ("plus sign"-shaped, not tau-shaped)
3. Peter denying Jesus
4. Suicide of Judas
5. Jesus on the cross
6. Women at the empty tomb
7. Jesus risen and interacting with disciples

One side of the Maskell Passion Ivories. Along with the Santa Sabina doors, this is one of the two oldest Christian images of Christ crucified. The ivory is housed in the British Museum. (Thomas W. McGovern)

These relief carvings demonstrate deliverance from death more than the fact of death, thus continuing the theme in early Christian art of picturing Christ as triumphant in death and not succumbing to death. They contain intricate details suggesting a highly developed pictorial narrative tradition of the Passion,[41] meaning that it is unlikely the ivories were the first time such a depiction was attempted.

These carvings were produced nearly 400 years after Christ's crucifixion and 100 years after the practice of crucifixion ended in the Roman Empire. They remain consistent with early images of crucifixion by demonstrating arms stretched out horizontally and feet side by side without a foot support (*suppedaneum*). A titulus describes Jesus' crime ("REX IVD" stands for Rex Iudaeorum, or "King of the Jews"). While Jesus is nearly naked, he does wear a loincloth. (The Roman concept of "stripped" [*nudus*] allowed for such a covering, which was called the perizoma.)[42] Nails are shown in the palms, and a spear is being thrust at his left side (the right side of the image). We see the irony of the dead Judas hanging on a live tree juxtaposed with a live Jesus hanging on a dead tree.

The emphasis in the Maskell ivories is the revelation of Christ's divinity, not the specifics of his trial and death. As mentioned earlier, funerary art from this period focused on instances of deliverance from death, not on the fact of death itself.[43]

Conclusions Regarding Crucifixion in Archaeology, Graffiti, Epigraphy, and Art

In the first several centuries of the Christian Church, there was a reluctance to portray Jesus' crucifixion in artwork. Once Christ's crucifixion was depicted, there was no established convention in the early Church for portraying it. Still, by compiling the similarities among the images and the evidence of the inscriptions and archaeology, we can list certain findings that likely point to actual crucifixion practice:

- Arms are uniformly depicted stretched out horizontally in images.
- Feet are uniformly depicted side by side, not with one foot on top of the other, in images and by archaeological finding.
- The head of the victim is uniformly depicted at or above the level of the *patibulum* (crossbeam), and the body is not depicted hanging down with arms above the head.
- Hands are attached to the *patibulum* at the wrist (earlier and more often) or palm (later and less often) by nails or fetters.
- A *patibulum* was carried with outstretched arms separate from — and almost certainly prior to — crucifixion.
- Scourging and other forms of torture such as burning preceded or accompanied crucifixion.

Bibliography

Agence France Press. "The Treasures of Notre Dame." France 24, April 16, 2019. https://www.france24.com/en/20190416-treasures-notre-dame.

Akin, Jimmy. "7 Clues Tell Us *Precisely* When Jesus Died (the Year, Month, Day, and Hour Revealed)." *National Catholic Register.* April 10, 2013. http://www.ncregister.com/blog/jimmy-akin/when-precisely-did-jesus-die-the-year-month-day-and-hour-revealed.

Ball, David A. "The Crucifixion and Death of a Man Called Jesus." *Journal MSMA* 30, no. 3 (1989): 77–83.

_____. "The Crucifixion Revisited." *Journal MSMA* 49 (2008): 67–73.

Barbet, Pierre. *A Doctor at Calvary: The Passion of Our Lord Jesus Christ as Described by a Surgeon.* Translated by the Earl of Wicklow. Garden City, NY: Image Books, 1963.

Benedict XVI. *Jesus of Nazareth: Holy Week — From the Entrance into Jerusalem to the Resurrection.* San Francisco: Ignatius Press, 2011.

Bergeron, Joseph W. "The Crucifixion of Jesus: Review of Hypothesized Mechanisms of Death and Implications of Shock and Trauma-Induced Coagulopathy." *J Forensic Legal Med* 19 (2012): 113–16.

Bevilacqua, M., G. Fanti, M. D'Arienzo, and R. De Caro. "Do We Really Need New Medical Information about the Turin Shroud?" *Injury, Int J Care Injured* 45 (2014): 460–64.

Bevilacqua, M., G. Fanti, M. D'Arienzo, A. Porzionato, V. Macchi, and R. De Caro. "How Was the Turin Shroud Man Crucified?" *Injury, Int J Care Injured* 45, supp. 6 (December 1, 2014): S142–48.

Bhattacharya, Subham, Mrinal Kanti Das, Suman Sarkar, and Avizhek De. "Hematidrosis." *Indian Pediatrics* 50 (2013): 703–4.

Blackmore, C. C., W. C. Black, R. V. Dallas, and H. C. Crow. "Pleural Fluid Volume Estimation: A Chest Radiograph Prediction Rule." *Acad Radiol* 3, no. 2 (1996): 103–9.

Bodidharma. *The Zen Teaching of Bodidharma.* Translated by Red Pine. New York: North Point Press, 1989.

Bond, Helen K. *Pontius Pilate in History and Interpretation.* Cambridge: Cambridge University Press, 1998.

Bordes, Stephen, Skyler Jenkins, Lexian McBain, Amgad Hanna, Marios Loukas, and R. Shane Tubbs. "The Clinical Anatomy of Crucifixion." *Clin Anat* 33 (2020): 12–21.

Boron, Walter. *Medical Physiology: A Cellular and Molecular Approach.* Amsterdam: Elsevier/Saunders, 2004.

Brathwaite, C. E., A. Rodriguez, S. Z. Turney, C. M. Dunham, and R. Cowley. "Blunt Traumatic Cardiac Rupture: A 5-Year Experience." *Annals of Surgery* 212 (1990): 701–4.

Broshi, Magen. "Estimating the Population of Ancient Jerusalem." *Biblical Archaeology Review* 4, no. 2 (June 1978).

Brown, Raymond E. *The Death of the Messiah: A Commentary on the Passion Narratives in the Gospels.* 2 vols. New Haven, CT: Yale University Press, 1994.

Bucklin, Robert. "An Autopsy of the Man of the Shroud." Shroud of Turin website, 1997. Accessed August 5, 2020. https://www.shroud.com/bucklin.htm.

Caja, V. L., and M. M. Reverte-Vinaiza. "Do We Really Need New Medical Information about the Turin Shroud?" *Injury* 45 (2014): 1804–5 .

Carvalho, Ana Carolina da Silva, Jackson Machado-Pinto, Gustavo Carneiro Nogueira, Luiz Maurício Costa Almeida, and Maurício Buzelin Nunes. "Hematidrosis: A Case Report and Review of the Literature." *Int J Dermatol* 47 (2008): 1058–59.

Case, Anne, and Angus Deaton. *Deaths of Despair and the Future of Capitalism.* Princeton, NJ: Princeton University Press, 2020.

Castelli, Francesco. *Padre Pio under Investigation: The Secret Vatican Files.* San Francisco: Ignatius Press, 2011.

Ching, Randal P. "Technical Brief: Relationship between Head Mass and Circumference in Human Adults." University of Washington, Applied Biomechanics Laboratory, July 20, 2007.

Cigna. "Research Puts Spotlight on the Impact of Loneliness in the U.S. and Potential Root Causes." News release, May 1, 2018. https://www.cigna.com/newsroom/news-releases/2018/new-cigna-study-reveals-loneliness-at-epidemic-levels-in-america.

Cook, John Granger. "Crucifixion as Spectacle in Roman Campania." *Novum Testamentum* 54 (2012): 68–100.

_____. *Crucifixion in the Mediterranean World*. Tübingen, Germany: Mohr Siebeck, 2014.

_____. *Crucifixion in the Mediterranean World*. 2nd ed., extended. Tübingen, Germany: Mohr Siebeck, 2019.

_____. "Review of *Crucifixion in Antiquity: An Inquiry into the Background and Significance of the New Testament Terminology of Crucifixion*, by Gunnar Samuelsson." *Review of Biblical Literature* 4 (2014).

_____. "John 19:17 and the Man on the Patibulum in the Arieti Tomb." *Early Christianity* 4 (2013): 427–53.

_____. "Matthew 5.39 and 26.67: Slapping Another's Cheek in Ancient Mediterranean Culture." *Journal of Greco-Roman Christianity and Judaism* 10 (2014): 68–89.

Crispino, Dorothy. "Questions in a Quandary." *Shroud Spectrum International* 31 (June 1989): 14–19.

Csikszentmihalyi, Mihaly. *Flow: The Psychology of Optimal Experience*. New York: Harper & Row, 1990.

De Stefano, V., P. Chiusolo, K. Paciaroni, and G. Leone. "Epidemiology of Factor V Leiden: Clinical Implications." *Semin Thromb Hemost* 24, no. 4 (1998): 367–79.

De Stefano, Valerio, Ida Martinelli, Pier Mannuccio Mannucci, Katia Paciaroni, et al. "The Risk of Recurrent Deep Venous Thrombosis among Heterozygous Carriers of Both Factor V Leiden and the G20210A Prothrombin Mutation." *N Engl J Med* 341 (1999): 801–6.

Donnadieu, Marie Louis Adolphe. *Le saint suaire de Turin devant la science.* Edited by Charles Mendel. Paris: C. Mendel, 1904.

Edwards, William D., Wesley J. Gabel, and Floyd E. Hosmer. "On the Physical Death of Jesus Christ." *J Am Med Assoc* 225 (1986): 1455–63.

Elliot, Elisabeth. *Passion and Purity: Learning to Bring Your Love Life under Christ's Control.* Grand Rapids: Fleming H. Revell, 1984.

Etheria. *The Pilgrimage of Etheria.* Edited and translated by M. L. Mc-Clure and C. L. Feltoe. London: Society for Promoting Christian Knowledge, 1919.

Evans, Craig A. "Hanging and Crucifixion in Second Temple Israel." In *Qumran und die Archäologie*, edited by Jörg Frey, Carsten Claussen, and Nadine Kessler, 481–501. WUNT 278. Tübingen, Germany: Mohr Siebeck, 2011.

Faccini, Barbara. "Scourge Bloodstains on the Turin Shroud: An Evidence for Different Instruments Used." University of Ferrara, 2009.

Faccini, Barbara, and Giulio Fanti. "New Image Processing of the Turin Shroud Scourge Marks." Proceedings of the International Workshop on the Scientific Approach to the Acheiropoietos Images, Frascati, Italy: ENEA, May 4–6, 2010. http://www.acheiropoietos.info/proceedings/FacciniWeb.pdf.

Fanti, Giulio, and Emanuela Marinelli. "Results of a Probabilistic Model Applied to the Research Carried Out on the Turin Shroud." Accessed August 5, 2020. http://www.shroud.com/fanti3en.pdf.

Fanti, Giulio, Emanuela Marinelli, and Alessandro Cagnazzo. "Computerized Anthropometric Analysis of the Man of the Turin Shroud." 1999. Accessed August 5, 2020. https://www.shroud.com/pdfs/marineli.pdf.

Finan, Patrick H., Burel R. Goodin, and Michael T. Smith. "The Association of Sleep and Pain: An Update and a Path Forward." *J Pain* 14, no. 12 (December 2013): 1539–52.

Gertoux, Gérard. "Dating the Last Passover of Jesus (by the Hour)." *In Herod the Great and Jesus: Chronological, Historical and Archaeological Evidence.* Self-published, Lulu, 2015.

Geva, Hillel. "Jerusalem's Population in Antiquity: A Minimalist View." *Tel Aviv* 41, no. 2 (2014): 131–60.

Gibson, Shimon. *The Final Days of Jesus: The Archaeological Evidence.* New York: HarperOne, 2009.

Górny, Grzegorz, and Janusz Rosikon. *Witnesses to Mystery: Investigations into Christ's Relics.* San Francisco: Ignatius Press, 2013.

Gould, Stephen Jay. *Wonderful Life: The Burgess Shale and the Nature of History.* New York: W. W. Norton & Co., 1989.

Gualdi-Russo, Emanuela, Ursula Thun Hohenstein, Nicoletta Onisto, Elena Pilli, and David Caramelli. "A Multidisciplinary Study of Calcaneal Trauma in Roman Italy: A Possible Case of Crucifixion?" *Archaeol Anthropol Sci* 11 (2019): 1783–91.

Guerrera, Vittorio. *The Shroud of Turin: A Case for Authenticity.* Rockford, IL: TAN Books, 2001.

Haas, N. "Anthropological Observations on the Skeletal Remains from Giv'at ha-Mivtar." *Israel Exploration Journal* 20, no. 1/2 (1970): 38–59, plates 18–24.

Hallett, C. *The Roman Nude: Heroic Portrait Statuary, 200 BC–AD 300*. Oxford: Oxford University Press, 2005.

Harley, F. "The Narration of Christ's Passion in Early Christian Art." In *Byzantine Narrative: Papers in Honour of Roger Scott*, edited by John Burke et al. Melbourne: Brill, 2006.

Harley-McGowan, F. "The Alexamenos Graffito." Chapter 66 in *The Reception of Jesus in the First Three Centuries*, edited by Chris Keith, 105–40. London: T&T Clark, 2019.

_____. "The Constanza Carnelian and the Development of Crucifixion Iconography in Late Antiquity." In *Gems of Heaven: Recent Research on Engraved Gemstones in Late Antiquity*, edited by C. Entwistle and N. Adams, 214–20. London: British Museum Press, 2011.

_____. "Death Is Swallowed Up in Victory: Scenes of Death in Early Christian Art and the Emergence of Crucifixion Iconography." *Cultural Studies Review* 17, no. 1 (March 2011): 101–24.

_____. Essay and catalogue entries. In *Picturing the Bible: The Earliest Christian Art*, by Jeffrey Spier, 227–32. New Haven, CT: Yale University Press, 2007.

_____. "The Maskell Passion Ivories and Greco-Roman Art: Notes on the Iconography of Crucifixion." Part I, chap. 1 in *Envisioning Christ on the Cross: Ireland and the Early Medieval West*. Dublin: Four Courts Press, 2013.

_____. "Picturing the Passion." Chap. 18 in *The Routledge Handbook of Early Christian Art*, edited by Robin M. Jensen and Mark D. Ellison. Abingdon-on-Thames,UK: Routledge: 2018.

Heller, John H., and Alan D. Adler. "Blood on the Shroud of Turin." *Applied Optics* 19, no. 16 (1980): 2742–44.

Hengel, Martin. *The Cross of the Son of God*. London: Forlag SCM Press, 1986.

_____. *Crucifixion*. Philadelphia: Fortress Press, 1977.

Heshmat, Shahram. "Anxiety vs. Fear." *Psychology Today*, December 3, 2018. https://www.psychologytoday.com/us/blog/science-choice/201812/anxiety-vs-fear.

Hitchens, Christopher. "Topic of Cancer." *Vanity Fair*, September 2010.

The Holy Bible: Revised Standard Version, Second Catholic Edition. San Francisco: Thomas Nelson Publishing for Ignatius Press, 2006.

Holoubek, J. E., and A. B. Holoubek. "Blood, Sweat and Fear: A Classification of Hematidrosis." *J Med* 27 (1996): 115–33.

Horwitz, Allan V. *Anxiety: A Short History*. Baltimore: Johns Hopkins University Press, 2013.

Hurtado, L. "The Staurogram: Earliest Depiction of Jesus' Crucifixion." *Biblical Archaeology Review* 39, no. 2 (2013): 49–52, 63.

Institute of Medicine (US), Committee on Military Nutrition Research. *Nutritional Needs in Hot Environments. Applications for Military Personnel in Field Operations*. Edited by Bernadette M. Marriott. Washington, DC: National Academies Press, 1993.

Jayaraman, A. R., P. Kansan, and V. Jayanthini. "An Interesting Case Report of Hematohidrosis." *Indian J Psychol Med* 39, no. 1 (2017): 83–85.

Jeremias, Joachim. *Jerusalem in the Time of Jesus: An Investigation into Economic and Social Conditions during the New Testament Peri-*

od. Philadelphia: Fortress Press, 1969.

Jerjani, H. R., B. Jaju, M. M. Phiske, and N. Lade. "Hematohidrosis — A Rare Clinical Phenomenon." *Indian Journal of Dermatology* 54 (2009): 290–92.

Jumper, Eric J., Alan D. Adler, John P. Jackson, Samuel F. Pellicori, John H. Heller, and James R. Druzik. "A Comprehensive Examination of the Various Stains and Images on the Shroud of Turin." In *Archaeological Chemistry* — III, vol. 205, edited by Joseph B. Lambert, 448–76. Washington, DC: American Chemical Society, 1984.

Kellogg, D. L., J. L. Zhao, U. Coey, and J. V. Green. "Acetylcholine-Induced Vasodilation Is Mediated by Nitric Oxide and Prostaglandins in Human Skin." *J Appli Physiol* (1985) 98, no. 2 (February 2005): 629–32.

Kilmon, Jack. "The Shroud of Turin: Genuine Artifact or Manufactured Relic?" *The Glyph* 1, no. 10 (September 1997); no. 11 (December 1997); and no. 12 (March 1998). Accessed at http://www.historian.net/shroud.htm.

Klawans, Jonathan. "Was Jesus' Last Supper a Seder?" *Bible Review* 17, no. 5 (October 2001). https://www.baslibrary.org/bible-review/17/5/9.

Kluger, Nicolas. "Hematidrosis (Bloody Sweat): A Review of the Recent Literature (1996–2016)." *Acta Dermatovenerol* APA 27 (2018): 85–90.

Koskenniemi, E., K. Nisula, and J. Toppan. "Wine Mixed with Myrrh (Mark 15.23) and Crurifragium (John 19.31–32): Two Details of the Passion Narratives." *Journal for the Study of the New Testament* 27, no. 4 (2005): 379–91.

Kubala, Mark. *The Execution of Jesus the Christ: The Medical Cause of Our Lord's Death during His Illegal Crucifixion.* Bloomington, IN: WestBow Press, 2017.

Lee, C., and K. M. Porter. "Prehospital Management of Lower Limb Fractures." *Emerg Med J* 22 (2005): 660–63.

Lewis, C. S. "Divine Omnipotence." Chap. 2 in *The Problem of Pain.* New York: Macmillan, 1940.

Lubov, D. C. "The Relics of Christ." Our Sunday Visitor, July 5, 2019.

Maglie, R., and M. Caproni. "A Case of Blood Sweating: Hematohidrosis Syndrome." *CMAJ* 189 (October 23, 2017): E1314.

Magness, J. "What Did Jesus' Tomb Look Like?" *Biblical Archaeology Review* 32, no. 1 (2006): 38–49, 70.

Maier, P. L. "The Episode of the Golden Roman Shields at Jerusalem." *Harvard Theological Review* 62, no. 1 (January 1969): 109–21

Majeres, K. "Anxiety and Prayer." Interview by Tom McGovern and Chris Stroud. *Doctor, Doctor* radio show and podcast, February 19, 2020.

Manounukul, J., W. Wisuthsarewong, R. Chantorn, A. Vonigirad, and P. Omeapinyan. "Hematidrosis: A Pathologic Process or Stigmata. A Case Report with Comprehensive Histopathologic and Immunoperoxidase Studies." *Am J Dermatopathol* 30 (2008): 135–39.

Manservigi, Flavia, and Enrico Morini. "The Hypotheses about the Roman Flagrum: Some Clarifications." Paper presented at St. Louis Shroud Conference: The Controversial Intersection of Faith and Science, October 9–12, 2014. https://www.academia.edu/10173083/Shroud_of_Turin_The_Controversial_Intersection_

of_Faith_and_Science._The_hypotheses_about_the_Roman_ flagrum._Some_clarifications.

Martinez, N. L., et al. "Recurrent Bleeding in an 18-Year-Old Girl." *Arch Dermatol* 148, no. 8 (2012): 960–61.

Maslen, Matthew W., and Piers D. Mitchell. "Medical Theories on the Cause of Death in Crucifixion." *J R Soc Med* 99 (2006): 185–88.

May, R. *Man's Search for Himself.* New York: Norton, 1953.

Merton, Thomas. *The Seven Storey Mountain.* New York: Harcourt, 1948.

Miller V. D., and S. F. Pellicori. "Ultraviolet Fluorescence Photography of the Shroud of Turin." *J Biol Photog* 49, no. 3 (1981): 71–85.

Mödder, H. "Die Todesursache bei Kreuzigung." *StdZ* 144 (1948): 50–59.

Mora, E., and J. Lucas. "Hematidrosis: Blood Sweat." *Blood* 121 (2013): 1493.

Mounce, W. D. *Mounce's Complete Expository Dictionary of Old and New Testament Words.* Grand Rapids, MI: Zondervan, 2006.

Murphy-O'Connor, Jerome. "The Geography of Faith: Tracing the Via Dolorosa." *Bible Review* 12, no. 6 (1996): 32–41, 52–53.

_____. "Where Was the Antonia Fortress?" *Revue Biblique* 111, no. 1 (2004): 78–89.

O'Rourke, David. *The Holy Land as Jesus Knew It: Its People, Customs, and Religion.* Liguori, MO: Liguori Publications, 1983. (Pages 8–9 mention cracked rock 30 feet high where Calvary is "fissure"-quarried around it.)

Orwa,C.,A.Mutua,R.Kindt,R.Jamnadass,andSAnthony."Zizyphusspi-na-christi." Agroforestree Database: A Tree Reference and Selection Guide Version 4.0, *World Agroforestry* (ICRAF), 2010. http://apps. worldagroforestry.org/treedb/AFTPDFS/Zizyphus_spina-christi. PDF.

Orwell, G. "Lear, Tolstoy and the Fool." *Polemic* 7 (March 1947): 2–17.

Paleotti, A. "Observations on the Wounds from the Crown of Thorns." Translated excerpt from 1599 edition of Esplicatione del sacro lenzuolo ove fu involto il Signore [Explanation of the holy sheet in which the Lord was wrapped]. Shroud Spectrum International 31 (June 1989): 8–10.

Paleotti, A. Esplicatione del sacro lenzuolo ove fu involto il Signore [Explanation of the holy sheet in which the Lord was wrapped]. 1598. Quoted in Dorothy Crispino, "Perceptions of an Antecessor," *Shroud Spectrum International* 23 (June 1987): 16–21.

Patel, R., and S. Mahajan. "Hematohidrosis: A Rare Clinical Entity." *Indian Dermatol Online J* 1 (2010): 30–32.

Pelliccia, F., G. Sinagra, P. Elliott, G. Parodi, C. Basso, and P. G. Camici. "Takotsubo Is Not a Cardiomyopathy." *Int J Cardiol* 254 (March 1, 2018): 250–53.

Pontifical Biblical Commission. *Sancta Mater Ecclesia: Instruction Concerning the Historical Truth of the Gospels.* Translated by Joseph Fitzmyer. April 21, 1964. Accessed at http://www.piercedhearts.org/ scriptures/historical_truth_gospels_pont_biblical_com.htm.

Praveen, B., and J. Vincent. "Hematidrosis and Hemolacria: A Case Report." *Indian J Pediatr* 79 (2012): 109–11.

Ratzinger, J. *Introduction to Christianity.* San Francisco: Ignatius Press, 1990.

Readers Reply. *Bible Review* 5, no. 6 (1989).

Regan, J., K. Shahlaie, and J. Watson. "Crucifixion and Median Neuropathy." *Brain Behavior* 3 (2013): 243–48.

Retief, F., and L. Cilliers. "The History and Pathology of Crucifixion." *SAMJ* 93 (2003): 938–41.

Rich, A. *A Dictionary of Roman and Greek Antiquities: With Nearly 2000 Engravings on Wood from Ancient Originals Illustrative of the Industrial Arts and Social Life of the Greeks and Romans.* London: Longmans, Green & Company, 1860.

Rogers, R. N. "Studies on the Radiocarbon Sample from the Shroud of Turin." *Thermochimica Acta* 425 (2005): 189–94.

Samuelsson, Gunnar. *Crucifixion in Antiquity: An Inquiry into the Background and Significance of New Testament Terminology of Crucifixion.* Tübingen, Germany: Mohr Siebeck, 2011.

_____. "Crucifixion Reconsidered." Accessed January 23, 2015. https://www.academia.edu/4167188/Crucifixion_Reconsidered.

_____. "The Historical Background of Crucifixion." 2011. Accessed January 23, 2015. https://www.academia.edu/4167152/The_Historical_Background_of_Crucifixion.

_____. "The Historical Background of Crucifixion Reconsidered: A Critical Use of Classical Greek Texts in Search of Crucifixions." Accessed January 23, 2015. https://www.academia.edu/4167165/The_Historical_Background_of_Crucifixion_Reconsidered_A_Critical_Use_of_Classical_Greek_Texts_in_Search_of_Crucifixions_.

Sato, H., H. Tateishi, K. Dote, T. Uchida, and M. Ishihara. "Tako-tsubo-like Left Ventricular Dysfunction due to Multivessel Coronary Spasm." In *Clinical Aspect of Myocardial Injury: From Ischemia to Heart Failure*, edited by K. Kodama, K. Haze, and M. Hori, 56–64. Tokyo: Kagakuhyoronsha, 1990.

Shahgholi, E. "A Case Series of Hematohidrosis: A Puzzling Medical Phenomenon." *Turkish J Pediatr* 60 (2018): 757–61.

Sheckler, A. E., and M. J. W Leith. "The Crucifixion Conundrum and the Santa Sabina Doors." *Harvard Theological Review* 103 (2010): 67–88.

Shorr, R., M. Crittenden, M. Indeck, S. Hartunian, and A. Rodriguez. "Blunt Thoracic Trauma: Analysis of 515 Patients." *Ann Surg* 206 (1987): 200–5.

Smith, W. S*mith's Bible Dictionary* (also cited as *A Dictionary of the Bible*). Revised and edited by Rev. F. N. Peloubet and M. A. Peloubet "with the latest researches and references to the Revised Version of the New Testament." Philadelphia: Porter and Coates, 1884. Accessed at biblehub.com/dictionary/smith.htm.

Thayer, J. *Greek-English Lexicon of the New Testament.* New York: Harper & Brothers, 1889.

Tshifularo, M. "Blood Otorrhea: Blood Stained Sweaty Ear Discharges: Hematohidrosis; Four Case Series (2001–2013)." *Am J Otolaryngol* 35 (2014): 271–73.

Tzaferis, V. "Crucifixion — The Archaeological Evidence." *Biblical Archaeology Review* 11, no. 1 (1985): 44–53.

Uner, B., O. Oyar, A. Var, and O. Altnta. "Effect of Thinning on Density of Pinus nigra Tree Using X-ray Computed Tomography." *J Environment Biol* 30 (2009): 359–62.

Vachon, D. *How Doctors Care: The Science of Compassionate and Balanced Caring in Medicine.* San Diego: Cognella, 2019.

Vermes, G. "Was Crucifixion a Jewish Penalty?" *Standpoint Magazine*, April 2013.

Vine, W. E. *The Expanded Vine's Expository Dictionary of New Testament Words.* Minneapolis: Bethany House, 1984.

Wang, Z., Z. Yu, J. Su et al. "A Case of Hematidrosis Successfully Treated with Propranolol." *Am J Clin Dermatol* 11 (2010): 440–43.

Ware, L., and M. Matthay. "The Acute Respiratory Distress Syndrome." *N Engl J Med* 342 (2000): 1334–49.

Wedeman, Ben. "Archaeologist: Jesus Took a Different Path." CNN, April 10, 2009. https://www.cnn.com/2009/WORLD/meast/04/10/wedeman.via.dolorosa/index.html.

Wells, H. G. *The Shape of Things to Come.* New York: Macmillan, 1933.

White N. "Mechanisms of Trauma-Induced Coagulopathy." *Hematol* 2013: 660–63.

Witherington, B. III. "Biblical Views: Images of Crucifixion: Fresh Evidence." *Biblical Archaeology Review* 39, no. 2 (2013): 28, 66–67.

Wittgenstein, L. *Philosophical Investigations*, 4th edition. Oxford: Wiley-Blackwell, 2009.

Young, Thomas R. "The Alexamenos Graffito and Its Rhetorical Contribution to Anti-Christian Polemic." Last revised January 21, 2015. https://ssrn.com/abstract=2546438.

Zaninotto, G. "The Penalty of the Cross." *Shroud Spectrum International* 25 (December 1987): 3–12.

Zhang, F. K. et al. "Clinical and Laboratory Study of a Case of Hematidrosis." *Zhognhua Xue Ye Xue Za Zhi* 25 (2004): 147–50.

Zias, J. "Crucifixion in Antiquity." Accessed January 23, 2015. https://www.academia.edu/588244/Crucifixion_in_Antiquity.

Zias, J., and E. Sekeles. "The Crucified Man from Giv'at ha-Mivtar: A Reappraisal." *Israel Exploration Journal* 35, no. 1 (1985): 22–27, plates 5–7.

Zugibe, Frederick T. *The Crucifixion of Jesus: A Forensic Inquiry.* New York: M. Evans and Company, 2005.

_____. "The Man of the Shroud Was Washed." *Sindon N. S.* 1 (1989): 18–24. Accessed at https://www.shroud.com/zugibe2.htm.

_____. "Pierre Barbet Revisited." *Sindon N. S.* 8 (1995): 25–40. Accessed at https://www.shroud.com/zugibe.htm.

_____. "Two Questions about Crucifixion: Does the Victim Die of Asphyxiation? Would Nails in the Hand Hold the Weight of the Body?" *Bible Review* 5, no. 2 (1989): 34–43.

Notes

Introduction

1. Matthew W. Maslen and Piers D. Mitchell, "Medical Theories on the Cause of Death in Crucifixion," *Journal of the Royal Society of Medicine* 99, no. 4 (April 2006): 185–88, https://www.ncbi.nlm.nih.gov/pmc/articles/PMC1420788/.

Chapter 1

1. Miroslav Volf, Theology of Joy and the Good Life project, Yale Divinity School, accessed June 15, 2020, https://faith.yale.edu/joy/about.

2. Ed Vulliamy, "Peter Singer" Observer profile, *The Guardian*, February 14, 2009, www.theguardian.com/books/2009/feb/15/peter-singer-profile.

3. John Paul II, *Salvifici Doloris*, accessed June 15, 2020, Vatican.va, par. 2. (Hereafter cited as SD.)

4. Elisabeth Elliot, *Passion and Purity* (Grand Rapids: Fleming H. Revell, 1984).

5. Stephen Jay Gould, *Wonderful Life: The Burgess Shale and the Nature of History* (New York: W. W. Norton & Company, 1989), 323.

6. Christopher Hitchens, "Topic of Cancer," *Vanity Fair*, September 2010, https://www.vanityfair.com/culture/2010/09/

hitchens-201009.

7. George Orwell, "Lear, Tolstoy and the Fool," *Polemic* 7 (March 1947).

8. H. G. Wells, *The Shape of Things to Come* (New York: Macmillan, 1933).

9. SD 3.

10. C. S. Lewis, *The Problem of Pain* (New York: Macmillan, 1940).

11. Thomas Merton, *The Seven-Storey Mountain* (New York: Harcourt, 1948).

12. SD 4.

13. SD 5.

14. SD 7.

15. SD 6.

16. SD 7.

17. Augustine of Hippo, *Confessions,* trans. Albert C. Outler (London: Westminster Press, 1955), bk. 7, chap. 12.

18. SD 7.

19. See SD 8.

Chapter 2

1. SD 2.

2. Thomas Rosica, "Upcoming Extraordinary Jubilee 1st since 1983," *Zenit*, March 18, 2015, https://zenit.org/articles/catholic-jubilees-date-back-to-year-1300/.

3. Jimmy Akin, "7 Clues Tell Us *Precisely* When Jesus Died (the Year, Month, Day, and Hour Revealed)," *National Catholic Register*, April 10, 2013, https://www.ncregister.com/blog/jimmy-akin/when-precisely-did-jesus-die
-the-year-month-day-and-hour-revealed.

4. Gérard Gertoux, "Dating the Last Passover of Jesus (by the Hour)," in *Herod the Great and Jesus: Chronological, Historical and Archaeological Evidence* (self-pub., 2015), Lulu.

5. "Hours," Chabad.org, accessed July 22, 2020, https://www.chabad.org/library/article_cdo/aid/526872/jewish/Hours.htm.

6. Benedict XVI, *Jesus of Nazareth: Holy Week — From the Entrance into Jerusalem to the Resurrection* (San Francisco: Ignatius, 2011), 106–15.

7. See also Jonathan Klawans, "Was Jesus' Last Supper a Seder?," *Bible Review* 17, no. 5 (October 2001). In this article, the author agrees with Pope Benedict XVI that the Last Supper was an ordinary Jewish meal with the addition of the Eucharist. He emphasizes that the three Synoptic Gospels actually draw on a single tradition, so that they do not represent three traditions against the one tradition of John.

8. Tacitus, *Annals*, 15.44.

9. Helen K. Bond, *Pontius Pilate in History and Interpretation* (Cambridge: Cambridge University Press, 1998), 7–8.

10. "Jerusalem, Israel," Israeli Meteorological Service, https://www.weatherbase.com.

11. Hillel Geva, "Jerusalem's Population in Antiquity: A Minimalist View," *Journal of the Institute of Archaeology of Tel Aviv University* 41, no. 2 (2014): 131–60.

12. Joachim Jeremias, *Jerusalem in the Time of Jesus: An Investigation into Economic and Social Conditions during the New Testament Period* (Philadelphia: Fortress Press, 1969).

13. Magen Broshi, "Estimating the Population of Ancient Jerusalem," *Biblical Archaeology Review* 4, no. 2 (June 1978).

14. Eric H. Cline, *Jerusalem Besieged: From Ancient Canaan to Modern Israel* (Ann Arbor: University of Michigan, 2004), 2.

Chapter 3

1. Weather average for April 2 in Jerusalem, www.weather.com. This is the modern-day average; for our purposes in this book, we will presume that temperatures 2,000 years ago were roughly the same.

2. Pierre Barbet, *A Doctor at Calvary: The Passion of Our Lord Jesus Christ Described by a Surgeon* (New York: Image Books, 1963), 69 (emphasis added).

3. Ibid., 74 (emphasis added). Repeated in William D. Edwards,

Wesley J. Gabel, and Floyd E. Hosmer, "On the Physical Death of Jesus Christ," *JAMA* 225 (1986): 1455–63; Frederick T. Zugibe, *The Crucifixion of Jesus: A Forensic Inquiry* (New York: M. Evans and Company, 2005); David A. Ball, "The Crucifixion Revisited," *Journal MSMA* 49 (2008): 67–73; Mark J. Kubala, *The Execution of Jesus the Christ: The Medical Cause of Our Lord's Death during His Illegal Crucifixion* (Bloomington, IN: WestBow Press, 2017); and Elham Shahgholi, "A Case Series of Hematohidrosis: A Puzzling Medical Phenomenon," *Turkish J Pediatr* 60 (2018): 757–61.

4. Kubala, *Execution of Jesus the Christ*, 96.

5. J. E. Holoubek and A. B. Holoubek, "Blood, Sweat and Fear: A Classification of Hematidrosis," *J Med* 27, no. 3–4 (1996): 115–33.

6. Nicolas Kluger, "Hematidrosis (Bloody Sweat): A Review of the Recent Literature (1996–2016)," *Acta Dermatovenerologica* 27 (2018): 85–90.

7. Summary of data from F. K. Zhang et al., "Clinical and Laboratory Study of a Case of Hematidrosis," *Zhognhua Xue Ye Xue Za Zhi* 25 (2004): 147–50; N. L. Martinez et al., "Recurrent Bleeding in an 18-Year-Old Girl," *Arch Dermatol* 148, no. 8 (2012): 960–61; Anu Rita Jayaraman et al., "An Interesting Case Report of Hematohidrosis," *Indian Journal of Psychological Medicine* 39, no. 1 (2017): 83–85; Roberto Maglie and Marzia Caproni, "A Case of Blood Sweating: Hematohidrosis Syndrome," *CMAJ* 189, no. 42 (2017): E1314; Kluger, "Hematidrosis (Bloody Sweat)"; and Shahgholi, "Case Series of Hematohidrosis."

8. Barbet, *Doctor at Calvary*, 69.

9. Kubala, *Execution of Jesus the Christ*, 69; Barbet, *Doctor at Calvary*, 73.

10. Kubala, *Execution of Jesus the Christ*, 69.

11. *Strong's Concordance*, 85.

12. Ibid., 1568.

13. Allan V. Horwitz, *Anxiety: A Short History* (Baltimore: Johns Hopkins University Press, 2013).

14. Ibid.

15. Shahram Heshmat, "Anxiety vs. Fear," *Psychology Today*,

December 3, 2018, https://www.psychologytoday.com/us/blog/science-choice/201812
/anxiety-vs-fear.

16. Kevin Majeres, "Anxiety Is Prayer Waiting to Happen," interview by Tom McGovern and Chris Stroud, *Doctor, Doctor* radio show and podcast, February 19, 2020.

17. National Institute of Mental Health, "Any Anxiety Disorder," November 2017, accessed July 9, 2020, https://www.nimh.nih.gov/health/statistics/any
-anxiety-disorder.shtml.

18. Mihaly Csikszentmihalyi, *Flow: The Psychology of Optimal Experience* (New York: Harper & Row, 1990).

19. John Geirland, "Go with the Flow," *Wired*, September 1, 1996, https://www.wired.com/1996/09/czik/.

Chapter 4

1. Jeremias, *Jerusalem in Time of Jesus*, 83.

2. "April 33 — Moon Phase Calendar," *Moon Giant*, accessed June 18, 2020, https://www.moongiant.com/calendar/April/33/.

3. Josephus, *Antiquities of the Jews*, 18.2.2.

4. *Strong's Concordance*, 4474, 75.

5. *Navarre Bible New Testament* (Scepter Press, 2008), 473.

6. W. E. Vine, *Vine's Expository Dictionary of New Testament Words* (Reformed Church Publications, 2015), 1:86.

7. Liddell-Scott-Jones Greek-English Lexicon.

8. "Flogging," Jewish Virtual Library, accessed June 22, 2020, https://www
.jewishvirtuallibrary.org/flogging.

9. Shira Schoenberg, "Ancient Jewish History: The Sanhedrin," Jewish Virtual Library, accessed June 22, 2020, https://www.jewishvirtuallibrary.org
/jsource/Judaism/Sanhedrin.html.

10. SD 16.

Chapter 5

1. Bond, *Pontius Pilate in History*.

2. Barbet, *Doctor at Calvary*, 91.

3. Edwards, Gabel, and Hosmer, "On the Physical Death," 1456.

4. Kubala, *Execution of Jesus the Christ*, 76.

5. "Praetorium," Merriam-Webster.com Dictionary, https:// www.merriam -webster.com/dictionary/praetorium.

6. Kubala, *Execution of Jesus the Christ*, 46.

7. Thayer (1889), quoted in "Praitorion," *The KJV New Testament Greek Lexicon*, BibleStudyTools.com, accessed July 23, 2020, https://www.biblestudytools .com/lexicons/greek/kjv/praitorion.html.

8. Jerome Murphy-O'Connor, "Where Was the Antonia Fortress?" *Revue Biblique* 111, no. 1 (2004): 78–89.

9. Shimon Gibson, *The Final Days of Jesus: The Archaeological Evidence* (New York: HarperOne, 2009), 91.

10. P. L. Maier, "The Episode of the Golden Roman Shields at Jerusalem," *Harvard Theological Review* 62, no. 1 (1969): 109–21.

11. "Pilate was one of the emperor's lieutenants, having been appointed governor of Judaea. He, not more with the object of doing honor to Tiberius than with that of vexing the multitude, dedicated some gilt shields in the palace of Herod, in the holy city [Jerusalem]." Philo of Alexandria, *On the Embassy to Gaius*, trans. Charles Duke Yonge (London: H. G. Bohn, 1854–1890), par. 299 (emphasis added), http://www.earlychristianwritings.com/yonge/book40.html.

12. Philo of Alexandria, *On the Embassy to Gaius*, pars. 299–306.

13. Josephus, *Wars of the Jews*, 2.14.9.

14. Robin Ngo, "Tour Showcases Remains of Herod's Jerusalem Palace—Possible Site of the Trial of Jesus," *Biblical History Daily*, July 6, 2020, https://www.biblicalarchaeology.org/daily/news/herods-jerusalem-palace-trial-of -jesus/.

15. Raymond Brown, *The Death of the Messiah: A Commentary on the Passion Narratives in the Gospels* (New Haven, CT: Yale University Press, 1994), 1:865.

16. Ibid.

17. Edwards, Gabel, and Hosmer, "On the Physical Death," 1457.

18. Hengel's book was surpassed in breadth and depth in 2014 by John Granger Cook's *Crucifixion in the Mediterranean World*.

19. Brown, *Death of the Messiah*, 851.

20. Dionysius of Halicarnassus, *Roman Antiquities*, 5.51.3

21. Xenophon, *Hellenica*, 3.3.11.

22. Plato, *Laws*, 9.872b–c.

23. Josephus, *Wars of the Jews*, 12.256.

24. Cicero, *Against Verres*, 2.5.14.

25. Livy, *History of Rome*, 22.13.8–9.

26. Ibid., 28.37.2.

27. Brown, *Death of the Messiah*, 852.

28. Livy, *History of Rome*, 33.36.1–3.

29. *Lex Puteolana*, par. 2, col. 2, 8–9.

30. Seneca the Younger, *Dialogues*, 6.20.3.

31. Josephus, *Wars of the Jews*, 2.306–8.

32. Ibid., 5.449–50.

33. Cicero, *Against Verres*, 2.5.160–61.

34. Livy, *History of Rome*, 1.8.

35. Aemilius Macer, *On Criminal Proceedings*, in *Digest of Justinian* 48.19.10 (c. 210 AD).

36. *Codex Theodosianus*, 16.5.40.7.

37. Prudentius, poem 10, lines 116, 121.

38. Flavia Manservigi and Enrico Morini, "The Hypotheses about the Roman Flagrum: Some Clarifications" (paper presented at St. Louis Shroud Conference: The Controversial Intersection of Faith and Science, October 9–12, 2014), https://www.academia.edu/10173083/Shroud_of_Turin_The_Controversial_Intersection_of_Faith_and_Science._The_hypotheses_about_the_Roman_flagrum._Some_clarifications.

39. Ibid.

40. Eric J. Jumper et al., "A Comprehensive Examination of the Various Stains and Images on the Shroud of Turin," *Archaeological Chemistry* III 205 (1984): 447–76.

41. V. D. Miller and S. F. Pellicori, "Ultraviolet Fluorescence Photography of the Shroud of Turin," *Journal of Biological Photography* 49, no. 3 (July 1981): 71–85.

42. John H. Heller and Alan D. Adler, "Blood on the Shroud of Turin," *Applied Optics* 19, no. 16 (1980): 1742–44.

43. Barbara Faccini, "Scourge Bloodstains on the Turin Shroud: An Evidence for Different Instruments Used," University of Ferrara, January 2009; Barbara Faccini and Giulio Fanti, "New Image Processing of the Turin Shroud Scourge Marks," in Proceedings of the International Workshop on the Scientific Approach to the Acheiropoietos Images (Frascati, Italy: ENEA, May 4–6, 2010), http://www.acheiropoietos.info/proceedings/FacciniWeb.pdf.

44. Flavia Manservigi, email message to author, December 16, 2015.

45. Grzegorz Górny and Janusz Rosikon, *Witnesses to Mystery: Investigations into Christ's Relics* (San Francisco: Ignatius, 2013), 261.

46. Etheria, *The Pilgrimage of Etheria*, ed. and trans. M. L. McClure and C. L. Feltoe (London: Society for Promoting Christian Knowledge, 1919). Now spelled "Egeria" by most scholars.

47. Deborah Castellano Lubov, "The Relics of Christ," Our Sunday Visitor, July 5, 2019, https://osvnews.com/2019/07/05/the-relics-of-christ/.

48. Górny and Rosikon, *Witnesses to Mystery*, 260.

49. Manservigi and Morini, "Hypotheses about the Roman Flagrum," 5.

50. C. C. Blackmore, W. C. Black, R. V. Dallas, and H. C. Crow, "Pleural Fluid Volume Estimation: A Chest Radiograph Prediction Rule," *Academic Radiology* (1996).

51. Benedict XVI, *Spe Salvi*, accessed June 15, 2020, Vatican.va, par. 2.

Chapter 6

1. Edwards, Gabel, and Hosmer, "On the Physical Death," 1455–63.

2. Barbet, *Doctor at Calvary*, 94.

3. *Strong's Concordance*, 4735.

4. Zugibe, *Crucifixion of Jesus*, 28–29.

5. C. Orwa et al., "Zizyphus spina-christi," Agroforestree Database: A Tree Reference Selection Guide Version 4.0, *World Agroforestry* (ICRAF), 2010, http://apps.worldagroforestry.org/treedb/AFTPDFS/Zizyphus_spina-christi.PDF.

6. Barbet, *Doctor at Calvary*, 94.

7. Zugibe, *Crucifixion of Jesus*, 29.

8. Vincent of Lerins, quoted in Barbet, *Doctor at Calvary*, 93.

9. Dorothy Crispino, ed., "Questions in a Quandary," *Shroud Spectrum International* 31 (June 1989): 14–19; Górny and Rosikon, *Witnesses to Mystery*, 274–75.

10. Barbet, *Doctor at Calvary*, 94.

11. Agence France Press, "The Treasures of Notre Dame," France 24, April 16, 2019, https://www.france24.com/en/20190416-treasures-notre-dame.

12. Randal P. Ching, "Technical Brief: Relationship between Head Mass and Circumference in Human Adults," University of Washington, Applied Biomechanics Laboratory, July 20, 2007, https://smf.org/docs/articles/pdf/chingtechbrief.pdf.

13. Barbet, *Doctor at Calvary*, 94–97.

14. William D. Mounce, *Mounce's Complete Expository Dictionary of Old and New Testament Words* (Grand Rapids, MI: Zondervan, 2006).

15. Christopher M. Harris, "Scalp Anatomy," Medscape.com, May 10, 2013, https://emedicine.medscape.com/article/834808-overview.

16. Note that the Synoptic Gospels state that Jesus was mocked after Pilate condemned him to die; John places the mocking before the condemnation.

17. SD 18.

Chapter 7

1. Barbet, *Doctor at Calvary*, 39.

2. Edwards, Gabel, and Hosmer, "On the Physical Death," 1459.

3. Ibid.

4. Dionysius of Halicarnassus, *Roman Antiquities*, 7.69.2.

5. Chariton of Aphrodisias, *Callirhoe*, 4.2.6.

6. Ibid., 3.4.18.

7. Plutarch, *Moralia*, On the Delays of the Divine Vengeance, 554B.

8. Plautus, *Mostellaria*, 359–60.

9. Plautus, *Miles Gloriosus*, 359–60.

10. Plautus, *Carbonaria*, 2 (emphases added).

11. John Granger Cook, *Crucifixion in the Mediterranean World* (Tübingen, Germany: Mohr Siebeck, 2014), 370 (emphases added).

12. John Granger Cook, personal communication to author.

13. Firmicus Maternus, *Mathesis*, 6.31.38, 59 (emphases added).

14. Macrobius, *Saturnalia*, 1.11.3–5.

15. *Thesaurus Linguae Latinae*, X/1.706.70–75, s.v. "patibulum"; translation as in Cook, *Crucifixion in the Mediterranean World*, 16.

16. Seneca the Younger, *De Vita Beata*, 19.3.

17. Ambrose, *On Abraham*, 1.8.72.

18. Edwards, Gabel, and Hosmer, "On the Physical Death," 1459.

19. I do not have access to the *Wycliffe Bible Encyclopedia*, so I have not been able to verify Dr. Edwards et al.'s reference to this work.

20. This number is offered as the actual width of the relic in Rome by Giulio Fanti and Emanuela Marinelli, "Results of a Probabilistic Model Applied to the Research Carried Out on the Turin Shroud," accessed August 3, 2020, https://www.shroud.com/fanti3en.pdf.

21. Patrick H. Finan, Burel R. Goodin, and Michael T. Smith,

"The Association of Sleep and Pain: An Update and a Path Forward," *J Pain* 14, no. 12 (December 2013): 1539–52.

22. Cook, *Crucifixion in the Mediterranean World*, 22.

23. Francesco Castelli, *Padre Pio under Investigation: The Secret Vatican Files* (San Francisco: Ignatius, 2011).

24. Jerome Murphy-O'Connor, "The Geography of Faith: Tracing the Via Dolorosa," *Bible Review* 12, no. 6 (1996): 32–41, 52–53.

25. David O'Rourke, *The Holy Land as Jesus Knew It: Its People, Customs, and Religion* (Liguori Publications, 1983), 8–9.

26. B. Bitton-Ashkelony et al., "Origeniana Duodecima: Origen's Legacy in the Holy Land — A Tale of Three Cities: Jerusalem, Caesarea and Bethlehem," Proceedings of the 12th International Origen Congress, Jerusalem, June 25–29, 2017.

27. Erik Koskenniemi, Kirsi Nisula, and Jorma Toppari, "Wine Mixed with Myrrh (Mark 15.23) and Crurifragium (John 19:31–32): Two Details of the Passion Narratives," *Journal for the Study of the New Testament* 27, no. 4 (2005): 379–91.

28. Augustine, *The Harmony of the Gospels*, 3:11.

29. Elie Wiesel, *US News & World Report*, October 27, 1986.

30. National Academies of Sciences, Engineering, and Medicine, "Health Impacts of Social Isolation and Loneliness on Morbidity and Quality of Life," chap. 3 in *Social Isolation and Loneliness in Older Adults: Opportunities for the Health Care System* (Washington, DC: National Academies Press, 2020), 3–12.

31. Julianne Holt-Lunstad et al., "Loneliness and Social Isolation as Risk Factors for Mortality: A Meta-Analytic Review," *Perspectives on Psychological Science* 10, no. 2 (2015): 227–37.

32. Ibid.

33. SD 13.

34. Fyodor Dostoevsky, *The Dream of a Ridiculous Man* (1877).

35. Tertullian, *Apology*, 39.

36. SD 14.

37. SD 18.

Chapter 8

1. Today, Calvary is located within the Church of the Holy Sepulchre.

2. Edwards, Gabel, and Hosmer, "On the Physical Death," 1459.

3. Ibid., 1460.

4. Raymond Brown, *Death of the Messiah*, 2:945.

5. Cook, *Crucifixion in the Mediterranean World*, 418.

6. Ludwig Wittgenstein, *Philosophical Investigations* (Oxford: Wiley-Blackwell, 2009), par. 67.

7. John Granger Cook, *Crucifixion in the Mediterranean World*, 2nd ed. (Tübingen, Germany: Mohr Siebeck, 2019), 418.

8. Justin Martyr, *Dialogue with Trypho*, 90.1.

9. Arnobius, *Against the Pagans*, 1.36.

10. Pliny the Elder, *Natural History*, 28.11.

11. Xenophon, *History of Ephesus*, 4.2.3.

12. Philo of Alexandria, *On Joseph*, 156.

13. Eusebius, *Church History*, 8.8.1.

14. Augustine, *Tractates on John*, 36.4.

15. Josephus, *Wars of the Jews*, 5.449–51.

16. Barbet, *Doctor at Calvary*; Zugibe, *Crucifixion of Jesus*; and Kubala, *Execution of Jesus the Christ*.

17. Alfonso Paleotti, quoted in Dorothy Crispino, "Perceptions of an Antecessor," *Shroud Spectrum International* 23 (June 1987).

18. Zugibe, *Crucifixion of Jesus*, 107–22.

19. M. Bevilacqua et al., "How Was the Turin Shroud Man Crucified?" *Injury* 45, supp. 6 (December 1, 2014).

20. Barbet, *Doctor at Calvary*, 117.

21. Bevilacqua et al., "How Was Shroud Man Crucified?"

22. Stephen Bordes et al., "The Clinical Anatomy of Crucifixion," *Clin Anat* 33 (2020): 12–21.

23. Edwards, Gabel, and Hosmer, "On the Physical Death," fig. 4, 1459.

24. Barbet, *Doctor at Calvary*, 105.

25. Zugibe, *Crucifixion of Jesus*, 95.

26. Encyclopedia Britannica online, s.v. "Crucifixion: Capital

Punishment," accessed August 5, 2020, https://www.britannica.com/topic/crucifixion-capital-punishment.

27. Edwards, Gabel, and Hosmer, "On the Physical Death," fig. 5, 1460.

28. Paleotti, *Esplicatione del sacro lenzuolo*; Bevilacqua et al., "How Was Shroud Man Crucified?".

29. M. Bevilacqua et al., "Do We Really Need New Medical Information about the Turin Shroud?" *Injury* 45 (2014): 460–64.

30. Zugibe, *Crucifixion of Jesus*, 97.

31. Plautus, *Bacchides*, 361–62.

32. Zugibe, *Crucifixion of Jesus*, 117.

33. SD 25.

34. SD 1.

Chapter 9

1. Edwards, Gabel, and Hosmer, "On the Physical Death," 1455.

2. A. A. LeBec, "The Death of the Cross: A Physiological Study of the Passion of Our Lord Jesus Christ," *Catholic Medical Guardian* 3 (1925): 126–32.

3. Barbet, *Doctor at Calvary*, 80.

4. R. W. Hynek, Golgotha, *Wissenschaft und Mystik — eine medizinisch-apologetische Studie über das heilige Grablinnen von Turin* (Karlsruhe, Germany: Badenia Verlag, 1936).

5. Barbet, *Doctor at Calvary*, 81.

6. Ibid., 82.

7. Philo of Alexandria, *On Joseph*, 156. See also Cook, *Crucifixion in the Mediterranean World*, 236.

8. Eusebius, *Church History*, 8.8.1.

9. Augustine, *Tractates on John*, 36.4.

10. Zugibe, *Crucifixion of Jesus*, 101–22.

11. Ball, "Crucifixion Revisited," 67–73.

12. Hermann Mödder, "Die Todesursache bei der Kreuzigung," *Stimmen der Zeit* (March 1949).

13. Barbet, *Doctor at Calvary*, 211.

14. Joseph W. Bergeron, "The Crucifixion of Jesus: Review of

Hypothesized Mechanisms of Death and Implications of Shock and Trauma-Induced Coagulopathy," *Journal of Forensic Legal Medicine* (2012): 113–16.

15. V. De Stefano et al., "Epidemiology of Factor V Leiden: Clinical Implications," *Semin Thromb Hemost* 24, no. 4 (1998): 367–79.

16. Valerio De Stefano et al., "The Risk of Recurrent Deep Venous Thrombosis among Heterozygous Carriers of Both Factor V Leiden and the G20210A Prothrombin Mutation," *New England Journal of Medicine* (September 9, 1999).

17. Bergeron, "Crucifixion of Jesus."

18. Francesco Pellicia et al., "Takotsubo Is Not a Cardiomyopathy," *International Journal of Cardiology* (March 1, 2018): 250–53.

19. Richard P. Dutton, "Pathophysiology of Traumatic Shock," *International TraumaCare* 18, no. 1: 12–15.

20. Barbet, *Doctor at Calvary*, 210–11.

21. Bergeron, "Crucifixion of Jesus."

22. In an unstressed adult, this amounts to just under a pint (400 ml) daily. See Kerry Brandis, "Fluid Physiology: 3.2 Insensible Water Loss," accessed August 5, 2020, https://www.anaesthesiamcq.com/FluidBook/fl3_2.php.

23. This amounts to the loss of another pint or more (500 ml) daily. See Institute of Medicine, Committee on Military Nutrition Research, *Nutritional Needs in Hot Environments: Applications for Military Personnel in Field Operations*, ed. Bernadette M. Marriott (Washington, DC: Institute of Medicine, National Academies Press, 1993).

24. Barbet, *Doctor at Calvary*; Bevilacqua et al., "Do We Really Need?"

25. Rolf Rossaint et al., "Management of Bleeding Following Major Trauma: An Updated European Guideline," *Critical Care*, April 6, 2010, http://www.ccforum.com/content/14/2/R52/table/T2.

26. Bergeron, "Crucifixion of Jesus."

27. N. White, "Mechanisms of Trauma-Induced Coagulopa-

thy," *Hematol* (2013): 660–63.

28. Kubala, *Execution of Jesus the Christ*, 103.

29. Eustace Fernandes, personal communication to author, January 11, 2016.

30. Maslen and Mitchell, "Medical Theories," 185–88.

31. Barbet, *Doctor at Calvary*, 87–88.

32. SD 26.

33. SD 20.

Chapter 10

1. Edwards, Gabel, and Hosmer, "On the Physical Death," 1461.

2. Cook, *Crucifixion in the Mediterranean World*, 429.

3. Eusebius, *Church History*, 5.21.3.

4. "Crurifragium," Wiktionary.com.

5. Plautus, *Poenulus*, 884–86.

6. Sextus Aurelius Victor, *De Caesaribus*, 41.4.

7. Firmicus Maternus, *Matheseos*, 8.6.11, quoted in Cook, *Crucifixion in the Medterranean World*, 429n65.

8. Plautus, *The Comedy of Asses*, 474.

9. Plautus, *The Braggart Warrior*, 722.

10. Zugibe, *Crucifixion of Jesus*, 106.

11. François Pieter Retief and Louise Cilliers, "The History and Pathology of Crucifixion," *South African Medical Journal* 93 (2003): 938–41.

12. C. Lee and K. M. Porter, "Prehospital Management of Lower Limb Fractures," *Emergency Medicine Journal* 22 (2005): 660–63.

13. Edwards, Gabel, and Hosmer, "On the Physical Death."

14. Robert Bucklin, "An Autopsy on the Man of the Shroud," Shroud of Turin website, 1997, accessed July 23, 2020, https://www.shroud.com/bucklin.htm.

15. Barbet, *Doctor at Calvary*, 140.

16. Zugibe, *Crucifixion of Jesus*.

17. Bevilacqua et al., "Do We Really Need?"

18. Cook, *Crucifixion in the Mediterranean World*, 429.

19. Ibid., 387.

20. Ibid., 385.

21. Ibid., 294, 336.

22. L. Y. Rahmani, "Ancient Jerusalem's Funerary Customs and Tombs: Part Three," *Biblical Archaeologist* 45, no. 1 (Winter 1982): 43–53.

23. Richard Neitzel Holzapfel et al., "Jesus and the Ossuaries: First-Century Jewish Burial Practices and the Lost Tomb of Jesus," in *Behold the Lamb of God: An Easter Celebration*, ed. Richard Neitzel Holzapfel, Frank F. Judd Jr., and Thomas A. Wayment (Provo, UT: Religious Studies Center, Brigham Young University, 2008), 201–36.

24. SD 29.

Chapter 11

1. SD 30.

2. SD 31.

3. SD 24.

4. Ibid.

5. Thomas Aquinas, *Summa Theologiae*, I-II, q.70, a.3, resp.

6. SD 24.

7. SD 19.

8. SD 30.

9. Dominic Vachon, *How Doctors Care: The Science of Compassionate and Balanced Caring in Medicine* (San Diego: Cognella Academic Publishing, 2019), 38.

10. Ibid.

11. Aquinas, *Summa Theologiae*, II-II, q.26, a.6.

12. SD 30.

Appendix 1

1. Maslen and Mitchell, "Medical Theories," 186 (emphases added).

2. Cook, *Crucifixion in the Mediterranean World*, 3.

3. John Granger Cook, "Review of *Crucifixion in Antiquity: An Inquiry into the Background and Significance of the New Testament*

Terminology of Crucifixion, by Gunnar Samuelsson," *Review of Biblical Literature* 4 (2014).

4. Ibid., 3.

5. Ibid., 4–5.

6. Seneca the Younger, *Dialogues*, 6.20.3.

7. Herodotus, *The Histories*, 7.194.1–3.

8. Ibid., 9.120.4.

9. Cook, *Crucifixion in the Mediterranean World*, 2nd ed. (2019), 226–27.

10. Ibid. See also Joel M. Hoffman, "Was Haman Hanged or Impaled in the Book of Esther?" God Didn't Say That, March 14, 2011, https://goddidntsaythat .com/2014/03/11/was-haman-hanged-or-impaled-in-the-book-of-esther/.

11. Plato, *Republic*, 2.361E–362A.

12. Joseph Ratzinger, *Introduction to Christianity* (San Francisco: Ignatius, 1990), 292.

13. Cook, *Crucifixion in the Mediterranean World*, 2nd ed. (2019), 272.

14. Philo of Alexandria, *On Joseph*, 156.

15. Cook, *Crucifixion in the Mediterranean World*, 236.

16. Josephus, *Antiquities of the Jews*, 12.256.

17. Ibid., 13.380.

18. Josephus, *Wars of the Jews*, 4.317.

19. Ibid., 7.202–3.

20. Plutarch, *Life of Antony*, 499D.

21. Plutarch, *Sera*, 554A–B (emphasis added).

22. Plutarch, *Life of Fabius Maximus*, 6.5.

23. Artemidorus, *Oneirocritica*, 2.53.

24. Cassius Dio, 11, I.165.12–14.

25. Ibid., 12, 1.173.9–10.

26. Plautus, *The Comedy of the Asses*, 940, and others. Also see *Oxford Latin Dictionary* entry for crux.

27. Plautus, *The Braggart Warrior*, 372–73.

28. Ibid., 359–60 (emphases added).

29. Plautus, *Miles Gloriosus*, Latin Texts & Translations, Perseus Digital Latin Library, http://perseus.uchicago.edu/cgi-bin/philologic/getobject.pl?c.187:7.LatinAugust2012.

30. Plautus, *Mostellaria*, 359–61.

31. Plautus, *Bacchides*, 361–62; Cook, *Crucifixion in the Mediterranean World*, 57.

32. Cook, *Crucifixion in the Mediterranean World*, 57.

33. Cicero, *Against Verres*, 2.5.14 (emphases added).

34. Ibid., 2.5.161.

35. Ibid., 2.5.169.

36. Cicero, *For Rabirius on a Charge of Treason*, chap. 3, 4, and 10.

37. Livy, *History of Rome*, 22.33.1–2.

38. Cicero, "Letter to Quintus," 1.2.6.

39. Cicero, *Against Verres*, 2.5.119.

40. Cicero, *Philippics*, ed. and trans. C. D. Yonge (London: George Bell & Sons, 1903), 13.27n1. Perseus Digital Library, http://www.perseus.tufts
.edu/hopper/text?doc=Perseus%3Atext%3A1999.02.0021%3A-speech%3D13%
3Asection%3D27#note-link1.

41. Gaius Maecenas, poetic fragment 4, quoted in Seneca the Younger, *Epistles*, 101.10.

42. Livy, *Periochae*, 17.

43. Livy, *History of Rome*, 22.13.9.

44. Ibid., 33.36.3.

45. Seneca the Younger, *Dialogues*, 7.19.3.

46. Ibid., 1.3.9–10.

47. Ibid., 6.20.3.

48. Ibid., 3.2.2.

49. Ibid., 5.3.6.

50. Valerius Maximus, *Factorum et Dictorum Memorabilium Libri Novem*, 6.2, 3.

51. Pseudo-Quintilian, *Minor Declamations*, 274.13.

52. Ibid., 380.1–2.

53. Pseudo-Quintilian, *Major Declamations*, 6.9.

54. Tacitus, *Annals*, 15.44.

55. Apuleius, *Metamorphoses*, 6.32.1.

56. Cook, *Crucifixion in the Mediterranean World*, 131–32.

57. Juvenal, *Satires*, 6.219–23.

58. Ibid., 14.77–78.

59. Firmicus Maternus, *Matheseos*, 6.31.58–59.

60. Augustine, *Tractates on John*, 36.4.

61. Livy, *History of Rome*, 22.33.1–2.

62. Valerius Maximus, *Memorable Deeds and Sayings: One Thousand Tales from Ancient Rome*, 2.7.12.

63. Livy, *History of Rome*, 33.36.2–3.

64. Appian, *The Civil Wars*, 1.120. Translation of Greek *ekremasthesan* as a form of *kremanymmi* (suspend — "to hang on, hang upon, be suspended" — according to *Strong's Greek-English Concordance*). The same verb is used in Luke 23:39: "One of the criminals who were hanged [*krematai*] railed at him, saying, "Are you not the Christ?"

65. Cicero, *Against Verres*, 2.5.168–69.

66. Lactantius, *Divine Institutes*, 4.18.7.

67. Paulus Orosius, *Seven Books of History against the Pagans*, 6.18.33.

68. Cassius Dio, *Roman History*, 54.3.7. The Greek word *grammaton* (as found in "Tetragrammaton" [YHWH or JHVH]) is translated as "inscription."

69. Josephus, *Wars of the Jews*, 2.75.

70. Tacitus, *Annals*, 1.61.4.

71. Ibid., 4.72.3.

72. Josephus, *Antiquities of the Jews*, 18.63–64.

73. Philo of Alexandria, *Against Flaccus*, 83.

74. Tacitus, *Annals*, 15.44.4.

75. Tertullian, *Scorpiace*, 15.

76. Eusebius, *Church History*, III.1.

77. Josephus, *Wars of the Jews*, 2.306–8.

78. Ibid., 5.449–51.

79. Josephus, *The Life of Flavius Josephus*, 420–21.

80. Eusebius, *Church History*, 8.8.1.

81. Eusebius, *Martyrs of Palestine*, 11.24.

82. Aurelius Victor, *De Caesaribus*, 41.4–5.

Appendix 2

1. N. Haas, "Anthropological Observations on the Skeletal Remains from Giv'atha-Mivtar," *Israel Exploration Journal* 20, no. 1/2 (1970): 38–59; J. Zias and E. Sekeles, "The Crucified Man from Giv'at ha-Mivtar: A Reappraisal," *Israel Exploration Journal* 35 (1985): 22–27.

2. Emanuela Gualdi-Russo et al., "A Multidisciplinary Study of Calcaneal Trauma in Roman Italy: A Possible Case of Crucifixion?" *Archaeological and Anthropological Sciences* 11 (2019): 1783–91.

3. Ibid.

4. John Granger Cook, email to author, July 20, 2020.

5. Cook, *Crucifixion in the Mediterranean World*, 224.

6. Ibid., 203–4.

7. Ibid.

8. Ibid.

9. Justin Martyr, *Dialogue with Trypho*, chap. 91.

10. Tertullian, *To the Nations*, 1.12.4.

11. Irenaeus, *Against Heresies*, 2.24.4.

12. Thomas R. Young, "The Alexamenos Graffito and Its Rhetorical Contribution to Anti-Christian Polemic," last revised January 21, 2015, https://ssrn.com/abstract=2546438.

13. Tertullian, *To the Nations*, 1.11.7.

14. John Granger Cook, "Crucifixion as Spectacle in Roman Campania," *Novum Testamentum* 54, no. 1 (2012): 68–100.

15. In Latin, *Cumis gl(adiatorum) p(aria) XX*.

16. Cook, "Crucifixion as Spectacle," 71.

17. Translated in Gino Zaninotto, "The Penalty of the Cross According to the Tabula Puteolana," *Shroud Spectrum International* 25 (December 1987): 3–12.

18. Translated by John Granger Cook, *Crucifixion in the Mediterranean World*, 370 (emphases added).

19. Ibid. (emphasis added).

20. F. Harley-McGowan, essay and catalogue entries in *Picturing the Bible: The Earliest Christian Art*, by Jeffrey Spier (New Haven, CT: Yale University Press, 2007), 227–32.

21. Origen, *Against Celsus*, bk. 1, chap. 6.

22. F. Harley-McGowan, "The Constanza Carnelian and the Development of Crucifixion Iconography in Late Antiquity," in *Gems of Heaven: Recent Research on Engraved Gemstones in Late Antiquity*, ed. C. Entwistle and N. Adams (London: British Museum Press, 2011), 214–20.

23. F. Harley-McGowan, essay and catalogue entries in *Picturing the Bible*.

24. Clement of Alexandria, Paedagogus, 3.57.1–3.60.1.

25. Eusebius, *Martyrs of Palestine*, par. 1.

26. Cicero, *For Rabirius on a Charge of Treason*, chap. 16.

27. Martin Hengel, *The Cross of the Son of God* (Forlag SCM Press, 1986), 138–42.

28. F. Harley, "The Narration of Christ's Passion in Early Christian Art," in *Byzantine Narrative: Papers in Honour of Roger Scott*, ed. John Burke et al. (Melbourne, 2006), 221–32, 536–38.

29. ChurchPOP editor, "A Tour of the Ancient Christian Art of the Roman Catacombs," ChurchPOP, July 26, 2015, https://churchpop.com/2015/07/26
/the-ancient-christian-art-of-the-roman-catacombs/.

30. Harley-McGowan, essay and catalogue entries in *Picturing the Bible*.

31. Harley, "Narration of Christ's Passion."

32. The Nicene Creed was modified in 381 at the Council of Constantinople, when among other changes, the line "For our sake he was crucified under Pontius Pilate" was added. Philip Schaff, *The Creeds of Christendom, with a History and Critical Notes* (New York: Harper & Brothers, 1877), 28–29.

33. Ibid.

34. John Granger Cook, "John 19:17 and the Man on the Patibulum in the Arieti Tomb," *Early Christianity* (Tübingen, Germany: Mohr Siebeck, 2013), 4:427–53.

35. Ibid.

36. Harley-McGowan, essay and catalogue entries in *Picturing the Bible*.

37. A. E. Sheckler and M. J. W. Leith, "The Crucifixion Conundrum and the Santa Sabina Doors," *Harvard Theological Review* 103 (2010): 67–88.

38. Ibid.

39. Tertullian, *On Prayer*, 14.

40. F. Harley-McGowan, "The Maskell Passion Ivories and Greco-Roman Art: Notes on the Iconography of Crucifixion," part 1, chap. 1 in *Envisioning Christ on the Cross: Ireland and the Early Medieval West*, ed. Juliet Mullins, Jenifer Ni Ghradaigh, and Richard Hawtree (Dublin: Four Courts Press, 2013), 13–33.

41. Ibid.

42. C. Hallett, *The Roman Nude: Heroic Portrait Statuary, 200 BC–AD 300* (Oxford: Oxford University Press, 2005), 61.

43. Harley-McGowan, "Maskell Passion Ivories."

About the Author

A native of Escanaba, Michigan, Tom completed his MD at Mayo Medical School and spent eight years in the U.S. Army that included biological warfare research and a dermatology residency at Fitzsimons Army Medical Center, Denver. He trained in Mohs surgery and cutaneous oncology at the Yale University School of Medicine and has practiced  Mohs surgery and reconstruction in Fort Wayne since 2000. He serves on the CMA national board and chairs both the CMA Annual Leadership Training Meeting and Young Member Advisory Committee. He is "living the dream," cohosting *Doctor, Doctor*, the official weekly radio program and podcast of the CMA that airs on EWTN. He and his wife, Sally, of 30 years, are raising seven homeschooled children who gladly get a break from his "Dad jokes" when he speaks at conferences.